This is a real gem. It provides an easy-to-follow bird's eye view of those developments and aspects of linguistics that may be helpful for better understanding the source texts of the Bible. It is a must read for students and exegetes who are serious about understanding the richness but also fascinating complexity of the Biblical texts that are so dear to us.

Professor Christo van der Merwe, Stellenbosch University

LINGUISTICS & BIBLICAL EXEGESIS

LEXHAM METHODS SERIES

LINGUISTICS & BIBLICAL EXEGESIS

——

Edited by Douglas Mangum & Josh Westbury

LEXHAM PRESS

Lexham Methods Series: Volume 2: Linguistics & Biblical Exegesis
Copyright 2017 Lexham Press

Lexham Press, 1313 Commercial St., Bellingham, WA 98225
http://www.lexhampress.com

Print ISBN 9781577996644
Digital ISBN 9781577997054

Lexham Editorial Team: Brandon Benziger, Claire Brubaker, and Randy Ferreiro
Design: Brittany Schrock
Typesetting: ProjectLuz.com

CONTENTS

Series Preface   ix

Abbreviations   xiii

1 | Introduction to Linguistics and the Bible   1
WENDY WIDDER

2 | Linguistic Fundamentals   11
WENDY WIDDER

3 | Language in Use   51
JEREMY THOMPSON & WENDY WIDDER

4 | Language Universals, Typology, and Markedness   67
DANIEL WILSON & MICHAEL AUBREY

5 | Major Approaches to Linguistics   87
JEREMY THOMPSON & WENDY WIDDER

6 | Linguistic Issues in Biblical Hebrew   135
WENDY WIDDER

7 | Linguistic Issues in Biblical Greek   161
MICHAEL AUBREY

8 | The Value of Linguistically Informed Exegesis   191
MICHAEL AUBREY

Bibliography   203

Subject Index   223

Scripture Index   231

SERIES PREFACE

The Lexham Methods Series introduces a variety of approaches to biblical interpretation. Due to the field's long history, however, the coverage is necessarily selective. This series focuses on the major areas of critical biblical scholarship and their development from the 19th century to the early 21st century. While we recognize that theological approaches to interpretation have played an important role in the life of the Church, this series does not engage the wide variety of hermeneutical approaches that arise from specific theological readings of the biblical text.

The methods discussed here include the broad movements in biblical criticism that have helped define how biblical scholars today approach the text. Understanding the basics of textual criticism, source criticism, form criticism, tradition history, redaction criticism, linguistics, social-scientific criticism, canonical criticism, and contemporary literary criticism (rhetorical, structural, narrative, reader-response, post-structural) will help illuminate the assumptions and conclusions found in many scholarly commentaries and articles.

Each approach to biblical interpretation—even those that are not explicitly theological—can be defined according to a guiding presupposition that informs the method.

- **Textual criticism**: Reading the text to identify *errors in transmission* and determine the best text

- **Source criticism**: Reading the text to find the *written sources* the author(s) used

- **Form criticism**: Reading the text to find the *oral traditions* the author(s) used

- **Tradition-historical criticism**: Reconstructing the *historical development of the traditions* identified by form criticism

- **Redaction criticism**: Reading the text to understand *how it was put together* and what message the text was meant to communicate

- **Canonical criticism**: Reading the final form of the text *as Christian Scripture*

- **Rhetorical criticism**: Analyzing the text for the *rhetorical effect of the literary devices* the writers used to communicate and persuade

- **Structural criticism**: Analyzing the text *in terms of contrast and oppositions*, recognizing that contrast is believed to be the essence of meaning within a cultural, linguistic, or literary system

- **Narrative criticism**: Reading the text *as a narrative* and paying attention to aspects including plot, theme, and characterization

- **Linguistic approach**: Analyzing the text *using* concepts and theories developed by *linguistics*

- **Social-scientific approach**: Analyzing the text *using* concepts and theories developed in the *social sciences*

The Lexham Methods Series defines these approaches to biblical interpretation, explains their development, outlines their goals and emphases, and identifies their leading proponents. Few interpreters align themselves strictly with any single approach. Contemporary Bible scholars tend to use an eclectic method that draws on the various aspects of biblical criticism outlined above. Many of these methods developed in parallel, mutually influenced each other, and share similar external influences from literary theory and philosophy. Similarly, ideas and questions arising from one approach often directly influenced the field as a whole and have become common currency in biblical studies, even though the method that generated the concepts has been radically reshaped and revised over the years.

In introducing a variety of methods, we will address each method as neutrally as possible, acknowledging both the advantages and limitations of each approach. Our discussion of a particular method or attempts to demonstrate the method should not be construed as an endorsement of that approach to the text. The Lexham Methods Series introduces you to the world of biblical scholarship.

ABBREVIATIONS

AEL	*Ancient Egyptian Literature*. M. Lichtheim. 3 vols. 1971–1980.
ANET	*Ancient Near Eastern Texts Relating to the Old Testament*. J. B. Pritchard. 1954.
AYBD	*Anchor Yale Bible Dictionary* (formerly *Anchor Bible Dictionary*). D. N. Freedman. 1992.
BDAG	W. Bauer, F. W. Danker, W. F. Arndt, and F. W. Gingrich. *A Greek-English Lexicon of the New Testament and Other Early Christian Literature*. 3d ed. 1999.
BDB	*Enhanced Brown-Driver-Briggs Hebrew and English Lexicon*
BEB	*Baker Encyclopedia of the Bible*. W. A. Elwell. 2 vols. 1988.
BHRG	*A Biblical Hebrew Reference Grammar*. Christo van der Merwe, Jackie Naudé, and Jan Kroeze. 1999.
COS	*The Context of Scripture*. W. W. Hallo and K. L. Younger. 3 vols. 1997–2003.
DCH	*Dictionary of Classical Hebrew*. D. J. A. Clines. 1993.
DDD	*Dictionary of Deities and Demons in the Bible*. K. van der Toorn, B. Becking, and P. W. van der Horst. 1995.
DJG	*Dictionary of Jesus and the Gospels*. J. B. Green and S. McKnight. 1992.
DLNT	*Dictionary of the Later New Testament and Its Developments*. R. P. Martin and P. H. Davids. 1997.
DPL	*Dictionary of Paul and His Letters*. G. F. Hawthorne and R. P. Martin. 1993.

DNTB	*Dictionary of New Testament Background.* S. E. Porter and C. A. Evans. 2000.
EDB	*Eerdmans Dictionary of the Bible.* D. N. Freedman. 2000.
EDNT	*Exegetical Dictionary of the New Testament.* H. Balz and G. Schneider. 1990–1993.
GKC	*Gesenius' Hebrew Grammar.* E. Kautzsch (ed.) and A. E. Cowley (trans.). 1910.
HALOT	*The Hebrew and Aramaic Lexicon of the Old Testament.* L. Koehler, W. Baumgartner, and J. J. Stamm. 1994–1999.
IBHS	*An Introduction to Biblical Hebrew Syntax.* B. K. Waltke and M. O'Connor. 1990.
IGEL	*An Intermediate Greek-English Lexicon.* 1888.
ISBE	*International Standard Bible Encyclopedia.* Revised ed. G. W. Bromiley. 4 vols. 1979–1988.
JM	*A Grammar of Biblical Hebrew.* P. Joüon and T. Muraoka. Rev. English ed. 2006.
LBD	*Lexham Bible Dictionary.* John D. Barry. 2012.
LEH	J. Lust, E. Eynikel, and K. Hauspie. *A Greek-English Lexicon of the Septuagint.* Revised ed. 2003.
L&N	J. P. Louw and E. A. Nida. *Greek-English Lexicon of the New Testament: Based on Semantic Domains.* 1989.
LSJ	H. G. Liddell, R. Scott, and H. S. Jones. *A Greek-English Lexicon.* 9th ed. with rev. supp. 1996.
MM	J. H. Moulton and G. Milligan. *The Vocabulary of the Greek Testament.* 1930.
NBD	*New Bible Dictionary,* 3rd ed. D. R. W. Wood. 1996.
NIDNTT	*New International Dictionary of New Testament Theology.* C. Brown. 4 vols. 1975–1985.
NIDOTTE	*New International Dictionary of Old Testament Theology and Exegesis.* W. A. VanGemeren. 5 vols. 1997.
OTP	*Old Testament Pseudepigrapha.* J. H. Charlesworth. 2 vols. 1983–85.
ODCC	*The Oxford Dictionary of the Christian Church.* F. L. Cross and E. A. Livingstone. 2nd ed. 1983.
TDNT	*Theological Dictionary of the New Testament.* G. Kittel and G. Friedrich. 10 vols. 1964–1976.

TLNT	*Theological Lexicon of the New Testament.* C. Spicq. 3 vols. 1994.
TLOT	*Theological Lexicon of the Old Testament.* E. Jenni and C. Westermann. 3 vols. 1997.
TWOT	*Theological Wordbook of the Old Testament.* R. L. Harris and G. L. Archer Jr. 2 vols. 1980.
ZEB	*The Zondervan Encyclopedia of the Bible.* Moisés Silva and M. C. Tenney. 5 vols. 2009.

COMMENTARIES

ACCS	Ancient Christian Commentary on Scripture
AYBC	Anchor Yale Bible Commentary (formerly Anchor Bible Commentary)
BCBC	Believers Church Bible Commentary
BKC	*Bible Knowledge Commentary*
BNTC	Black's New Testament Commentaries
CCS	Continental Commentary Series
FOTL	The Forms of the Old Testament Literature
IBC	Interpretation: A Bible Commentary for Teaching and Preaching
ICC	International Critical Commentary
ITC	International Theological Commentary
K&D	Keil, C. F., and F. Delitzsch. *Commentary on the Old Testament.* 1857–1878. Reprint 1996.
NAC	New American Commentary
NICNT	New International Commentary on the New Testament
NICOT	New International Commentary on the Old Testament
NIGTC	New International Greek Testament Commentary
NIVAC	The NIV Application Commentary
OTL	Old Testament Library
PNTC	The Pillar New Testament Commentary
TNTC	Tyndale New Testament Commentaries
TOTC	Tyndale Old Testament Commentaries
UBCS	Understanding the Bible Commentary Series (formerly the New International Biblical Commentary)
WBC	Word Biblical Commentary

| ZIBBCNT | Zondervan Illustrated Bible Backgrounds Commentary (New Testament) |
| ZIBBCOT | Zondervan Illustrated Bible Backgrounds Commentary (Old Testament) |

JOURNALS

ATJ	Ashland Theological Journal
BA	Biblical Archaeologist
BAR	Biblical Archaeology Review
BBR	Bulletin for Biblical Research
BSac	Bibliotheca sacra
CBQ	Catholic Biblical Quarterly
CurBS	Currents in Research: Biblical Studies
CurTM	Currents in Theology and Mission
EQ	Evangelical Quarterly
HUCA	Hebrew Union College Annual
JAAR	Journal of the American Academy of Religion
JBL	Journal of Biblical Literature
JETS	Journal of the Evangelical Theological Society
JHS	Journal of Hebrew Scriptures
JNES	Journal of Near Eastern Studies
JNSL	Journal of Northwest Semitic Languages
JSOT	Journal for the Study of the Old Testament
JSNT	Journal for the Study of the New Testament
JSSR	Journal for the Scientific Study of Religion
JR	Journal of Religion
MSJ	The Master's Seminary Journal
NovT	Novum Testamentum
PRSt	Perspectives in Religious Studies
RevExp	Review and Expositor
RBL	Review of Biblical Literature
Them	Themelios
TS	Theological Studies
TynBul	Tyndale Bulletin
USQR	Union Seminary Quarterly Review
VT	Vetus Testamentum

WTJ	*Westminster Theological Journal*

BIBLE VERSIONS

AMP	The Amplified Bible. 1987.
ASV	American Standard Version. 1901.
BHK	*Biblia Hebraica.* R. Kittel. 1905–1973.
BHS	*Biblia Hebraica Stuttgartensia.* K. Elliger and W. Rudolph. 1977–1997.
BHQ	*Biblia Hebraica Quinta.* A. Schenker. 2004–.
CEB	Common English Bible. 2011.
CEV	Contemporary English Version. 1995.
DRB	Douay-Rheims Bible.
ESV	English Standard Version. 2001.
GNT	Good News Translation. 1992.
HCSB	Holman Christian Standard Bible. 2009.
JPS	Jewish Publication Society. 1917.
KJV	King James Version.
LEB	Lexham English Bible. 2012.
LES	Lexham English Septuagint. 2012.
LHB	Lexham Hebrew Bible. 2012.
LXX	Septuagint
MT	Masoretic Text
MSG	*The Message.* 2005.
NA27	Nestle-Aland *Novum Testamentum Graece.* 27th edition. 1993.
NA28	Nestle-Aland *Novum Testamentum Graece.* 28th edition. 2012.
NAB	New American Bible. 1970.
NASB	New American Standard Bible. 1995.
NCV	New Century Version. 2005.
NET	New English Translation. 2005.
NIV	New International Version. 2011.
NIV84	New International Version. 1984.
NJPS	*Tanakh.* Jewish Publication Society. 1985.
NKVJ	New King James Version. 1982.
NLT	New Living Translation. 2007.
NRSV	New Revised Standard Version. 1989.
RSV	Revised Standard Version. 1971.

SBLGNT   Greek New Testament: SBL Edition. 2011.
UBS4   United Bible Societies' *Greek New Testament*. 4th edition. 1998.

1

INTRODUCTION TO LINGUISTICS AND THE BIBLE

Wendy Widder

1.1 UNDERSTANDING LANGUAGE

Everyone knows what language is, and many people have studied it formally at some point by learning the grammar of their native language or by learning another language. Through that study of language, many people likely became familiar with general concepts of language such as parts of speech, sentences, vocabulary, and the like. Fewer people know what linguistics is. Linguistics is the study of language as language—that is, how language works as a system.

In this volume, we introduce the field of linguistics and show how it can be used to understand the Bible better. Most of the Bible was written in two languages that the majority of modern readers do not know, and many of those who have studied biblical Hebrew and Greek likely have limited proficiency. A basic understanding of linguistics and how it applies to the Bible will help people better evaluate biblical interpretations based on language usage and reinforce even rudimentary language skills in Hebrew and Greek.

Language is remarkably simple and extraordinarily complex at the same time. Aside from those with physical or cognitive impairments, all humans speak at least one language fluently, and they did not have to work very hard to acquire their skill. Children learn to speak and use their native language simply by hearing it spoken. However, anyone who has tried to master another language, especially as an adult, realizes how complicated languages are. Learning an overwhelming list of vocabulary is the first step, followed by mastery of paradigms and learning to decode the syntax of full sentences and paragraphs. At every turn one encounters idiomatic language, connotations the dictionary does not include, and endless cultural elements that affect meaning. Learning vocabulary is the easy part.

One way to think about language is that it is the means by which we express thoughts or emotions. By this definition, language encompasses speech, text, and even body movement (e.g., sign language, gestures, or body language). It is a medium of communication. Another way to think about language is that it is a collection of meaningful sounds strung together in linear fashion to form words and then create sentences that will be vocalized by one person and understood by another—that is, language is speech. Speech becomes the basis for a written language. A third way to define language is that it is the specific communication system of a certain people group, such as the French, the English, or the deaf communities.

1.2 UNDERSTANDING LINGUISTICS

Language in all its nuances is the object of study for linguists. No linguist could reasonably explore every area of language, but "the field as a whole attempts to break down the broad questions about the nature of language and communication into smaller, more manageable questions"[1] and then address these questions in scientific ways to reach reasonable, reproducible results. Linguistics is interested in language as language—that is, language as structured systems of human communication. In the process of studying patterns of language, linguists have discovered "that language is a system so organized that by learning a manageable set of elements and the rules for their combination, we can produce an indefinite variety of particular messages."[2]

Linguists ask several questions of languages. First, they are interested in how a language encodes meaning. "Meaning" is a multifaceted concept

---

1. Adrian Akmajian, et al., *Linguistics: An Introduction to Language and Communication*, 5th ed. (Cambridge, MA: MIT Press, 2001), 5–6.

2. David Alan Black, *Linguistics for Students of New Testament Greek: A Survey of Basic Concepts and Applications*, 2nd ed. (Grand Rapids: Baker, 1995), 10.

that we will discuss more in chapter 2 (see §2.3 Semantics). For now we can say that meaning encompasses more than words, though it very often does include words. Words have particular sounds and grammatical shapes, and they are arranged in certain orders and then fit into larger contexts. But meaning also involves the people engaged in communication. They have particular roles and motives, and they speak within the contexts of relationships and situations. Words, situations, gestures, intonation—all of these and more affect how we encode meaning when using language. When linguists study language systems, they want to understand how every part of the communication process contributes to meaning.

A second question that drives linguistic study involves the ambiguity that a language allows and the multiple, related meanings it permits a given word to have. For example, the English word "diamond" can refer to a geometric shape, and it can also refer to a baseball infield, which has the same shape. This phenomenon is known properly as "polysemy," and it occurs cross-linguistically. For non-native speakers of a language, polysemous words cause endless difficulty, but native speakers have no trouble understanding and correctly using different senses of the same word (largely due to their greater familiarity with the socio-cultural context). Linguists are interested in how such related meanings develop and what the relationships between them are.

A third issue of interest to linguists is the significance of linguistic choices. In every language, there is more than one way to say what appears to be the same thing. For example, consider the following sentences:

> Let's have lunch at the café.
> I want to have lunch with you at the café.
> Do you want to go to the café for lunch?
> You and I should have lunch at the café.
> The café for lunch?

Each sentence expresses one person's desire to have lunch with another person at the café, but each statement has a slightly different emphasis or nuance.

Some sentences can use almost all the same words but in a different order. Consider the following set of sentences:

> I teach math to Jack once a week.
> I teach Jack math once a week.
> Once a week, I teach math to Jack.
> I teach math once a week to Jack.
> Once a week Jack is taught math by me.
> Jack is taught math once a week by me.

This is not an exhaustive list of options, but it illustrates the versatility of language and the fact that every speaker makes linguistic choices. Linguists are interested in how these differences affect meaning and what motivates a speaker's choice of one combination of words over another.

These are just three examples of questions that linguists want to answer when they study a language. Finding the answers helps them understand the structure of a language, and understanding the structure of language allows them to compare languages. When several languages can be compared and contrasted, linguists are able to formulate general principles of language.

1.3 LINGUISTIC ANALYSIS EXPLAINED

In this volume we are not solely concerned with linguistics, but with linguistic analysis of biblical texts; that is, analyzing a text according to linguistic principles in order to make decisions about the structure and meaning of the text's language. The serious study of any text must begin with textual criticism, that is, determining the most authentic reading of a text based on an evaluation of the available textual variants. Linguistic analysis focuses on trying to understand the language of the text. If we misunderstand a language, we will also misunderstand a text. With respect to biblical study, this means analyzing the text in order to understand the Hebrew and Greek languages. Black summarizes the importance of linguistic analysis for biblical studies: "If the student of the Bible is to become something more than a well-trained technician, he must sooner or later develop a solid perspective on linguistic study and on the nature of language itself."[3]

---

3. Black, *Linguistics for Students of New Testament Greek*, 21.

1.4 STUDYING THE BIBLICAL LANGUAGES

Biblical scholars have been studying language for nearly as long as there has been a text. Most of these studies fall more properly under philology, not linguistics—a distinction we address below and more extensively in chapter 5 (see §5.1 Comparative Philology).

1.4.1 PHILOLOGY: THE TRADITIONAL APPROACH TO LANGUAGES

Modern linguistics developed out of research on language from the late nineteenth and early twentieth centuries, but biblical scholarship did not incorporate its advances until the latter half of the twentieth century. Biblical scholars largely continued using traditional ways to study the languages. These traditional methods of study can be broadly categorized as philology, though scholars of biblical Hebrew and Greek understand "philology" differently.

The word "philology," (*philologia*) meaning "love of learning and literature,"[4] is commonly associated with the historical study of literary texts, specifically those in the classical languages (Latin and Greek). More specifically, the word is used to refer to the study of a language through the history of its usage and through languages related to it. This is the way it is used with respect to biblical Hebrew. Since biblical Hebrew and other classical languages have no native speakers, scholars are dependent on written texts, from which they have tried to determine how the languages developed over time.

Within biblical Hebrew study, philology involves trying to understand difficult aspects of the language through a careful reconstruction and categorization of words and grammatical structures. This is primarily accomplished through comparing related words and grammatical structures in cognate languages. Arabic was widely used as a comparative language for biblical Hebrew, mainly because of its long documented history and large vocabulary. Aramaic also provided a good point of comparison because of its similarity to Hebrew and its widespread use in the ancient Near East. As archaeologists discovered texts from other ancient Semitic languages, comparative studies grew to include languages such as Akkadian and Ugaritic.

---

4. Konrad Koerner, "Linguistics vs Philology: Self-definition of a Field or Rhetorical Stance?," *Language Sciences* 19, no. 2 (1997), 168.

One of the purposes of philology was to identify the genetic relationships between languages so scholars could use data from one language to clarify features of related languages. For example, if English were a dead language, philologists could use information from other Germanic languages to suggest explanations for obscure English words or even grammatical and syntactical features.

By contrast, when New Testament scholars use the word "philology," they are not referring to the study of comparative languages. Rather, they mean studying words according to their etymology—that is, the meaning of a word based on its past usage and development. New Testament scholars also use the term "philology" to describe the study of a word's grammatical function (e.g., its part of speech).

Finally, philology also draws on knowledge of other stages of the same language. For example, biblical Hebrew is an earlier stage of Hebrew than rabbinic Hebrew, and Koine Greek is a later stage of Greek than Attic Greek. When a word or language feature is unclear in biblical Hebrew or Greek, scholars have used what they know about classical Hebrew or Greek from other texts to hypothesize about the biblical language.

1.4.2 LINGUISTICS AND PHILOLOGY: WHAT'S THE DIFFERENCE?

There is a longstanding discussion in biblical scholarship about the differences between philology and linguistics. Bodine summarizes "generally recognized" distinctions between the two fields:

> "Philology gives attention to particular texts (usually of a literary nature and written), seeks to elucidate features of these texts which are more-or-less language specific, emphasizes the content of the texts, and draws implications that are related to the culture in which the texts were produced. Linguistics, on the other hand, studies speech with an eye to language *qua* language, attends more to features of its texts and other sources of information which are shared among languages rather than language specific, is concerned more with the structure of language than the content of texts, and is more theoretically than culturally oriented."[5]

---

5. Walter R. Bodine, "Linguistics and Philology in the Study of Ancient Near Eastern Languages," in *Working With No Data: Semitic and Egyptian Studies Presented to Thomas O.*

Thus, we can say that philology largely focuses on the reconstruction of the form and meaning of words and grammatical structures, and the categorization of these elements. Linguistics, on the other hand, focuses on the linguistic systems, taking into account the accumulated evidence and hypotheses of contemporary theories of language. Both contribute to our understanding of the Bible, and since the scope of linguistics is broader than that of philology, it can even include philology.

1.4.3 THE BENEFIT OF DRAWING ON LINGUISTICS

Biblical scholars have been slowly integrating the findings of modern linguistics into their biblical scholarship beginning in the second half of the twentieth century. In what follows, we provide one example of how linguistics has advanced our knowledge of biblical Hebrew and provided a plausible explanation for a long-running debate.

One of the first vocabulary words students of biblical Hebrew learn is the particle הִנֵּה (hinnē). English translations typically translate הִנֵּה (hinnē) with the interjections "behold!" or "lo!" or "look!" (see, e.g., Gen 1:29; Exod 7:17; 1 Sam 26:24). However, the simplicity of these translations is misleading. In fact, a great deal of uncertainty has long surrounded the meaning and function of the word. *The Hebrew and Aramaic Lexicon of the Old Testament* (HALOT) explains that הִנֵּה (hinnē) is a "deictic and interrupting interjection," but the 10 glosses that follow this explanation highlight the difficulty of explaining the meaning of הִנֵּה (hinnē) in its wide variety of contexts.[6]

However, a recent study by biblical Hebrew linguists incorporates linguistic methodology to offer a clearer perspective on the meaning and function of הִנֵּה (hinnē). In their 2011 study, Cynthia Miller-Naudé and Christo van der Merwe draw on a linguistic idea, mirativity, that appears in many other languages, and they hypothesize that this same idea can explain the function of הִנֵּה (hinnē) in biblical Hebrew.[7] Mirativity "refers to the linguistic marking for indicating that the information conveyed is new or unexpected to the speaker."[8]

Lambdin, ed. David M. Golomb (Winona Lake, IN: Eisenbrauns, 1987), 40.

6. *HALOT*, s.v. הִנֵּה.

7. Cynthia L. Miller-Naudé and Christo H. J. van der Merwe, "הִנֵּה and Mirativity in Biblical Hebrew," *Hebrew Studies* 52 (2011): 53–81.

8. Miller-Naudé and van der Merwe, "הִנֵּה and Mirativity in Biblical Hebrew," 57.

Some languages indicate mirativity grammatically, but it can be expressed in other ways, too. For example, English can express surprise lexically (e.g., the English expressions "I'm really surprised that" or "Surprisingly") or even intonationally. Miller-Naudé and van der Merwe illustrate the concept with two examples of English speech patterns that indicate the speaker's surprise. The first "involves stressing and lengthening the relevant word in the sentence in order to express surprise as a compliment," as in, "Your daughter plays *really* well." The second speech strategy uses what they call "question intonation," as in, "You're not coming? (meaning 'I'm surprised that you're not coming, because I thought you were')."[9]

Miller-Naudé and van der Merwe concluded in their exhaustive study of הִנֵּה (*hinnē*) that the "most typical and central use" of the biblical Hebrew particle is indicating mirativity,[10] and in cases where it does not, their study explains how the word functions instead. By using a characteristic of other language systems, they have been able to offer a better explanation for a difficult feature of biblical Hebrew than what has been previously available.

1.5 OVERVIEW

Linguistics is a broad discipline. We are not able—nor is it necessary—to cover all facets of the field in this introductory volume. Neither do we intend to teach readers to do linguistic analysis for themselves, since it is a field that requires expertise in the languages of the Bible as well as in at least one area of formal linguistics. Rather, we will introduce you to the aspects of linguistics that most apply to biblical study so that you can better understand commentaries and other resources that include linguistic discussions. Further, a working knowledge of the field will help you appreciate the complexity of language study and the rigor required of scholars to understand biblical Hebrew and Greek.

Chapter 2 introduces four fundamental aspects of linguistic study: phonology, morphology, semantics, and syntax. These branches of linguistics look at language at the word or sentence level—how words and sentences are constructed. Chapter 3 surveys several areas of linguistics focused on language use; that is, studying how language is used in context. The

---

9. Miller-Naudé and van der Merwe, "הִנֵּה and Mirativity in Biblical Hebrew," 57.
10. Miller-Naudé and van der Merwe, "הִנֵּה and Mirativity in Biblical Hebrew," 53.

branches of linguistics concerned with analyzing language in context (e.g., especially samples of language larger than a sentence, such as paragraphs and longer discourses) are pragmatics, discourse analysis, and sociolinguistics. Chapter 4 gives a concise overview of a few of the more complicated linguistic topics that are relevant for analyzing the biblical languages: language universals, linguistic typology, and markedness. Chapter 5 provides a brief introduction to the field of linguistics and the main schools of thought in linguistics, such as structuralism, functionalism, generative grammar, and cognitive linguistics.

In chapter 6, we turn our attention to particular linguistic issues facing scholars of biblical Hebrew, and chapter 7 does the same with NT Greek. In chapter 8 we conclude the volume by reflecting on the value of linguistically informed exegesis for the church.

1.6 RESOURCES FOR FURTHER STUDY

Akmajian, Adrian, Richard A. Demers, Ann K. Farmer, and Robert M. Harnish. *Linguistics: An Introduction to Language and Communication.* 6th ed. Cambridge, MA: MIT Press, 2010.

This book is a widely used textbook on linguistics and includes material on all the key topics of linguistic inquiry, as well as discussions of how children acquire language and how the brain processes language. Its foundations are in generative grammar.

Bodine, Walter R., ed. *Linguistics and Biblical Hebrew.* Winona Lake, IN: Eisenbrauns, 1992.

Bodine's edited volume provides an excellent overview of how scholars of biblical Hebrew are integrating modern linguistics into their research. The book includes chapters on phonology, morphology, syntax, semantics, discourse analysis, historical/comparative linguistics, and graphemics. (In this volume, we address all of these areas except graphemics.)

Cotterell, Peter, and Max Turner. *Linguistics and Biblical Interpretation.* Downers Grove, IL: InterVarsity Press, 1999.

Cotterell and Turner's introduction to how linguistics contributes to biblical interpretation is an engaging, readable resource. They

provide ample illustrations to explain linguistic concepts for
the beginner.

Poythress, Vern Sheridan. *In the Beginning Was the Word: Language-A
God-Centered Approach*. Wheaton, IL.: Crossway, 2009.

Vern Poythress presents a theology of language in his cross-
disciplinary study of how language reveals God. Poythress writes
for those with no linguistics knowledge and provides insight for
Christians to think biblically about language.

Silva, Moisés. *God, Language and Scripture: Reading the Bible in the Light of
General Linguistics*. Foundations of Contemporary Interpretation
4. Grand Rapids: Zondervan, 1990.

Silva introduces readers who are unfamiliar with linguistics
to general linguistic concepts and how they are important for
biblical studies. He includes an overview of the development of
modern linguistics, and he highlights many examples of how
language is mishandled.

2
——

LINGUISTIC FUNDAMENTALS

Wendy Widder

Linguistics is a diverse discipline. New Testament Greek scholar David Alan Black compares it to "the proverbial hydra—a monster with an end-less number of heads."[1] The wide-ranging nature of the discipline can be overwhelming, but a basic understanding of the field will enable you to navigate more effectively the material in the rest of this book. In this chapter, we introduce several key components of linguistic study and describe how each has influenced biblical scholarship. These key components of linguistics include phonology, the study of the sounds of a language; morphology, the study of how languages form words; semantics, the study of how words convey meaning; and syntax, the study of how words are formed into phrases and clauses.

2.1 PHONOLOGY

Sounds are the building blocks of spoken language. The study of sounds and their organization in language systems is called phonology. The number of sounds in a language differs from language to language. For example, American English has 39 sounds, while Hawaiian has 13, and Georgian, a language of the Caucasus region northeast of Turkey, has 90.[2] Often speakers of one language have difficulty making unfamiliar sounds

---

1. David Alan Black, *Linguistics for Students of New Testament Greek: A Survey of Basic Concepts and Applications,* 2nd ed. (Grand Rapids: Baker, 1995), xiv.

2. Adrian Akmajian, et al., *Linguistics: An Introduction to Language and Communication,* 5th ed. (Cambridge, MA: MIT Press, 2001), 85.

of other languages. This is the case when English speakers encounter the guttural letters (*aleph* and *ayin*) of biblical Hebrew or the clicks of many African languages.

2.1.1 PHONOLOGY EXPLAINED

A particular sound or group of sounds that perform the same phonetic function is known as a phoneme, such as the "k" sound in "**c**at" or "**sk**ill" or the "d" sound in "**d**o" or "ben**d**." The phonemes "k" and "d" are the same in each set of examples, although we pronounce the actual letters "c/k" and "d" in slightly different ways.[3] In phonology, multiple sounds belonging to the same phoneme are called allophones (lit. "other sound").[4] A phoneme does not carry any meaning, but phonemes are important parts of a language because they distinguish between words. For example, the words "pit" and "bit" only differ in their first phoneme, and while "p" and "b" do not carry meaning in themselves, they create two distinct words when added to "-it."

2.1.1.a Articulation

We produce sounds using our vocal tract, the organs of the mouth and throat. Sounds are created by the shape of the tract, the position of the tongue, and the restriction of air as we push it from our lungs through our mouth or nose. The diagram on the next page shows the speech apparatus.

2.1.1.a.1 Consonants

Consonants vary based on where the air is blocked (totally or partially) in the vocal tract. This is known as the "place of articulation." When both lips touch, the resulting phoneme is a p, b, or m. These are called "bilabial" (lit. "two lips") consonants. When the top teeth touch the bottom lip during speech, a "labiodental" results (lit. "lip-teeth"): f or v. The tip of the

---

3. Although it is often difficult for the native speaker to detect a difference in the sounds of the letters in these examples, linguists are able to draw a distinction based on specific criteria, such as how the particular sound in pronounced. For example, the "k" sound in "cat" is aspirated, while the sound in "skill" is unaspirated.

4. Phonologists represent phonemes and allophones in different ways. Generally, a phoneme is enclosed by slashes: e.g., /t/. Allophones, that is, different articulations of the same phoneme, are enclosed by brackets. Thus, /t/ in "stunt" is represented as [t], but the /t/ in "pitted" is more d-like and is represented with a special symbol: [ɾ]. A phonetics chart (such as the IPA chart) provides a fuller range of sound representations. In this volume we will not distinguish between these representations.

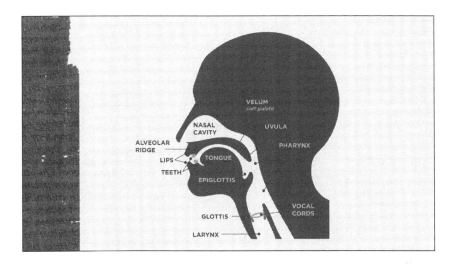

tongue between the teeth creates an "interdental" consonant (lit. "between teeth"): "th." If the tip of the tongue is on or near the alveolar ridge of the upper mouth, the sounds are t, d, n, s, z, r, or l: "alveolars" (if the tongue touches the teeth, the term "dental" is also used). "Velars" result when the back of the tongue is on or near the velum (soft palate): k, g, ng. The phoneme "h" is a "glottal," articulated in the space between the vocal folds, the glottis. Two places of articulation not typically used in English are the uvula, the fleshy projection at the back of the throat, and the pharynx, the space between the mouth and the larynx. "Uvulars" include the French "r," and "pharyngeals" include the Hebrew ח (het).[5]

Consonants also vary based on how the air travels through the vocal tract. When air travels from the lungs to the vocal tract, it goes through the larynx—the "voice box." Some sounds are made by vibrating vocal chords: b, d, g, v, th, z, and dz. If you place your fingers on your throat as you make these sounds, you will feel the "buzz" or vibration of the vocal chords. These consonants are called "voiced" consonants. Other consonants are "unvoiced," that is, you will not feel any vibration on your throat when you say them: p, t, k, f, s, and ts. In English, voicing is the essential

---

5. Some linguists contend that these categories have been based primarily on English and other Indo-European languages. They propose more generic categories that can be applied more universally. See the discussion, e.g., in Akmajian et al., *Linguistics: An Introduction to Language and Communication*, 112–20.

difference between several pairs of sounds that are otherwise identical: b and p, d and t, g and k, v and f, z and s, dz and ts.

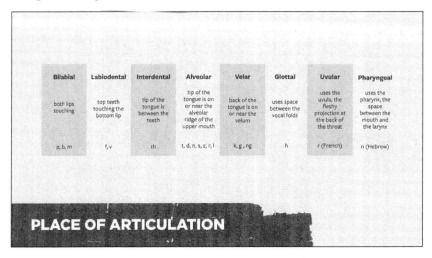

Bilabial	Labiodental	Interdental	Alveolar	Velar	Glottal	Uvular	Pharyngeal
both lips touching	top teeth touching the bottom lip	tip of the tongue is between the teeth	tip of the tongue is on or near the alveolar ridge of the upper mouth	back of the tongue is on or near the velum	uses space between the vocal folds	uses the uvula, the fleshy projection at the back of the throat	uses the pharynx, the space between the mouth and the larynx
p, b, m	f, v	th	t, d, n, s, z, r, l	k, g , ng	h	r (French)	n (Hebrew)

PLACE OF ARTICULATION

As air moves from the throat to the front of the mouth, we restrict its flow in different places and to different degrees to create sounds. When we temporarily block the flow completely at the place of articulation and then release a puff of air, we create a "stop" (also known as a "plosive"): p, t, k, b, d, g. If we stop air from entering the mouth but let it escape through the nose instead, we make a "nasal" sound: m, n, ng. In a "fricative" sound, the air goes through a narrow opening: f, s, v, z. An "affricative" sound is made by a "stop" and then a "fricative": ch ("chair") and j ("jump"). The "l" sound is a "lateral," so named because air escapes over the sides of the tongue. The English "r" is a "liquid" (air goes out over the tongue's center), and it is sometimes classified with "w" and "y" as a "glide," a sound in which airflow is barely obstructed.

2.1.1.a.2 Vowels

Vowels are more difficult to describe because they do not involve the obstruction or restriction of the airflow in the same way as consonants do. Rather, the shape of the vocal tract as air passes through determines the sound of the vowel. Vowels are classified according to how "high" or "low" the sound is made in the mouth, a position determined by the movement of the tongue: notice how your tongue moves from high to low when you

Stop	Nasal	Fricative	Affricative	Lateral	Liquid	Glide
block flow completely and release a puff of air	stop air from entering mouth but let it escape through the nose	force air through a narrow opening	combine a stop and a fricative	let air escape over the sides of the tongue	let air escape over the center of the tongue	barely obstruct airflow
p, t, k, b, d, g	m, n, ng	f, s, v, z	ch, j	l	r	w, y (r)

MANNER OF ARTICULATION

say "reed," "rid," "raid," "red," and "rad."[6] Vowels also differ according to whether they are made in the front, center, or back of the mouth: "if you start with your tongue forward and fairly close to the roof of your mouth, and slowly lower your tongue and jaw, you will pronounce, in order, [ē] (as in *beet*), [ā] (as in *babe*), [ĕ] (as in *bet*), and finally, with the tongue and jaw in the lowest position, [ah] (as in *pot*)."[7] A vowel may be articulated with rounded or spread lips (contrast "ooo" with "eee") or with neither (e.g., "ahhh"). Muscle tension in the mouth and throat also affects the sound of the vowel; compare "bait" with "bet." Like consonants, vowels are voiced and, in some languages, unvoiced (e.g., Japanese[8]).

2.1.1.b Sound Change

Language is constantly changing, and one of the ways it changes is how words or phrases are pronounced. Consider how different Shakespearean English sounds to speakers of modern English. Consider also the English slang expression "got you," widely pronounced as "gotcha." Linguists generally believe that many sounds change in predictable ways, regardless of the actual language. A variety of factors cause sound change, but one significant reason is that speakers tend to simplify speech; that is, language

---

6. Peter James Silzer and Thomas John Finley, *How Biblical Languages Work: A Student's Guide to Learning Hebrew and Greek* (Grand Rapids: Kregel, 2004), 52–53.

7. Black, *Linguistics for Students of New Testament Greek*, 35–36.

8. Black, *Linguistics for Students of New Testament Greek*, 35.

	Front	Center	Back
High	heed hid	(none)	cool book
Mid	paid red	pun	snow

VOWEL SOUNDS

tends to take the path of least resistance. Some of the more common changes are described below:

- **Assimilation.** One sound becomes like a nearby, often adjacent, sound: e.g., English "in" + "possible" becomes "impossible" because the "m" phoneme is more similar than the "n" to the "p" phoneme; English "in" + "legal" becomes "illegal."

- **Deletion.** A sound (usually a vowel) drops out from a word. Deletion can happen in the middle of a word (known as "syncope"), at the beginning of a word (known as "aphaeresis"), or at the end of a word (known as "apocope").

  - "fam-i-ly" is pronounced "fam-ly"

  - "stic-ca" in Old English is pronounced "stick" in Modern English[9]

  - "around" becomes "round"

  - Greek διά αὐτοῦ (dia autou, "through him") becomes δι' αὐτοῦ

---

9. Lyle Campbell, *Historical Linguistics: An Introduction*, 2nd. ed. (Cambridge, MA: MIT Press, 2004), 34. Many nicknames from full names with an unaccented final vowel sound could also fall under the category of apocope: "Bonnie" becomes "Bon;" "Jenny" becomes "Jen;" "Becca" becomes "Bec(k)."

- **Contraction** is a kind of deletion that occurs when two words are joined together.

  - "did not" becomes "didn't"

- **Elision** is a kind of deletion that occurs when a sound drops out in a word or between words, and the words run together in pronunciation.

  - Compare the pronunciation of "the" in "the chair" and "the elephant," where the words run together.

  - "pine nuts" is pronounced as if there is one "n"

- **Insertion**. A sound is inserted in a word: e.g., "ath-lete" > "ath-i-lete." This sound change is also known as "epenthesis" (lit. "up in" + "I place" = "I insert"[10]).

- **Apophony**. Vowel sounds in forms of the same root word change the meaning: e.g., the English verb forms "sing," "sang," "sung," and then the noun "song."

- **Metathesis**. Two sounds transpose, or switch, places. Sometimes this is an accidental occurrence, as when someone says "irrevelant" but means "irrelevant," but many transpositions are not: e.g., "asteriks" for "asterisk" or "axe" for "ask," a pronunciation that dates back to Old English.[11]

2.1.2 PHONOLOGY AND THE BIBLICAL LANGUAGES

Understanding the basics of phonology and sound change can help with learning biblical Hebrew and Greek. Knowing why different forms look the way they do may aid in recognizing and remembering vocabulary and paradigms.

---

10. Black, *Linguistics for Students of New Testament Greek*, 45.
11. Black, *Linguistics for Students of New Testament Greek*, 48.

2.1.2.a Phonology and Biblical Hebrew

Many students have memorized Hebrew paradigms and vocabulary forms with the mistaken impression that the differences (and difficulties) are "just the way it is" with Hebrew. However, many "irregularities" in biblical Hebrew are probably the result of regular sound changes.[12] For example, the word מֶלֶךְ (melek, "king") occurs in a number of forms with different vowels. The plural form is מְלָכִים (mělākîm), and the masculine singular form with a possessive suffix is מַלְכּוֹ (malkô). What accounts for the different vowels? Most scholars of biblical Hebrew believe that early in the development of the language, the word for "king" was *מַלְכּוּ (*malku),[13] formed from the root מלך (mlk), a short "a" vowel, and a short "u" ending representing a nominative case ending. When case endings dropped off in the language (called apocope), the word was *מַלְךְ (*malk). This form picked up an extra vowel sound between the "l" and "k," presumably because it made the word easier to pronounce. The easiest vowel sound to insert (epenthesis) in an unstressed syllable is "e," so the word became *מַלֶךְ (*malek), and then the "a" of the accented syllable assimilated to the second "e," creating the form we know in biblical Hebrew: מֶלֶךְ (melek). The suffixed form מַלְכּוֹ (malkô) preserves the original "a" vowel of *מַלְכּוּ (*malku). Scholars cannot prove that this is what happened, especially since we have no native speakers of the ancient Hebrew language. However, this is how they hypothesize the development of the word—and of other Hebrew segolates (the name for the pattern of words like melek)—based on what we know about sound changes:

$$\text{מֶלֶךְ} > \text{מַלֶךְ} > \text{מַלְךְ} > \text{מַלְכּוּ}$$

   The hypothesis for how plural forms of Hebrew segolates formed also follows known sound change patterns. The plural of מֶלֶךְ (melek,"king") is מְלָכִים (mělākîm). Scholars think the base form of the plural was *מַלַךְ (*malak), and the masculine plural suffix ‑ים (-îm) gets added to that to form

---

12. Because there are no native speakers of biblical Hebrew to consult and because the linguistic data is limited, linguists cannot be sure how words developed. Based on the data available and their knowledge of how sounds change, biblical Hebrew scholars have hypothesized the development of the language.

13. Asterisks indicate unattested, hypothetical forms used to describe the possible historical development of an attested form.

מַלְכִים* (*malakîm). The stress shifts to the last syllable, ים (-îm), and this shift affects the earlier vowel sounds. Consider what happens to the first syllable of the English noun "pro-duce" in the verb form "pro-duce." The shift of stress shortens or, technically, reduces the earlier vowel from "ō" to the schwa, "ə." In Hebrew nouns the general sound-change rule is that the shift of stress shortens a vowel that is two syllables removed from the stressed syllable (the "propretonic syllable"), but it lengthens the vowel immediately preceding the stressed syllable (the "pretonic syllable"). Thus the shift of stress with the masculine plural suffix of מַלְכִים* (*malakim) causes the first vowel to reduce to *shewa* and the second vowel to lengthen from a *patach* to a *qamets*: מְלָכִים (*mĕlākîm*).

2.1.2.b Phonology and New Testament Greek

Greek verbal paradigms reflect a great deal of sound change, and there is also sound change as verb forms become nouns. The sound change known as apophony, the changing of a vowel sound in forms of the same root word to change the meaning, is one common way Greek creates forms with different meanings. Black provides the following illustrations of apophony in Greek verbs and nouns:[14]

The verb λείπω (*leipō*, "I leave"):
- Present: λείπω (*leipō*)

- Aorist: ἔλιπον (*elipon*)

- Perfect: λέλοιπα (*leloipa*)

The alternation of *epsilon* (ε) and *omicron* (o) to form nouns from verbs:
- φέρω (*pherō*, "I carry") becomes φορός (*phoros*, "burden").

- λέγω (*legō*, "I speak") becomes λόγος (*logos*, "word").

Sound changes are normal and often predictable processes in languages. Understanding why and how sounds change can help with learning Greek and Hebrew because the changes will no longer appear to be so random.

---

14. Black, *Linguistics for Students of New Testament Greek*, 43–44.

2.1.3 RESOURCES FOR FURTHER STUDY

Black, David Alan. "Phonology: The Sounds of Greek." Pages 23–52 in
    Linguistics for Students of New Testament Greek: A Survey of Basic
    Concepts and Applications. 2nd ed. Grand Rapids: Baker, 1995.

> Black's introduction to linguistics is quite thorough in its
> treatment of each subfield. His chapter on phonology details how
> consonant and vowel sounds are made, which phonemes occur
> in Greek, and some of the important phonological changes that
> occur in NT Greek.

Blau, Joshua. "Phonetics." Pages 63–71 in *Phonology and Morphology*
    of Biblical Hebrew: An Introduction. Winona Lake, IN:
    Eisenbrauns, 2010.

> Blau's chapter on phonetics provides a helpful overview of the
> main sounds used in biblical Hebrew. He explains how the
> sounds are formed and distinguishes sounds based on duration,
> place of articulation, resonance, and voicing.

Silzer, Peter James, and Thomas John Finley. "Can You Spell That?
    Reading and Writing." Pages 39–73 in *How Biblical Languages Work:*
    A Student's Guide to Learning Hebrew and Greek. Grand Rapids:
    Kregel, 2004.

> Silzer and Finley's introduction to the biblical languages works
> through each area of linguistics and how it applies to Hebrew
> and Greek. Their treatment of each area is readable and amply
> illustrated, and since they address both biblical languages, they
> do not include the level of detail that Black does.

2.2 MORPHOLOGY

The first building blocks of a language are its phonemes, the sounds that
are strung together to form words. But words do not result from randomly
running sounds together. Rather, words are meaningful constructions that
each language creates by following its own rules and patterns. Morphology
is the study of how languages form their words.

2.2.1 MORPHOLOGY EXPLAINED

We often think of words as the smallest units of meaning in a language, but words often contain several units of meaning. Consider how the meaning of the word "dog" changes when an "s" is added to the end: "dogs." Then consider the difference between "dogs" and "dog's." These examples have three distinct units of meaning: the word "dog," the letter "s," and the letter "s" with an apostrophe.[15] Each unit of meaning is called a "morpheme." The term "lexeme" indicates a basic lexical unit—a word and all its morphological forms. The preceding examples are all morphological changes applied to the lexeme "dog." However, the lexeme "dog" is also a morpheme. In other words, morphemes may or may not be complete words. The morpheme "dog" can stand alone; it is a "free morpheme." But the morpheme "s" must be attached to another morpheme to have meaning; it is a "bound morpheme."

Morphemes are also categorized according to whether they are roots or affixes. A root morpheme carries the main content of a word's meaning (e.g., "dog"), while an affix adds meaning or grammatical information (e.g., "s" or apostrophe "s"). A root in English is most commonly a free morpheme, though it may also be bound (e.g., "cran-" of "cranberry"). By contrast, both Greek and Hebrew have many roots that are bound morphemes. However, an affix is always a bound morpheme, though it can be attached in several places. When an affix is attached to the front of a root, it is a prefix, while one attached to the end of a root is a suffix. Many languages, including Greek and Hebrew (but not English), allow affixes to be inserted into the roots (i.e., "infixes") and even around the root (i.e., "circumfixes").

Some affixes change the grammatical category (or part of speech) of a word. These are called "derivational affixes." For example, adding the suffix "-tion" to a verb creates a noun: "produce" + "-tion" = "production." Other affixes are "inflectional"; they add grammatical information (e.g., tense, number) that does not change a word's function as derivational affixes do (e.g., "s" added to "dog" makes the singular word plural).

---

15. While the letter "s" is always a phoneme because it represents a sound, in this case it is also a morpheme because it changes the meaning of "dog."

2.2.1.a Nominal Morphology

Every word encodes meaning, and depending on the complexity of its morphology, a word may encode several components of meaning. Nouns and pronouns identify people, objects, and ideas, and the forms may encode answers to several questions: How many (i.e., number)? What kind (i.e., grammatical gender)? How does it relate to me (i.e., person)? How is it functioning in this sentence (i.e., case)?[16]

Nouns can be singular or plural, and in some languages, dual. In English, the most common way to form a plural noun is to add the affix "-s" to the singular root. However, not all nouns follow this pattern. For example, the singular "child" has a morpheme "-ren" affixed to it to make the plural "children."

Nouns in many languages have gender—that is, they are grammatically masculine, feminine, or even neuter. (Grammatical gender applies to non-animate nouns as well as animate ones.) While English does not assign gender to all its nouns, some gender-specific suffixes have traditionally indicated biological gender: e.g., "-er"/"-or" and "-ress," as in "waiter" and "waitress" or "actor" and "actress." Many English pronouns also indicate gender: he, she, his, hers (but compare "you," "they," and "we").

Pronouns in English, as well as in Hebrew and Greek, carry grammatical information about their relationship to the speaker. This is known as "person." The speaker is "first person": I, we, us, our. The person addressed is "second person," and unlike many languages, English does not distinguish between number (singular or plural) or gender: you, your, yours. "Third person" is the person being talked about, and some English pronouns distinguish gender while others do not. Compare the masculine, feminine, and neuter forms "he/she/it" and "his/hers/its," with the non-gendered forms "they/them/theirs."

The final piece of grammatical information that a noun encodes is its role in the sentence—that is, is it a subject or an object? This grammatical category is called "case." A noun that performs the action (i.e., the subject) is in the nominative case (e.g., "I" or "girl"). When a noun receives the action (i.e., the object), it is in the accusative case (e.g., "me" or "girl"). A noun that possesses something is in the genitive case (e.g., "my" or "girl's").

---

16. Silzer and Finley, *How Biblical Languages Work*, 87.

New Testament Greek marks case with suffix morphemes, and it includes a fourth case, the dative case, the noun (or pronoun) to which something is given. (The comparable form in English is the indirect object: "The girl gave *me* the book.") For the most part, biblical Hebrew does not mark case, though earlier forms of the language did.

Biblical Greek has three grammatical categories for gender: masculine, feminine, and neuter. Biblical Hebrew only distinguishes grammatically between masculine and feminine. Hebrew has several morphemes to indicate number, but unlike English, these morphemes also encode the gender and role of the noun in the sentence. For example, the masculine plural morpheme is םי- (-*îm*) or י- (-*ēy*), depending whether the noun is absolute or in construct with another noun. Similarly, Greek nouns indicate gender, number, and case by their endings. Pronouns in both languages also indicate person.

2.2.1.b Verbal Morphology

The morphology of verbs is typically more complex than that of nouns. They incorporate much of the same information as nouns (i.e., gender, number, person), but verbs of many languages encode a great deal more information. They may indicate the timing of the action—that is, whether something happens in the past, present, or future (i.e., tense): e.g., I slept, I sleep, I will sleep. Verbs also can indicate whether an action is complete or is in process: e.g., "I slept" is a complete action; "I was sleeping"

TERM	QUESTION IT ANSWERS	KINDS OF ANSWERS
Number	How many?	singular, plural, (dual)
Gender	What kind?	masculine, feminine, (neuter)
Person	Relation to the speaker?	first, second, third
Case	How is it functioning?	subject, object

NOMINAL MORPHOLOGY

or "I have been sleeping" is an incomplete action. This verbal category is called "aspect." Verbs may encode "voice," that is, whether the subject controls the action (active voice) or is being controlled by it (passive voice): e.g., "The dog walked" (active) and "The dog was walked" (passive). Verbs also include information about "mood" (also "modality"), a category that indicates the degree of certainty with which something is said or that expresses the statement's relationship to reality. In English grammar, the most common modal categories are declarative, imperative, interrogative, and subjunctive—although these are not necessarily indicated grammatically. Similarly, biblical Hebrew does not grammatically indicate many of its modal categories. The common exceptions are imperative forms and unique jussive forms. Verbs in biblical Greek are morphologically marked as one of four moods: indicative, imperative, subjunctive, or optative.

As with nouns, particular verbal morphemes carry meaning. Most are bound morphemes, such as the past tense suffix "-ed," although free morphemes are not unknown in English (i.e., the word "will" of the future tense). In both Greek and Hebrew, verbal paradigms indicate which affixes attach to the root morphemes to conjugate the verbs properly. Some morphemes may change their "phonetic shape," depending on the surrounding morphemes. For example, the past tense suffix "-ed" is added to "walk" to make "walked," but if a verb already ends in "e," such as "receive," then the past tense morpheme is simply "-d." The past tense suffixes "-ed" and "-d" are allomorphs.

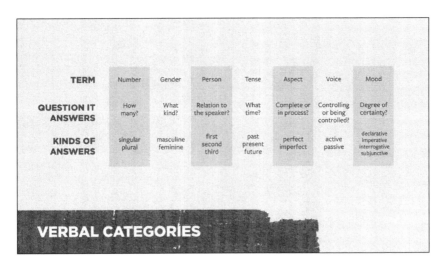

TERM	Number	Gender	Person	Tense	Aspect	Voice	Mood
QUESTION IT ANSWERS	How many?	What kind?	Relation to the speaker?	What time?	Complete or in process?	Controlling or being controlled?	Degree of certainty?
KINDS OF ANSWERS	singular plural	masculine feminine	first second third	past present future	perfect imperfect	active passive	declarative imperative interrogative subjunctive

VERBAL CATEGORIES

2.2.2 MORPHOLOGY AND THE BIBLICAL LANGUAGES

Understanding how morphology works can help with learning biblical Hebrew and Greek. Recognizing morphemes and their meanings can make it easier to remember vocabulary and parse Hebrew and Greek forms.

2.2.2.a Morphology and Biblical Hebrew

It is daunting to face the pages of paradigms in standard biblical Hebrew textbooks. However, mastering a handful of paradigms can help you recognize morphemes that are used across the language. For example, the following paradigm of suffixes on the *lamed* preposition is easy to learn and provides a guide for recognizing the suffix morphemes that express gender, number, and person on prepositions, nouns, pronouns, and even direct objects attached to verbs. Phonology and other factors may cause differences in certain forms that include these morphemes, but learning the paradigm is a good place to start.

Pronominal Suffixes with the *Lamed* Preposition				
לוֹ	*lô*	*to him*	The third-masculine singular suffix is וֹ (-ô).	Compare noun סוּסוֹ (*sûsô*; "his horse") and verb דִּבְּרוֹ (*dibběrô*; "he spoke it").
לָהּ	*lâ*	*to her*	The third-feminine singular suffix is הָ (-â).	Compare noun סוּסָהּ (*sûsâ*; "her horse") and verb שִׁלְּחָהּ (*šilěhāh*; "he sent her").
לְךָ	*lᵉkā*	*to you* (masc.)	The second-masculine singular suffix is ךָ (-kā).	Compare noun סוּסְךָ (*sûsěkā*; "your horse") and verb קִבֶּצְךָ (*qibbeṣkā*; "he gathered you").
לָךְ	*lāk*	*to you* (fem.)	The second-feminine singular suffix is ךְ (-k).	Compare noun סוּסֵךְ (*sûsēk*; "your horse") and verb שְׁלָחֵךְ (*šělāhēk*; "he sent you").
לִי	*lî*	*to me*	The first-common singular suffix is י (-î).	Compare noun סוּסִי (*sûsî*; "my horse") and verb שְׁלָחָנִי (*šělāhanî*; "he sent me").

Pronominal Suffixes with the *Lamed* Preposition				
לָהֶם	*lāhem*	*to them (masc. pl.)*	The third-masculine plural suffix is הֶם (-hem).	Compare noun סוּסָם (*sûsām*; "their horse,") and verb שְׁלָחָם (*šĕlāḥām*; "he sent them").
לָהֶן	*lāhen*	*to them (fem. pl.)*	The third-feminine plural suffix is הֶן (-hen).	Compare noun סוּסָן (*sûsān*; "their horse") and verb קִבְּצָן (*qibbĕṣān*; "he gathered them").
לָכֶם	*lākem*	*to you (masc. pl.)*	The second-masculine plural suffix is כֶם (-kem).	Compare noun סוּסְכֶם (*sûsĕkem*; "your horse") and verb אֲלַמֶּדְכֶם (*'ălammedkem*; "I will teach you").
לָכֶן	*lāken*	*to you (fem. pl.)*	The second-feminine plural suffix is כֶן (-ken).	Compare noun סוּסְכֶן (*sûsĕken*; "your horse"). The suffix is never used with a finite verb in Biblical Hebrew; it appears once with an infinitive: יַלֶּדְכֶן (*yalledken*).
לָנוּ	*lānû*	*to us*	The first-common plural suffix is נוּ (-nû).	Compare noun סוּסֵנוּ (*sûsēnû*; "our horse") and verb שְׁלָחָנוּ (*šĕlāḥānû*; "he sent us").

2.2.2.b Morphology and New Testament Greek

The vocabulary of New Testament Greek is limited to several thousand words, but it is still quite difficult to master. Learning Greek vocabulary becomes much simpler when you memorize certain morphemes and understand how the language constructs words. In his handbook for learning New Testament vocabulary, Robert Van Voorst provides lists of well-known NT words with lists and meanings of their affixes. Learning the general pattern allows a student to transfer knowledge to vocabulary they have not memorized yet. The examples below are excerpted from Van Voorst's information:[17]

Nominal Suffix Morpheme	Typical Significance/ Meaning	Example NT Word
-ος (-os)	person, thing	θεός (theos) "god, God"
-της (-tēs)	person, agent	κριτής (kritēs) "judge"
-τις (-tis)	activity	πίστις (pistis) "faith"
-μα (-ma)	result of an activity	γράμμα (gramma) "letter"
-ια (-ia)	abstraction, quality	σωτηρία (sōtēria) "salvation"
-ιον (-ion)	diminution	παιδίον (paidion) "infant"

2.2.3 RESOURCES FOR FURTHER STUDY

Black, David Allan. "Morphology: The Anatomy of Greek Words." Pages 53–95 in *Linguistics for Students of New Testament Greek: A Survey of Basic Concepts and Applications*. 2nd ed. Grand Rapids: Baker, 1995.

Black's introduction to linguistics is quite thorough in its treatment of each subfield. His chapter on morphology includes the basics of word construction, and then he provides a lengthy itemization of Greek roots and affixes, as well as some of the rules behind putting them together.

Blau, Joshua. "Morphology." Pages 156–283 in *Phonology and Morphology of Biblical Hebrew*. Winona Lake, IN: Eisenbrauns, 2010.

Blau offers a dense and comprehensive look at Hebrew morphology. His chapter devoted to morphology runs over 125 pages. Advanced students with a deep interest in the workings of Hebrew morphology will find his work indispensable.

Silzer, Peter James, and Thomas John Finley. "Putting It into Words: How Words Are Made." Pages 74–117 in *How Biblical Languages Work:*

---

17. Robert E. Van Voorst, *Building Your New Testament Greek Vocabulary*, 3rd ed. (Atlanta: Society of Biblical Literature, 2001), 5.

A Student's Guide to Learning Hebrew and Greek. Grand Rapids: Kregel, 2004.

Silzer and Finley's introduction to the biblical languages works through each area of linguistics and how it applies to Hebrew and Greek. Their treatment of each area is readable and amply illustrated, and since they address both biblical languages, they do not include the level of detail found in either Black or Blau.

Van Voorst, Robert E. "Basic Principles of Greek Word Building." Pages 4–11 in *Building Your New Testament Greek Vocabulary*. 3rd ed. Atlanta: Society of Biblical Literature, 2001.

Van Voorst's handbook uses principles of morphology in conjunction with cognate relationships of Greek vocabulary to help students memorize and remember the words more easily.

2.3 SEMANTICS

Semantics is the study of how a language creates meaning, an enterprise that Cotterell and Turner describe as "far more complex than we might initially suppose."[18] When we try to determine what a word, phrase, or sentence means, we encounter the question, "Whose meaning?" The author meant something, although without direct access to an author, we cannot be certain we have correctly understood what that was. Deciding what the author meant requires a degree of subjectivity. A second kind of meaning is the meaning of the text, that is, what the words and phrases themselves mean—apart from what the author may have intended. Determining this meaning involves a more objective analysis of a text, based on word definitions and rules of grammar and syntax.

A third meaning that can sometimes help us get at the author's meaning is the perceived meaning, that is, what the original audience may have understood the author/speaker to mean. This can be especially helpful with the biblical text, since the distance in time and culture between the author and a modern audience is enormous. Cotterell and Turner illustrate

---

18. Peter Cotterell and Max Turner, *Linguistics & Biblical Interpretation* (Downers Grove, IL: InterVarsity Press, 1989), 38.

this kind of meaning with Jesus' response to his accusers in Luke 22:70. They asked if he was the Son of God, and he replied, "You say that I am," a response they understood as affirmative: "Why do we have need of further testimony? For we ourselves have heard it from his mouth" (Luke 22:71). Cotterell and Turner remark,

> The situation being depicted is very dramatic but linguistically unclear. Any credible attempt to understand what Luke signals when he thus records the words of Jesus must take into account the way in which he describes the perception of those words by those who then heard it. For his hearers were well qualified to understand it, better qualified, indeed, than the modern exegete could possibly be.[19]

We cannot address all these aspects of meaning in the discussion that follows. Rather, we will focus on the second kind of meaning—namely, what the words and phrases themselves mean. We will focus primarily on meaning at or below the sentence level.

2.3.1 SEMANTICS EXPLAINED

Semantics is related to syntax, which we will discuss in the next section (see §2.4 Syntax), but unlike syntax, semantics is not concerned about the rules that dictate word arrangement. It cares about the meaning of words and what meaning their arrangement produces.

When we say a word "means" something, we are saying that it refers to something. Some words refer to tangible things, such as the word "chair" referring to an object on which people sit. Some refer to abstract things, like the word "anger," which refers to an emotion of strong displeasure. These words denote, or refer to, a particular thing, whether tangible or abstract. For the most part, they are arbitrary labels; that is, there is no good reason for the word "chair" instead of "cat" to refer to an object people sit on. At some point in the development of our language, "chair" became the verbal symbol for an object people sit on. In linguistics terminology, the object is the "signified" and the word "chair" is the "signifier."

Words often evoke more meaning than just the signified object. Consider the word "winter," which simply denotes the season of the year when a

---

19. Cotterell and Turner, *Linguistics & Biblical Interpretation*, 45.

given land region is farthest from the sun. For some people, "winter" connotes negative things, such as darkness, cold, and bad weather. For others, "winter" carries positive connotations, such as skiing, Christmas, and snow days. Connotations are the values and attitudes we associate with a given word. They are often culturally specific, and many are even individually determined. For example, the word "father" denotes a biological relationship, but it connotes something different for everyone depending on their own life experiences.

Some words have more than one meaning, and the meanings are unrelated. For example, the English word "bat" can refer to a baseball bat or a flying mammal. Words such as this are called homonyms, and they typically appear as separate entries in a dictionary. However, many words have more than one meaning, and the meanings are related. The word has a primary meaning and then secondary meanings that may have developed from it. These secondary meanings are often what we call figurative language or metaphoric. Consider the verb "roast." The primary meaning of "roast" refers to a cooking technique: "Bob roasted the potatoes." However, a person who is too warm might say, "I am roasting," a meaning that is obviously related to the primary meaning. The verb can also refer to severe criticism: "The president roasted the finance committee for falsifying its budget." Finally, a group of friends might "roast" a colleague with tongue-in-cheek ridicule at an occasion meant to honor him. "Roast" is "polysemous"; it has more than one meaning, but the meanings are related.

In each of these examples the only way to be certain of the word's meaning is through context. Unless the speaker intended to make a pun or use the word's ambiguity for rhetorical effect, no native speaker would read the sentence with the wrong meaning. Nor would anyone alter their understanding of the sentence based on all possible meanings of the word. Users of language understand how it "works"—and effective communication depends on people following the same unwritten rules.

Many people forget the rules of their own language when they approach Bible study. The authors of the Bible did make use of word play and ambiguity, but this does not give us the liberty to be vague whenever it is difficult to decide on an interpretation. D. A. Carson illustrates with Stephen's use of ἐκκλησία (ekklēsia; "assembly, church") in Acts 7:38:

It would be admittedly invalid to overload Acts 7:38 with all the senses in which ἐκκλησία [ekklēsia, "church"] is used by the apostles; some of these senses (e.g., reference to the so-called universal church) would actually be contradictory in this verse. However, it is easy, especially in the course of a sermon, to comment on the broad meanings of a word at the risk of obscuring its specific function in a given text.[20]

Moisés Silva provides a second illustration with Jesus' statement in Mark 11:22, "Ἔχετε πίστιν θεοῦ" (echete pistin theou): "have faith of God" or "have faith in God." Silva says,

> It is difficult for most of us, having been taught that possession is the "primary meaning" of the genitive, to take the construction exclusively as an objective genitive, "have faith in God." We may therefore be tempted somehow to combine both ideas: "to have true faith in God means to have God's own faith." Some interpreters may even argue that such an approach is its own best confirmation—the fuller the meaning, the more valid the interpretation is likely to be. As we have seen, however, language works differently—context serves to *eliminate* multiple meanings. ... In view of the nature of language and communication, however, we should assume *one* meaning unless there are strong *exegetical* (literary, contextual) grounds to the contrary.[21]

We are not free to pick the sense of the word we want—or to pick several senses. The meaning is dictated by context, a rule we readily recognize in our own language.

2.3.2 APPROACHES TO LEXICAL SEMANTICS

The branch of semantics that focuses its study on the word or phrase is lexical semantics.[22] However, lexical semantics is not interested in *all* words.

---

20. D. A. Carson, *Exegetical Fallacies*, 2nd ed. (Grand Rapids: Baker, 1996), 61.

21. Moisés Silva, *Biblical Words and Their Meaning: An Introduction to Lexical Semantics*, rev. and exp. ed. (Grand Rapids, Zondervan, 1994), 150-51. Emphasis original.

22. Lexical semantics is one of several approaches to studying meaning. Alan Cruse identifies four other approaches: grammatical semantics, logical semantics, and linguistic

Linguists often classify words into two groups (or classes): a closed group and an open group. The closed group of words in every language is small and it encompasses words that "do not refer to any sort of reality outside of the grammatical relations of the language." These "function words" include articles (e.g., a, an, the), prepositions (e.g., to, from, in), conjunctions (e.g., and, but), and pronouns (e.g., you, she, them). They carry grammatical meaning, but not content meaning or lexical meaning. Languages do not readily admit new words into this closed class.[24]

By contrast, the open class of words is always changing. Sometimes called "content words," these words refer to "people, things, ideas, actions, qualities, or quantities"[25]—that is, they are the nouns, verbs, adjectives, and adverbs of a language. A language can create as many new words as it needs to reflect its culture. Lexical semantics is the study of a language's content words.

Two approaches to lexical semantics have characterized the study of word and phrase meaning in biblical scholarship: componential analysis and conceptual (or cognitive) semantics. These are not the only ways linguists study meaning, but we will limit our discussion to them since they are the most relevant for linguistics in biblical studies.[26]

2.3.2.a Componential Analysis

One approach to defining words is the identification of features that are essential and non-essential to the word's meaning. For example, the definition of "car" requires, among other things, that the object have four wheels, but it does not include how many doors or windows it must have. This way of defining words is based on the ability to categorize, a function of all living creatures to some extent. Linguist John Taylor notes that even an animal "has to be able, at the very least, to distinguish between what is edible from what is inedible, what is benign from what is harmful. And in

---

pragmatics (*Meaning in Language: An Introduction to Semantics and Pragmatics*, 2nd. ed., Oxford Textbooks in Linguistics [Oxford: Oxford University Press, 2004], 14–15).

23. Silzer and Finley, *How Biblical Languages Work*, 82.

24. Grammatical semantics studies the meanings of words in a closed set.

25. Silzer and Finley, *How Biblical Languages Work*, 81.

26. Cruse details six approaches in his textbook (*Meaning in Language*, 93–99).

order to mate and reproduce, a creature must be able to recognize its own kind."[27] The human mind, especially, is wired for categorization.

The classic approach to categorization is known as "componential analysis." Aristotle distinguished between a thing's essence and its accidents, and from this distinction componential analysis defines a "thing" in terms of what is essential for membership and what is not (i.e., Aristotle's "accidents"). The combination of essential features gives a word its meaning. For example, the English word "spinster" includes four essential features: [human], [female], [adult], and [never married]. A spinster is someone who is [+human], [+female], [+adult], and [+never married]. (In compential analysis, meaning is described according to the presence or absence of distinguishing features, usually indicated by a plus or minus sign [+/-].) If any of these four features is absent [-], the entity cannot be a spinster; for example, a young girl is [+human], [+female], and [+never married], but since she is [-adult], she cannot qualify as a spinster. The meanings of words are based on relationships of binary opposition.

Componential analysis provided a helpful way for lexicographers to analyze the semantics of a language. It gave them a principled way to describe the relationships between words and thus better understand the semantic structure of a language. However, other linguists found several limitations of componential analysis. First, the sheer number of categories required to define all words in every language is unrealistic.[28] Further, componential analysis did not have a way to rank the relative importance of features. For example, how important is the ability to fly to the definition of a "bird"? Is it as important as the feature of having wings? Third, the rigid categorization of componential analysis is too simplistic to capture finer nuances of meaning. Consider the words *boy* and *girl*. They each are [+young] and [+human] and only differ with regard to gender. However, if you contrast *man* and *boy* and then *woman* and *girl*, you discover that the differences extend beyond gender: in English *girl* is often used interchangeably with *woman* (e.g., "The Golden Girls"), whereas it is less acceptable to use *boy* instead of *man*. Finally, componential analysis cannot account for figurative language. Consider Taylor's illustration: *Sally is a block of ice.*

---

27. John R. Taylor, *Linguistic Categorization*, 3rd ed., (Oxford: Oxford University Press), xi.
28. Taylor, *Linguistic Categorization*, 31.

According to componential analysis, "ice" is an inanimate object, and it is impossible for Sally, who is animate, to also be inanimate.[29]

2.3.2.b Conceptual or Cognitive Semantics

The limitations of componential analysis and advances in science about how the brain works led many linguists to think about meaning differently. Categories may be fundamental to the way we think, but their boundaries tend to be fluid instead of rigid (as in componential analysis). Such flexibility allows us to include penguins, robins, and ostriches in the category of "bird."

Twentieth-century philosopher Ludwig Wittgenstein proposed the idea of "family resemblance" to describe how we categorize: "members of a large family typically resemble one another in a variety of ways, but there are no features which they all have, and there may be members who share no features, but these will nonetheless be linked to the others by a chain of resemblance."[30] Others developed Wittgenstein's idea, observing that we do not think of members in a category equally. For example, many people would consider a robin to be more "bird-like" than a penguin. There are better and worse representatives in every category. The best representation of a category is a prototypical member, and the worst are considered marginal members (see §5.6.2.b Prototype Theory).

At the heart of this approach to semantics is the belief that humans think in broad concepts that are being continually shaped by life experiences. Meaning is not a set of static features that an entity has or does not have. Rather it is a dynamic network of events, situations, ideas, and so on. Taylor summarizes,

> We apprehend and learn categories (at least, many of them) holistically, in the context of our interaction with the world. We do not understand categories by breaking them down into their components, neither do we "build up", or "assemble" categories out of their defining features, of the kind that might be contained in definitions.[31]

---

29. Taylor, *Linguistic Categorization*, 133.
30. Alan Cruse, *Meaning in Language*, 98.
31. Taylor, *Linguistic Categorization*, 38.

The cognitive or conceptual approach to semantics falls within the broader field of cognitive linguistics and will be discussed in greater detail below (see §5.6 Cognitive Linguistics).

2.3.3 SEMANTICS AND THE BIBLICAL LANGUAGES

Biblical studies depend on the work of semantics. We read, study, and preach from a book written in two languages most people do not know—and many who do know them have limited skills. Even the experts in the fields of biblical Greek and Hebrew are limited by time and space from the original authors and audiences. The task of translating and interpreting the Bible for new generations and different cultures is ongoing, and so is our need for linguistically grounded semantic practice.

Those who study and teach the Bible typically learn the importance of semantic analysis when they work through a passage of Scripture. The kind of semantic analysis they learn is the word study, a process that is fundamental to exegesis. However, word studies are also landmines for bad exegesis. The definitive statement on "word studies" is D. A. Carson's chapter "Word-Study Fallacies" in his indispensable book, *Exegetical Fallacies*.[32] Carson discusses 16 fallacies that plague the study of Greek and Hebrew words. We detail just a few below:

2.3.3.a Semantics and Biblical Hebrew

It has been popular in studies of the biblical languages to link language and mentality, or worldview, and then make exegetical claims based on a supposed relationship. For example, the authors of an introductory textbook to the Bible describe the Hebrew language as having "biographical suitability," which presumably makes it a better language than others for recounting the stories of OT characters. Further, they agree with the statement that the Hebrew people "thought in pictures, and consequently [their] nouns are concrete and vivid. There is no such thing as neuter gender, for the Semite everything is alive."[33] Carson calls this the "linkage of language

---

32. D. A. Carson, *Exegetical Fallacies*, 2nd ed. (Grand Rapids: Baker, 1996), 27–64.

33. Norman L. Geisler and William E. Nix, *A General Introduction to the Bible* (Chicago: Moody, 1968), 219, quoted in Moisés Silva, *Biblical Words and Their Meaning: An Introduction to Lexical Semantics*, rev. and exp. ed. (Grand Rapids: Zondervan, 2010), 21. Silva notes that Geisler and Nix were, in fact, quoting "with approval" from an earlier work.

and mentality" fallacy: "The heart of this fallacy is the assumption that any language so constrains the thinking processes of the people who use it that they are forced into certain patterns of thought and shielded from others. Language and mentality thus become confused."[34] Another aspect of this fallacy is when exegetes contrast Hebrew and Greek and then draw significance from supposed differences.[35]

2.3.3.b Semantics and New Testament Greek

From morphology we know that roots carry the main content of a word's meaning (see §2.2.1 Morphology Explained above), but it is a mistake to think that the meaning of a root always determines a word's meaning. Carson calls this the "root fallacy" and describes it as follows: "the root fallacy presupposes that every word actually *has* a meaning bound up with its shape or its components. In this view, meaning is determined by etymology."[36] Even in English we can find examples, such as the word "butterfly," which no one thinks has anything to do with butter, even though "butter" is a component of the word "butterfly." Carson illustrates with the New Testament word ἀπόστολος (apostolos, "apostle"), which is related to the verb ἀποστέλλω (apostellō), which means "I sent." Based on the shared root, it has often been said that an apostle is "one who is sent." However, actual usage in the NT takes a different focus. Carson summarizes:

> New Testament use of the noun does not center on the meaning *the one sent* but on "messenger." Now a messenger is usually sent; but the word *messenger* also calls to mind the message the person carries, and suggests he represents the one who sent him. In other words, actual usage in the New Testament suggests that ἀπόστολος (apostolos) commonly bears the meaning a *special representative* or a *special messenger* rather than "someone sent out."[37]

Describing a related fallacy, Carson highlights how we combine the root fallacy with a change in language over time. The "semantic anachronism"

---

34. Carson, *Exegetical Fallacies*, 44.

35. See Carson's illustration about the purported superiority of Greek for New Testament revelation (*Exegetical Fallacies*, 45).

36. Carson, *Exegetical Fallacies*, 28.

37. Carson, *Exegetical Fallacies*, 30.

fallacy happens "when a late use of a word is read back into earlier literature."[38] A classic example of this is the Greek word δύναμις (dynamis, "power, miracle"), which Paul uses in Rom 1:16 to describe the gospel: "it is the δύναμις of God for salvation to everyone who believes." Many have used this verse to talk about the gospel being the "dynamite of God," since our word "dynamite" derives from the Greek word δύναμις (dynamis). Carson summarizes the problem:

> It is an appeal to a kind of reverse etymology, the root fallacy compounded by anachronism. Did Paul think of dynamite when he penned this word? ... The power of God concerning which Paul speaks he often identifies with the power that raised Jesus from the dead (e.g., Eph. 1:18–20); and as it operates in us, its goal is ... aiming for the wholeness and perfection implicit in the consummation of our salvation. ... Of course, what preachers are trying to do when they talk about dynamite is give some indication of the greatness of the power involved. Even so, Paul's measure is not dynamite, but the empty tomb.[39]

2.3.4 RESOURCES FOR FURTHER STUDY

Barr, James. *The Semantics of Biblical Language*. Oxford: Oxford University Press, 1961.

> James Barr's mid-twentieth-century critique of semantic methodology in biblical scholarship set the course for better approaches to understanding the languages. His classic book addresses arguments based on "Greek and Hebrew thought," etymology, morphological and syntactic phenomena, and other linguistic issues.

Black, David Allan. "Semantics: Determining Meaning." Pages 120–42 in *Linguistics for Students of New Testament Greek: A Survey of Basic Concepts and Applications*. 2nd ed. Grand Rapids: Baker, 1995.

---

38. Carson, *Exegetical Fallacies*, 33.
39. Carson, *Exegetical Fallacies*, 34.

Black's introduction to linguistics is quite thorough in its treatment of each subfield. His chapter on semantics includes a basic overview of concepts and then concentrated application to Greek.

Carson, D. A. "Word-Study Fallacies." Pages 27-64 in *Exegetical Fallacies*. 2nd ed. Grand Rapids: Baker, 1996.

Carson's classic book *Exegetical Fallacies* includes a lengthy chapter on word studies. He provides examples of 16 kinds of word study fallacies as well as a list of resources to help students do word study properly.

Cotterell, Peter, and Max Turner. *Linguistics & Biblical Interpretation*. Downers Grove, IL: InterVarsity Press, 1989.

Cotterell and Turner's book includes a helpful multi-chapter discussion of how meaning and texts correspond. The final chapter on meaning deals specifically with lexical semantics. Included in their treatment is a chapter on "The Use and Abuse of Word Studies in Theology."

Silzer, Peter James, and Thomas John Finley. "What Do You Mean? It's Just Semantics." Pages 160-93 in *How Biblical Languages Work: A Student's Guide to Learning Hebrew and Greek*. Grand Rapids: Kregel, 2004.

Silzer and Finley, in their introduction to semantics, overview general semantic vocabulary and concepts with respect to English. They then demonstrate how an understanding of semantics helps with learning biblical Hebrew and Greek. Their treatment is readable and amply illustrated.

Thiselton, Anthony C. "Semantics and New Testament Interpretation." Pages 74–100 in *New Testament Interpretation: Essays on Principles and Methods*. Edited by I. Howard Marshall. Waynesboro, GA: Paternoster, 2005.

Thiselton's chapter in a collection of essays on NT interpretation specifically addresses some of the pitfalls of semantics. He concludes with a semantic analysis of Paul's language on "justification by faith."

2.4 SYNTAX

"Syntax" comes from the Greek word σύνταξις (*syntaxis*, "ordering together"), and it is the study of how a language arranges its words into phrases, clauses, and sentences. No language creates sentences by simply stringing words together. Rather, every language follows its own rules for combining words, and syntax is interested in deciphering the structure these rules create.

2.4.1 SYNTAX EXPLAINED

Speakers combine words to create phrases, and they join phrases to form clauses. Some clauses are complete sentences, and others combine to form sentences. Phrases, clauses, and sentences are all "syntactic units," and understanding how these units are formed is a skill all native speakers have, whether or not they can explain the formal rules of grammar behind the process. In this section, we will detail some of the features of English syntax to provide an overview of general syntactic principles which should demonstrate the significance of syntax for the study of biblical Hebrew and Greek.

2.4.1.a Words and Phrases

One of the first things students learn when they study grammar is that there are different kinds of words—that is, the parts of speech: nouns, verbs, adjectives, adverbs, pronouns, prepositions, conjunctions, and interjections. The following chart identifies the most common parts of speech and their functions:[40]

Then students learn that certain kinds of words go together. For example, adjectives describe nouns: "the large brown grizzly bear," where "large" and "brown" are adjectives describing the noun "grizzly bear." Adjectives describe nouns in every language, but languages differ in their placement of adjectives in a phrase. In English, adjectives precede nouns: "the large

---

40. Adapted from Silzer and Finley, *How Biblical Languages Work*, 81.

PART OF SPEECH	FUNCTION	EXAMPLES
Noun	Identifies people, objects, ideas	John, book, love
Pronoun	Replaces a noun or a group of word (e.g., "it" can replace "the grizzly bear")	he, them, you, which, who
Adjective	Describes a noun	dry, sacred, red
Article (or determiner)	Identifies a particular noun	a, an, the
Verb	An action or state	read, go, be
Adverb	Describes a verb, adjective, or another adverb	slowly, however, not, very
Conjunction	Joins words or groups of words	and, but, or, because
Preposition	Indicates a relationship between words	to, for, in, over
Interjection	An exclamation	Oh! Wow!

PARTS OF SPEECH

brown grizzly bear," not "the grizzly bear brown large." However, both Hebrew and Greek prefer the adjective after the noun. A noun and the words describing it create a noun phrase: "the large brown grizzly bear" is a noun phrase comprised of a noun ("grizzly bear"), two adjectives ("large, brown"), and one article ("the"). Each of these components of the phrase is called a "constituent," a term also used to describe components made up of larger syntactic units (i.e., clauses and sentences).

Another kind of phrase is the prepositional phrase, which begins with a preposition and ends with a noun or pronoun: "across the green valley." Other phrase types include verb phrases and adjective phrases.

2.4.1.b Clauses and Sentences

The next level of syntactic unit is the clause, which typically has a subject and predicate, often involving a verb. Kroeger defines a predicate as "the element of meaning which identifies the property or relationship being described."[41] In other words, a predicate may indicate that a participant possesses a certain property, as in "Chris is **angry**", or that a certain relationship holds between two or more participants, as in "Chris **loves** Mary." Often the predicate is the same as the verb. For example, "loves" in "Chris loves Mary" is both the verb and the predicate of the clause. It would be a mistake, however, to assume that all predicates are verbs. For instance, in

---

41. Paul Kroeger, *Analyzing Grammar: An Introduction* (Cambridge: Cambridge University Press, 2005), 48.

the above example "Chris is angry", the predicate is not a verb, but an adjective.[42] This is an important distinction when we study Greek and Hebrew. Unlike English, Greek and Hebrew can form grammatical clauses without a verb. This type of construction is common in Greek and Hebrew, and is known as a "verbless clause." Although such clauses do not have verbs, they do have predicates. We discuss the verbless clause further below (see §2.4.2.a.1 The Verbless Clause).

When a single clause forms a complete sentence (that is, a complete grammatical unit), it is called an independent clause (or main clause). When it does not, it is a dependent (or subordinate) clause. For example, the clause "The bear climbed the tree" is an independent clause, forming a sentence. The clause "because the bear climbed the tree" is a dependent clause, not a sentence. A particular kind of dependent clause is the relative clause—a clause that describes a noun. Relative clauses often begin with the words "which," "who," or "that." For example, in the sentence "The dog, which had brown fur, chased the car," the independent clause is "the dog chased the car." The dependent clause, "which had brown fur," describes the dog and is a relative clause.

For our purposes, a simple sentence is an independent clause. For example, the clause "The dog chased the car" is a simple sentence. Unlike clauses, however, sentences may be complex sentences, composed of one or more independent clauses and modified by one or more dependent clauses. The sentence "John bought some donuts and he gave one to Jake, who had forgotten to eat breakfast" is a single complex sentence which consists of two independent clauses (e.g., "John bought some donuts" / "he gave one to Jake") and one dependent clause (e.g., "who had forgotten to eat breakfast").

2.4.1.c Organizing Words and Units

The way we organize clusters of words in phrases and clauses depends on which words control the syntactic unit. The controlling word is called a "head," and it governs the way words are arranged. For example, in an

---

42. Unlike Greek and Hebrew, English grammar stipulates that every clause must contain a verb. The word "is" in the example "Chris is angry" is grammatically the verb, although it contains virtually no semantic meaning. For this reason, it is commonly referred to as a "linking verb" or "copula." The meaning of the clause is determined by the word that occurs after the linking verb, the "predicate complement." In this case, the predicate complement is the adjective "angry."

English noun phrase, the noun is the head (even though it will always fall at the end of a noun phrase), and any words that occur with it will do so according to rules of English syntax. Consider the collection of words "block," "the," "wooden," and "green." The only correct way to arrange these is "the green wooden block." Native speakers of English intuitively know this order of article, adjectives,[43] and noun.

The verb is the head of the verb phrase, and it controls the nouns and adjectives associated with it. Some verbs require only a subject. Consider the sentence "she slept." The verb "slept" is called an intransitive verb. Other verbs require a subject and an object. For example, in the sentence "she threw the ball," the verb "threw" requires a subject ("she") and an object ("the ball"). The verb "threw" is called a *transitive*. Some verbs require a subject and two objects—what English calls a direct and an indirect object. The verb "gave" is such a verb: "The boy gave the dog a bone." This kind of verb is called a ditransitive verb. A final kind of verb is the linking verb, a verb that does not show action but says the subject *is* something else. In the clause "The bear is furry," the subject ("bear") is identified by the adjective ("furry"). Or consider the sentence "the professor is an accomplished linguist." The subject ("the professor") is identified with the noun phrase after the linking verb ("an accomplished linguist"). With translating a clause or sentence, knowing what kind of verb it has helps delimit what other elements are required.

Of great interest to linguists is the word order of a sentence—namely, the order of the three major components of a clause: the subject, the verb, and the object(s). For example, English syntax dictates that in a typical sentence the subject precedes the verb, and the verb precedes the object. English is what linguists call an "SVO" language (subject-verb-object). However, several other word order tendencies are evident in the languages of the world. Welsh and Tagalog are VSO (verb-subject-object) languages, while the Guatemalan language Cakchiquel is a VOS (verb-object-subject) language. Japanese, Korean, and Turkish are SOV (subject-object-verb) languages. Still other languages show OVS (object-verb-subject) and OSV

---

43. Silzer and Finley include a chart that details the English speaker's intuitive knowledge of how to order adjectives (*How Biblical Languages Work*, 133).

(object-subject-verb) order.[44] This is an important part of the structure of a language, yet linguists of biblical Hebrew and Greek continue to debate the word order of each language (see §6.4 Word Order for Hebrew and §7.4 Word Order for Greek).

The task of syntax is to determine the way words are arranged in units and the way these units function together. Analysis begins at the bottom—with individual words that form phrases—and it continues up a hierarchy until each part of a sentence is accounted for and understood in its relationship to the whole.

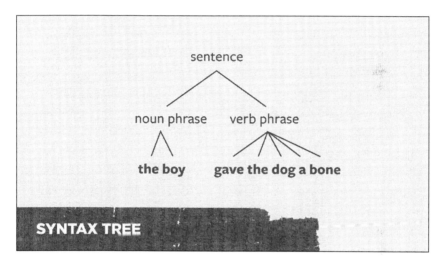

SYNTAX TREE

2.4.2 SYNTAX AND THE BIBLICAL LANGUAGES

For most students of the Bible, phonology, morphology, and semantics are simply means to an end—namely, actually translating and understanding what a verse or passage says. Once we have all these pieces, we must be able to sort out how they all work together in a biblical text. This "working together" in a text is *syntax*, and each language has its own rules. In what follows, we illustrate some of the syntactic features of biblical Hebrew and Greek.

---

44. Silzer and Finley, *How Biblical Languages Work*, 138.

2.4.2.a Syntax and Biblical Hebrew

Scholars have done a great deal of work trying to understand the syntax of biblical Hebrew. Probably the area of greatest attention/focus has been the issue of word order. Because of the importance of this discussion in the literature, we have devoted a section to it in chapter 6 (§6.4 Word Order). In this chapter, we will discuss two other matters of importance for biblical interpretation: the verbless clause and ellipsis.

2.4.2.a.1 The Verbless Clause

One of the first things a student of biblical Hebrew learns is the "verbless clause" construction. In biblical Hebrew, two non-verbal phrases can be set alongside each other and make a clause (or sentence).[45] For example, Gen 42:92 says מְרַגְּלִים אַתֶּם (*měraggělîm ’attem*), literally "spies [noun] you." While unacceptable in English, this is an acceptable construction in Hebrew. It forms a clause, which is also a sentence: "You are spies." In verbless clauses, the reader knows to fill in a form of the verb "to be."

There are several kinds of verbless clauses, and scholars are not certain how the syntax works for all of them. This uncertainty affects translation. For example, one of the most important texts in the Old Testament features an uncertain use of the verbless clause. The Shema in Deut 6:4 reads, שְׁמַע יִשְׂרָאֵל יְהוָה אֱלֹהֵינוּ יְהוָה אֶחָד (*šěma‘ yiśrā’ēl yhwh ’ělōhênû yhwh ’eḥād*), literally, "Hear, Israel, YHWH our God YHWH one." The traditional Jewish translation is, "Hear, O Israel, the LORD our God, the LORD is one." However, the syntax has the potential for three different verbless clauses: (1) "YHWH our God" could be "YHWH is our God" (e.g., NRSV, NASB) (2) "YHWH one" could be "YHWH is one" (e.g., ESV, NASB, NIV) (3) the entire clause could be "YHWH our God is one YHWH" (e.g., KJV, RSV). Miller-Naudé says the syntax "resists any simple solution."[46] This example illustrates the importance of linguistics and biblical study. As linguists understand the verbless

---

45. Not all biblical Hebrew scholars use the term "verbless clause." The most commonly used alternative is "nominal clause," because of the presence of noun phrases without a verb.

46. Cynthia L. Miller-Naudé, "Pivotal Issues in Analyzing the Verbless Clause," in *The Verbless Clause in Biblical Hebrew: Linguistic Approaches*, ed. Cynthia L. Miller-Naudé, Linguistic Studies in Ancient West Semitic 1 (Winona Lake, IN: Eisenbrauns, 1999), 4. Miller-Naudé discusses the possible translations of the Shema in her article. Daniel I. Block also discusses the issue, including its theological implications, in his article "How Many Is God? An Investigation into the Meaning of Deuteronomy 6:4–5," *JETS* 74.2 (2004): 193–212.

clause better, they will hopefully be able to resolve issues such as the syntax of Deut 6:4.

2.4.2.a.2 Ellipsis

Ellipsis is a literary phenomenon also known as "gapping," "elision," or "deletion."[47] It occurs when certain words (often the verb) are omitted from a sentence and the reader must fill in the blank mentally. Ellipsis is most common in poetry, where words are used economically. Native speakers of a language know when words can be omitted and when they are necessary. Consider the following English examples of acceptable ellipsis and then unacceptable ellipsis marked with an asterisk:

Bill ran a 5k, and Jenny (_____) a marathon.

Bill applied for (_____), but Jenny actually received, a loan for her tuition.

I write biographies; my brother (_____) novels.

*I write biographies; I novels.

*Bill arrives today, and Jenny yesterday.

Now consider how ellipsis creates ambiguity in the following example:

Bill ate the banana slowly and the monkey quickly.

The poetry of the Old Testament is filled with ellipsis, and the challenge for translators and interpreters is knowing what rules ellipsis in biblical Hebrew follows. Consider the following examples, where the omitted words are italicized in brackets:

Isa 1:27
    Zion by justice <u>shall be redeemed</u>,
    And her repentant ones by righteousness [*shall be redeemed*]

---

47. In this volume we reserve the term "deletion" for the phonological process in which sounds fall out of words.

Isa 60:2

> For behold, darkness <u>will cover</u> the earth,
> And thick darkness [*will cover*] the peoples.

Sometimes English translations will alert you to the fact that it has filled in a word by italicizing it, and other times it will just leave the gap. Compare the following translations of Psa 49:3, which may have a gap:

Psa 49:3. My mouth will speak wisdom, and the meditation of my heart understanding.

From this word-for-word rendering, two translations are equally possible in Hebrew syntax:

1. My mouth will speak wisdom, and the meditation of my heart (will be/is) understanding.

2. My mouth will speak wisdom, and the meditation of my heart (will speak) understanding.

Consider several English translations of 3b:

- "And the meditation of my heart <u>will be</u> understanding." (NASB; compare ESV, NRSV, KJV)

- "My heart's meditation <u>brings</u> understanding." (HCSB)

- "The utterance from my heart <u>will give</u> understanding." (NIV)

- "My <u>speech is full of</u> insight." (NJPS)

Which is better? Traditionally commentators and English translations have preferred the first ("the meditation of my heart <u>will be/is</u> understanding"), probably because we have a tendency "to read the exact words on the page [and this translation is closest to the "exact words on the page"], unless we are compelled to do otherwise."[48] However, consideration of the broader context of the psalm suggests that the psalmist is drawing a

---

48. Cynthia L. Miller-Naudé, "A Linguistic Approach to Ellipsis in Biblical Hebrew Poetry (Or, What to Do When Exegesis of What Is There Depends on What Isn't)," *BBR* 13 (2003): 266.

contrast between speech and thought, actually making the traditional reading the less preferable option. Consider the broader context:

vs. 1   Hear this, all you peoples;
         give ear, all inhabitants of the world

vs. 2   both low and high,
         rich and poor together.

vs. 3   My mouth <u>shall speak</u> wisdom;
         the murmuring of my intellect [*shall speak*] understanding.

vs. 4   I will incline my ear to a proverb;
         I will solve my riddle to the music of the harp.

Miller-Naudé explains what's going on:

This first section of the psalm plays upon the complementary actions of hearing and speaking. At the beginning of the stanza, vv. [1] and [2] are a command to everyone to hear. At the end of the stanza, v. [4] describes the fact that the psalmist himself will hear the proverb that he will pose in the remainder of the psalm. In v. [3] at the center of the stanza, the psalmist characterizes his own speech which will be presented in the remainder of the poem. In the same way that his mouth speaks wisdom, the murmuring of his heart speaks understanding. The first line focuses on the mouth as the locus of wise speech; the second line on the heart (or, intellect) as the source of insightful speech.[49]

There are several reasons why understanding ellipsis is important for students of the Bible. First, it refutes the idea that "word-for-word" translations are always the best. It also explains why translations can vary so much at times. Third, it reminds us that ellipsis has rules in every language, and just because we may prefer a particular translation does not mean it accurately represents the Hebrew. When we find the kind of disagreement between translations that Psa 49 illustrates, we should research and read commentaries to find out why.

---

49. Miller-Naudé, "A Linguistic Approach to Ellipsis," 266.

2.4.2.b Syntax and New Testament Greek

Sorting out the components of a long verse or rambling passage is difficult. It is helpful to think in terms of several sentence patterns in Greek, or
"kernel sentences," to which phrases and other clauses are added. Mastering
a handful of simple sentence types helps one dissect complicated sentences.
Cotterell and Turner describe the process: "Compound and complex sentences may be reduced back to a small number of basic sentence forms or
kernels by removing modifiers, eliminating the results of subordinating
and co-ordinating processes, turning negatives into positives and passives
into actives." Black identifies six basic sentence patterns, based on whether
the verb is intransitive or transitive, and whether it has a linking verb. A
simplified version of Black's patterns is charted below:[50]

Intransitive Verbs	Pattern	English Example
Pattern 1	Noun—Verb (subject—predicate)	He slept.
Pattern 2	Noun—Verb - Adverb	He slept peacefully.
Transitive Verbs		
Pattern 3	Noun—Verb—Noun (Subject—Verb—Direct Object)	He ate breakfast.
Pattern 4	Noun—Verb—Noun—Noun (Subject—Verb—Indirect Object—Direct Object)	He fed the cat breakfast.
Linking Verbs		
Pattern 5	Noun—Verb—Adjective	The cat is full.
Pattern 6	Noun—Verb—Noun	The cat is a tabby.

2.4.3 RESOURCES FOR FURTHER STUDY

Black, David Alan. "Syntax: The Architecture of the Greek Sentence."
    Pages 96–119 in *Linguistics for Students of New Testament Greek: A*

---

50. Black, *Linguistics for Students of New Testament Greek*, 102–106.

Survey of Basic Concepts and Applications. 2nd. ed. Grand Rapids: Baker, 1995.

Black's introduction to linguistics is quite thorough in its treatment of each subfield. His chapter on syntax includes a basic overview of concepts and then concentrated application to Greek. He especially focuses on how to analyze Greek sentences based on six basic sentence patterns.

Cotterell, Peter, and Max Turner. "Sentences and Sentence Clusters." Pages 188–229 in *Linguistics & Biblical Interpretation.* Downers Grove, IL: InterVarsity Press, 1989.

Cotterell and Turner's multi-chapter discussion of meaning includes a chapter on sentences and "sentence clusters." They discuss several basic sentence patterns and how learning to dissect sentences can help students understand the structure of the language. Their discussion includes several examples from the NT.

Miller-Naudé, Cynthia L. "A Linguistic Approach to Ellipsis in Biblical Hebrew Poetry (Or, What to Do When Exegesis of What Is There Depends on What Isn't)." *Bulletin for Biblical Research* 13 (2003): 251–270.

———. "Pivotal Issues in Analyzing the Verbless Clause." Pages 3–17 in *The Verbless Clause in Biblical Hebrew: Linguistic Approaches.* Winona Lake, IN: Eisenbrauns, 1999.

Linguist and biblical Hebrew scholar Cynthia Miller-Naudé has done extensive work with syntax and biblical Hebrew, particularly with the verbless clause and ellipsis.

Silzer, Peter James, and Thomas John Finley. "Putting Words Together: Phrases and Clauses." Pages 118–42 in *How Biblical Languages Work: A Student's Guide to Learning Hebrew and Greek.* Grand Rapids: Kregel, 2004.

Silzer and Finley's introduction to syntax overviews general vocabulary and concepts of syntax with respect to English. Then they demonstrate how an understanding of syntax helps with learning biblical Hebrew and Greek. Their treatment is readable and amply illustrated.

3
—
LANGUAGE IN USE

Jeremy Thompson & Wendy Widder

The study of language progresses logically from the sounds (phonology) that form words (morphology) to the meaningful combinations of words that form phrases and sentences (syntax and semantics). These fundamental components of linguistics were detailed in the previous chapter (see chap. 2, Linguistic Fundamentals). But language does not function as sentences or phrases in isolation. The communicative purpose of language is realized in various contexts of use. Sentences combine to form paragraphs. Paragraphs organize larger discourses. In use, language has different conventions based on whether it is oral or written, or whether it occurs in one social setting or another. In this chapter, we introduce the subfields of linguistics that are primarily concerned with language as it is actually used in literary and social contexts: pragmatics, discourse analysis, and sociolinguistics.

3.1 PRAGMATICS

3.1.1 PRAGMATICS EXPLAINED

We often speak of a pragmatist as a person who gets things done. One of the earliest works in the field of linguistic pragmatics was a book by J. L. Austin titled *How to Do Things with Words*.[1] Yet the field of pragmatics

---

1. John L. Austin, *How to Do Things with Words*, 2nd ed., ed. J. O. Urmson and Marina Sbisa (Cambridge, MA: Harvard University Press, 1975).

is broader than our presuppositions about the meaning of the term may imply. Pragmatics also focuses on meaning in context. Yan Huang defines pragmatics in such a way as to capture this broad meaning: "Pragmatics is the systematic study of meaning by virtue of, or dependent on, the use of language. The central topics of inquiry of pragmatics include implicature, presupposition, speech acts, and deixis."[2] We will come back to some of Huang's central topics shortly, but one might rightly be thinking at this point: *I thought* semantics *was the study of meaning.*

The question of where to draw the line between semantics and pragmatics is one of the more difficult areas within these two subdisciplines. Ronald Langacker pessimistically concludes, "I do not believe that a fixed boundary between semantics and pragmatics can be drawn on a principled basis."[3] A traditional distinction is that semantics focuses on meaning abstracted away from particular contexts, whereas pragmatics focuses on meaning in context. The problem emerges when we begin to ask what meaning that is not dependent on context would actually look like, since all natural language use occurs in a context. In light of this, it might be better to think of semantics as dealing with what a linguistic unit might mean in a default context. Pragmatics would then focus on meaning outside these default contexts. Those seeking additional details about the division of labor between the two fields might consult Alan Cruse's *Meaning in Language: An Introduction to Semantics and Pragmatics.*[4]

Having established the difficulty of separating semantics and pragmatics, we will offer a few examples to illustrate just how much context can influence meaning. Relevance theory is a modern approach to pragmatics that argues for a substantial gap between sentence meaning and speaker meaning.[5] Deirdre Wilson and Dan Sperber offer the two following examples:

2. Yan Huang, *Pragmatics*, Oxford Textbooks in Linguistics (Oxford: Oxford University Press, 2007), 2.

3. Ronald Langacker, *Cognitive Grammar: A Basic Introduction* (Oxford: Oxford University Press, 2008), 40.

4. Alan Cruse, *Meaning in Language: An Introduction to Semantics and Pragmatics*, 3rd ed., Oxford Textbooks in Linguistics (Oxford: Oxford University Press, 2011).

5. Deirdre Wilson and Dan Sperber, *Meaning and Relevance* (Cambridge: Cambridge University Press, 2012), 26.

(20) a. Peter: Is John a good accountant?

     b. Mary: John is a computer.

(21) a. Peter: How good a friend is John?

     b. Mary: John is a computer.[6]

In these examples, the response to both questions is the same: "John is a computer." Yet Mary is using the same phrase to communicate two entirely different meanings. In 20b, Mary is suggesting that John is a fantastic accountant because his mathematical computation skills are as reliable as a computer's. In 21b, Mary is suggesting that John is not a good friend because he lacks emotional substance. Referring back to the previous discussion, it is difficult to discern what the context-independent meaning of something like "John is a computer" would be. Wilson and Sperber suggest that examples like this are not isolated cases, but are common in natural language.

To briefly summarize, pragmatics is the study of meaning in context. The effects that context can have on language are substantial.

3.1.2 IMPORTANT CONCEPTS

We will now move into some subtopics within the field of pragmatics, several of which relate to the topics mentioned in Huang's definition given above. First, we will delve more deeply into what we mean by the word "context"; second, we will briefly introduce speech-act theory; and third, we will define what we mean by "discourse" as a preliminary to introducing discourse analysis and discourse grammar.

3.1.2.a Context

Alan Cruse divides context into three types: physical, human, and discourse.[7] He states that the physical context refers to what participants in an interaction "can see, hear, and so on, and each participant can assume is accessible to the other(s)." This plays a different role in the interpretation of text than it does in ordinary conversation. Cruse juxtaposes a face-to-face conversation with a phone conversation. In a face-to-face conversation, if

---

6. Wilson and Sperber, *Meaning and Relevance*, 21–22.

7. All references to Cruse in this section come from Cruse, *Meaning in Language*, 8.

the doorbell rings, one participant might simply say, "That'll be John." In a phone conversation, on the other hand, one participant may need to say, "There's someone at the door. It's probably John." In the phone conversation, one participant needs to fill in the details of the physical context. In the case of writing, there is more displacement in time and space, so the physical context may often be less important. Authors do, however, fill in details about their physical context to some extent. For example, the Apostle Paul occasionally mentions his "imprisonment," which makes up an important part of his physical context that the reader should keep in mind to understand his message more clearly (e.g., Phil 1:7).

Cruse describes human context as the "speaker's assessment of characteristics of the addressee(s) which are liable to affect their ability to comprehend the message ... such matters as the addressee's age, intelligence, and relevant knowledge." Examples of the effects of human context abound when interpreting an ancient text such as the Bible, since modern readers' knowledge base often differs drastically from that of the original audience. Incongruities arise because authors were not assessing us as addressees to consider our relevant knowledge; rather, they were assessing ancient people. Consider, for instance, the difficulties that emerge when a modern reader with no direct experience of animal sacrifice reads Leviticus, which also contains a significant amount of technical detail not directed at a layperson. Of course, this discussion of human context is not significantly different from what someone would find in a typical book about biblical interpretation, but it is important for the interpreter to take into account the background knowledge of both the author(s) and audience of a text when possible.

The final type of context that Cruse discusses is discourse context. He states, "The discourse context of an utterance consists of the utterance(s) which preceded it in the same discourse, whether a conversation or text." A simple demonstration of the importance of discourse context is the assignment of referents. Consider the following sentence: "She told her *she* needed to go to the store." Grammar instructors would say that sentences like this are ambiguous and should be avoided since it is impossible to tell who the first or second "she" refers to. However, sentences like this consistently occur in natural language. For example, imagine that the sentence occurred in a discourse like: "Old Mother Hubbard was telling her neighbor that her cupboard was bare. She told her she needed to go to the store." Our linguistic intuition will most likely guide us to identify Old Mother Hubbard as the one who needs to go to the store (unless we imagine her as a pushy person who would order her neighbor around). Discourse context provides a means to perform basic linguistic tasks such as assigning referents.

3.1.2.b Speech-Act Theory

Though we are moving on to speech-act theory, context will still play an important role in our discussion, since Austin's criteria for valid speech acts are contextual. For example, the statement, "I hereby sentence the defendant to thirty years in prison" only works if it is uttered by a judge in the context of a court proceeding. The types of conditions necessary for a speech act to be valid are called felicity conditions.[8] Having linked speech acts to context, we will next give a brief overview of speech-act theory and provide a taxonomy of speech acts.

Much early work in speech-act theory grew from dissatisfaction with the logical analyses of language popular at the time. Austin and others insist that in natural language use, speakers are often not attempting to establish truth relations between what they are thinking and what is the case in the real world. A widely used example is the question, "Can you pass the salt?" Here, the speaker is not trying to determine whether an addressee has the physical capability to pass the salt; rather, the speaker is trying to get the addressee to actually pass the salt. Austin's interest is in how speakers get someone to perform an action by using a question that is almost irrelevant if taken literally.

Early on, Austin distinguished between the types of speech acts that people use to compel action (e.g., "can you pass the salt?") and statements made to convey information (e.g., "the salt is on the table"). He called this first kind of speech act "performative." However, he later came to the position that conveying information is also something that people *do* with language. Thus, he claimed that all speech acts are performative.[9] Austin's

---

8. Ignacio Vazquez-Orta, "Doing Things with Words," in *Cognitive Exploration of Language and Linguistics*, ed. R. Dirven and M. Verspoor (Philadelphia: John Benjamins, 2004), 158.

9. Vazquez-Orta, "Doing Things with Words," 151–52.

student John Searle articulated an initial taxonomy of speech acts.[10] Ignacio Vazquez-Orta provides Searle's taxonomy as follows:

a) *assertive*   Sam smokes a lot

b) *directive*   Get out. I want you to leave.

c) *commissive*   I promise to come tomorrow.

d) *expressive*   Congratulations on your 60th birthday.

e) *declaration*   I hereby take you as my lawful wedded wife.[11]

Vazquez-Orta further elucidates these categories by dividing them into informative speech acts, obligative speech acts, and constitutive speech acts. Assertive speech acts, along with informative questions, are types of informative speech acts. Directive and commissive speech acts are types of obligative speech acts, with directives placing an obligation on an addressee and commissives placing obligations on speakers themselves. Expressives and declarations are types of constitutive speech acts because they involve some kind of ritualized social context.

Further classification of speech acts involves whether they are direct or indirect. This is especially true in the case of directives, where social factors often lead to indirect speech acts for the sake of politeness.[12] Consider again the example of, "Can you pass the salt?" A speaker could more directly say something like, "Pass me the salt," or "Give me the salt," but this would come across as an affront to the addressee. Thus, a question like, "Can you pass the salt?" is used to soften the more direct speech act. It is possible to see from this that pragmatics is very closely associated with the field of sociolinguistics, addressed later in this chapter (see §3.2 Sociolinguistics).

3.1.2.c Discourse Analysis

Just as we linked speech-act theory with the concept of context, it is necessary to link context with the concept of discourse. In the section on context, we discussed discourse context without really defining the term "discourse."

---

10. John R. Searle, *Expression and Meaning: Studies in the Theory of Speech Acts* (Cambridge: Cambridge University Press, 1979).

11. Vazquez-Orta, "Doing Things with Words," 152.

12. Betty Birner, *Introduction to Pragmatics* (Malden, MA: Wiley, 2013), 191–202.

In what follows, we define what discourse is and also discuss discourse analysis and discourse grammar. By way of definition, Betty Birner states, "Whereas morphology restricts its purview to the individual word, and syntax focuses on individual sentences, discourse analysis studies strings of sentences produced in a connected discourse."[13] This is something of an oversimplification, yet it is a helpful starting point. A discourse is a string of connected sentences, and discourse analysis is the field of study that focuses on analyzing strings of sentences connected in a discourse.

As a brief aside, Birner, among others, considers discourse analysis as distinct from, but overlapping with, the field of pragmatics. She states, "Because pragmatics concentrates on the use of language in context, and the surrounding discourse is part of the context, the concerns of the two fields overlap significantly."[14] Only those interested in reading further on discourse analysis need to be aware of this, since it may be necessary to look for texts that specifically deal with the topic.[15] Some introductory pragmatics texts will not explicitly cover discourse analysis.[16]

Discourse analysis, like any other field, is fairly varied, so here we discuss only two of the matters that discourse analysts look at—namely, frames (or schemas) and discourse markers. These are two relatively different types of analysis, so this should provide an idea of the range of work done by discourse analysts.

A famous example of the effects of frames comes from work on comprehension and recall by John Bransford and Marcia Johnson.[17] In an experiment, they read the following passage to participants:

> The procedure is actually quite simple. First you arrange things into
> different groups. Of course, one pile may be sufficient depending
> on how much there is to do. If you have to go somewhere else due

---

13. Birner, *Pragmatics*, 5.

14. Birner, *Pragmatics*, 5.

15. A good starting point with articles on a variety of topics is Deborah Tannen, Heidi E. Hamilton, and Deborah Schiffrin, eds., *The Handbook of Discourse Analysis*, 2nd ed. (Malden, MA: Wiley Blackwell, 2015).

16. For example, the topic is not explicitly mentioned in Huang, *Pragmatics*.

17. John Bransford and Marcia Johnson, "Contextual Prerequisites for Understanding: Some Investigations of Comprehension and Recall," *Journal of Verbal Learning and Behavior* 11 (1972): 722–25.

to lack of facilities that is the next step, otherwise you are pretty well set. It is important not to overdo things. That is, it is better to do too few things at once than too many. In the short run this may not seem important but complications can easily arise. A mistake can be expensive as well. At first the whole procedure will seem complicated. Soon, however, it will become just another facet of life. It is difficult to foresee any end to the necessity for this task in the immediate future, but then one never can tell. After the procedure is completed one arranges the materials into different groups again. Then they can be put into their appropriate places. Eventually they will be used once more and the whole cycle will then have to be repeated. However, that is part of life.

One group of participants is told prior to the experiment, "The paragraph you will hear will be about washing clothes." Another group was told, "It may help you to know that the paragraph was about washing clothes" after the experiment. A control group received no information about the topic. Participants who received information on the topic before the experiment demonstrated better comprehension and recall than either of the other two groups.[18] The topic provided a frame for understanding the discourse. One of the tasks of discourse analysis is to examine how framing works in language use.

Discourse analysts also look at discourse markers. One example of this kind of analysis in English is work on the quotative "like"—as in, "Then she was like, 'No way!'"[19] Here, "like" is used to introduce direct speech, much like the word "say" could: "Then she said, 'No way!'" To many people, this usage of "like" seems far removed from its normal usages, such as for comparing things: "My book looks just like your book." Discourse analysts examine the particular functions that words such as "like" perform in discourse. As a matter of further thought, the word *lēʾmōr* (לֵאמֹר; "to say") performs a somewhat similar function in biblical Hebrew. Much direct speech in biblical Hebrew is introduced as "Moses said to the people to

---

18. Bransford and Johnson, "Contextual Prerequisites," 722–25.

19. This linguistic phenomenon has received mention in the wider culture: Patricia T. O'Conner, "Language: Learning to Like Like," *New York Times*, July 15, 2007, accessed October 16, 2014, www.nytimes.com/2007/07/15/opinion/15iht-edoconnor.1.6661788.html.

say/saying (*lē 'mōr*) ...." Many modern English translations take *lē 'mōr* as a function word and, rather than giving it a lexical translation value, simply use quotation marks.

3.1.2.d Discourse Grammar

Discourse grammar is related to pragmatics and discourse analysis, though it is perhaps also another field unto itself. According to Steven Runge, the goal of discourse grammar is to describe "grammatical conventions based upon the discourse functions they accomplish."[20] One example Runge uses is the Greek historical present. Discourse grammar tries to answer what something like the historical present is doing at the level of the discourse.[21] This differs from traditional grammatical analysis, which focuses only on the word itself (morphology) or on what the word is doing at the sentence level (syntax). To some degree, this also distinguishes discourse grammar from discourse analysis, since those working within discourse analysis do not deal as explicitly with features more typically associated with syntax or morphology.

Work in discourse grammar is motivated by how traditional grammar that focuses on the word or sentence level often cannot make sense of some grammatical features. Runge states the following:

> Many of the devices described below involve the use of some gram-matical feature in a context where it does not formally belong, one that essentially "breaks" the grammatical rules. ... Consider the kinds of descriptions one finds in NT Greek grammars. We tra-ditionally label a present-tense verb used in context where a past-tense verb is expected in English as a "historical present." ... Although such labeling does describe the usage to some extent, it tells us little about why the Greek writer would use such a form or about the specific effect that it achieves. Traditional descriptive frameworks often tell us more about how Greek and English differ than they do about Greek *as Greek*.[22]

---

20. Steven Runge, *Discourse Grammar of the Greek New Testament: A Practical Introduction for Teaching and Exegesis* (Peabody, MA: Hendrickson, 2010), 3.

21. Runge, *Discourse Grammar*, 4.

22. Runge, *Discourse Grammar*, 4.

Discourse grammar attempts to address these inadequacies by providing an overarching framework for looking at the functions of these specific kinds of discourse features.

3.1.3 IMPORTANCE FOR BIBLICAL LANGUAGES

If we consider pragmatics, discourse analysis, and discourse grammar as distinct (though closely related), we will see that more work has been and currently is being done in the biblical languages on discourse analysis and discourse grammar. Though somewhat dated, a good place to start looking at discourse analysis is the volume edited by Robert Bergen titled *Biblical Hebrew and Discourse Linguistics*.[23] This volume provides an idea of the work being done and the names of scholars to look for to go further into discourse studies. For the more adventurous, Bryan Rocine has written a text for learning biblical Hebrew that employs discourse analysis.[24] In terms of discourse grammar, *The Lexham Discourse Hebrew Bible* marks for Hebrew many of the features discussed in Runge's work on Greek discourse grammar.[25]

For Greek, the works of Stephen Levinsohn and Runge offer the best place to start looking at discourse analysis and discourse grammar. Levinsohn and Rung have both published a significant amount of work related to these topics.[26] For those interested in dealing firsthand with the discourse features that Runge has identified, there is a corresponding database to *The Lexham Discourse Hebrew Bible* called *The Lexham Discourse Greek New Testament*.[27] Each of these resources has also been made accessible to those unfamiliar with the biblical languages in the form of *The Lexham High Definition Old Testament* and *The Lexham High Definition New Testament*.[28]

---

23. Robert Bergen, ed., *Biblical Hebrew and Discourse Linguistics* (Dallas: SIL, 1994).

24. Bryan M. Rocine, *Learning Biblical Hebrew: A New Approach Using Discourse Analysis* (Macon, GA: Smyth & Helwys, 2000).

25. Steve E. Runge and Joshua R. Westbury, eds., *The Lexham Discourse Hebrew Bible* (Bellingham, WA: Lexham Press, 2012–2014).

26. See Runge, *Discourse Grammar*; and Stephen H. Levinsohn, *Discourse Features of New Testament Greek*, 2nd ed. (Dallas: SIL, 2000).

27. Steven E. Runge, ed., *The Lexham Discourse Greek New Testament* (Bellingham, WA: Lexham Press, 2008–2014).

28. Steven E. Runge and Joshua R. Westbury, eds., *The Lexham High Definition Old Testament: ESV Edition* (Bellingham, WA: Lexham Press, 2012–2014); Steven E. Runge, ed., *The Lexham High Definition New Testament: ESV Edition* (Bellingham, WA: Lexham Press, 2008–2014).

3.2 SOCIOLINGUISTICS

3.2.1 SOCIOLINGUISTICS EXPLAINED

One of the most interesting ancient examples of the interaction between social context and language use comes from the Hebrew Bible. John Edwards relates the story from his perspective as a sociolinguist:

> A thousand years before the dawn of the modern era, some Ephraimites attempted to "pass" as Gileadites: they had been defeated and hoped to return home across the Jordan. They were detected, however, because of their inability when challenged to pronounce the word *shibboleth* in the Gileadite manner. In Judges 12:6, when the impostor "could not frame to pronounce it right ... they took him, and slew him at the passages of Jordan" (KJV). ... In both its ordinary and communicative role as the most immediate symbolic marker of human affiliation, language is preeminently a social phenomenon.[29]

Since a person's accent can provide clues to their group affiliation, it is not surprising that the study of accents falls within the field of sociolinguistics.

Sociolinguistics is the study of the interaction between language and society, or social context. This interaction is bidirectional. Someone can study how language users' choices are affected by a variety of social factors, such as geographical location, socioeconomic status, and gender. Someone can also study what language users' choices demonstrate about society. At least in introductory linguistics texts, the first of this pair of interests appears more common—namely, sociolinguists often focus on the effects that social factors have on the choices of language users.

3.2.2 IMPORTANT CONCEPTS

In this section, we will introduce two areas of study common among sociolinguists: the relationship between language, culture, and thought, and the topic of language variation and change.

---

29. John Edwards, *Sociolinguistics: A Very Short Introduction* (Oxford: Oxford University Press, 2013), 2.

3.2.2.a Language, Culture, and Thought

Language regularly appears in lists of cultural universals; however, linguists draw different conclusions about this.[30] The relationship between language, culture, and thought is a major topic of debate. Languages categorize the world differently; some use distinct words to label concepts that must be described with a phrase in another language. For example, Russian has different words for dark blue and light blue, English uses an adjective to modify the word "blue," and Korean uses the same word for both green and blue.[31] Every language also has words and expressions that relate to the cultural concerns of its speakers. The debate is whether a language forces speakers to think in particular ways.

The idea that language constrains or determines thought is known as linguistic determinism, also called linguistic relativity, the Sapir-Whorf hypothesis, or Whorfianism.[32] Edward Sapir claims that language "powerfully conditions all our thinking" and that people are "very much at the mercy of the particular language which has become the medium of expression for their society."[33] Whorf also held that language was "the shaper of ideas, the program and guide for the individual's mental activity."[34] Research thus far has not demonstrated that language places such strong constraints on our thinking.[35] However, since linguistic features can emphasize some aspects of reality over others and encode different cultural categories,[36] the effect that language has on how people perceive the world around them continues to be debated. Language can undoubtedly be used

---

30. Jon Shepard, *Sociology*, 9th ed. (Belmont, CA: Wadsworth/Thomson Learning, 2005), 83.

31. Victoria Fromkin, Robert Rodman, and Nina M. Hyams, *An Introduction to Language*, 9th ed. (Boston: Wadsworth, Cengage Learning, 2011), 311.

32. The last two labels in this list reflect the idea's association with Edward Sapir and his student Benjamin L. Whorf.

33. Edward Sapir, "The Status of Linguistics as a Science," *Language* 5, no. 4 (1929): 209.

34. Quoted by Fromkin et al., *Introduction to Language*, 311.

35. For an overview of the research, see Steven Pinker, *The Stuff of Thought: Language as a Window into Human Nature* (New York: Viking, 2007), 124-51. For a book-length debunking of the popular misconceptions about Whorfianism, see John H. McWhorter, *The Language Hoax: Why the World Looks the Same in Any Language* (Oxford: Oxford University Press, 2014).

36. This weaker version of the idea—that differences in language correlate with differences of conception—is sometimes called "linguistic relativity." Unlike linguistic determinism, it is not necessarily making the claim that language *causes* the differences in thinking (see Michael Cole and Sylvia Scribner, "Culture and Language," in *Issues in Cultural Anthropology: Selected Readings*, ed. David W. McCurdy and James P. Spradley [Boston: Little, Brown, 1979], 79).

actively to influence opinions about culturally sensitive topics, with different labels carrying different connotations (e.g., "freedom fighter" vs. "terrorist"). Language is one way that cultural values are reproduced, especially as common expressions serve to reinforce stereotypes and shared assumptions.[37] There is little evidence that "politically correct" language—substituting new "neutral" terms for those with negative connotations—actually has any effect on society, since those new labels generally acquire the negative cultural connotations of the terms they replaced.[38] Even Whorf, a linguist strongly associated with the idea that language determines thought, recognized that language and culture "have grown up together, constantly influencing each other."[39] The extent and nature of that mutual influence may be debated, but few today would deny that it exists.

3.2.2.b Language Variation and Change

Language variation and change is another area of research within the field of sociolinguistics; however, we are not leaving behind the topic of language and culture, since variation often involves aspects of culture. Under the topic of language variation and change we will discuss dialect and register. Dialect and register are two types of language variation.

The distinction between what constitutes a language or dialect is one of the more difficult topics within the field of linguistics as a whole. English is a typical example of a language, whereas British English and American English are well-known dialects. What is it about British English and American English that make them dialects and not separate languages? The traditional criterion for distinguishing languages from dialects is that dialects are mutually intelligible.[40] In other words, native speakers of British English and American English can understand each other, though there are some areas of nonoverlap. On the other hand, native speakers of English

---

37. Racist and sexist expressions are commonly cited as examples of how language reproduces negative cultural categories; see Michael Stubbs, "Language and the Mediation of Experience: Linguistic Representation and Cognitive Orientation," in *The Handbook of Sociolinguistics*, ed. Florian Coulmas (Oxford: Blackwell, 1998), 358–73.

38. Fromkin et al., *Introduction to Language*, 315.

39. Benjamin Lee Whorf, "The Relation of Habitual Thought and Behavior to Language," in *Issues in Cultural Anthropology: Selected Readings*, 65.

40. Fromkin et al., *Introduction to Language*, 430.

cannot readily understand a speaker of Mandarin Chinese; thus, English and Mandarin are separate languages.

However, in some cases the criterion of mutual intelligibility has been shown to be problematic. Mandarin Chinese provides a typical example: Speakers of some dialects of Mandarin cannot understand speakers of other dialects. Yet these dialects are grouped together under one language because there is political cohesion.[41] More recently, sociolinguists have begun to focus on a much larger set of criteria for determining whether they are dealing with two dialects of the same language or two separate languages, with no single criteria being definitive.[42]

Registers are similar to dialects, only more restrictive. Particular sets of social contexts produce different registers.[43] For example, the ways that doctors or computer programmers speak to each other are different from the ways friends might talk to each other on an outing to a movie theater. Some topics related to registers are taboo language, euphemism, and jargon.[44] Some social contexts allow more readily for explicit language while others more readily call for euphemism. A famous biblical example is that in a time of conflict it might be appropriate to refer to males as "wall-pissers" (1 Sam 25:22), whereas in other contexts euphemisms like "cover the feet" (1 Sam 24:3) might be used to refer to a person urinating. Much of the priestly language in the Hebrew Bible is identified based on a set of priestly "jargon." Sociolinguists have not done much research on this, so the research may refer to "style" rather than register; however, style and register are near synonyms in some linguistics texts.[45]

3.2.3 IMPORTANCE FOR BIBLICAL LANGUAGES

Some sociolinguistic work has been done on the Hebrew Bible and Greek NT over the last several decades, such as Louw's *Sociolinguistics and*

---

41. Fromkin et al., *Introduction to Language*, 431.

42. For an accessible discussion of the issues involved in distinguishing between dialects and languages, see John McWhorter, *The Power of Babel: A Natural History of Language* (New York: Perennial, 2003).

43. William O'Grady et al., *Contemporary Linguistics: An Introduction* (Harlow, UK: Longman, 1997), 579.

44. Fromkin et al., *Introduction to Language*, 470–76.

45. Fromkin et al., *Introduction to Language*, 469.

Communication[46] and Schniedewind's "Prolegomena for the Sociolinguistics of Classical Hebrew."[47] However, as Schniedewind notes, the field of sociolinguistics as a whole is relatively new, and the insights from this field have not been adequately applied to biblical Hebrew.[48] So, the application of the methods of sociolinguistics could be an area for significant future advancement. However, it is also important to note that some work has been done on sociolinguistics without explicitly claiming to be such. For example, as noted above, biblical scholars have for quite a long time been making statements about matters of authorship and composition based on the presence of jargon, such as priestly jargon in the Pentateuch. Therefore, one of the tasks of advancement in sociolinguistic study of the Bible is to make connections between a new methodology and this previous research.

3.3 RESOURCES FOR FURTHER STUDY

Matthews, Victor H. *More than Meets the Ear: Discovering the Hidden Contexts of Old Testament Conversations*. Grand Rapids: Eerdmans, 2008.

> In *More than Meets the Ear*, Matthews demonstrates how sociolinguistics, discourse analysis, and speech-act theory can be profitably applied to biblical exegesis. He distills complicated theories from the social sciences and linguistics and provides a model for how to use those concepts to elucidate OT narratives.

Polak, Frank. "Sociolinguistics: A Key to the Typology and the Social Background of Biblical Hebrew." *Hebrew Studies* 47 (2006): 115–62.

> Polak's lengthy article demonstrates how sociolinguistics can be used to explain style differences in Hebrew narratives and ultimately help scholars distinguish the stages of development in Biblical Hebrew.

Porter, Stanley E., and Jeffrey T. Reed, eds. *Discourse Analysis and the New Testament: An Introduction*. Sheffield: Sheffield Academic, 1999.

---

46. Johannes Louw, ed., *Sociolinguistics and Communication* (London: United Bible Societies, 1986).

47. William Schniedewind, "Prolegomena for the Sociolinguistics of Classical Hebrew," *Journal of Hebrew Scriptures* 5 (2004), www.jhsonline.org/Articles/article_36.pdf.

48. Schniedewind, "Prolegomena," §1.4.

This volume includes contributions by many important scholars who have worked at the intersection of discourse analysis and biblical exegesis, such as Robert Longacre, Eugene Nida, Johannes Louw, and Stephen Levinsohn.

Poythress, Vern Sheridan. "The Theory of Speech Acts." Pages 353–69 in *In the Beginning Was the Word: Language—A God-Centered Approach.* Wheaton, IL: Crossway, 2009.

In his book about God and language, Vern Poythress includes an appendix on speech-act theory. He offers an overview and a critique of its use in biblical studies.

Runge, Steven E. "Preface." In *Discourse Grammar of the Greek New Testament: A Practical Introduction for Teaching and Exegesis.*

Steven E. Runge is explicitly practical in his *Discourse Grammar.* His goal is to use the study of language and how languages are used in general to help explain why NT Greek uses certain language structures or constructions.

Schniedewind, William M. "Prolegomena for the Sociolinguistics of Classical Hebrew." *Journal of Hebrew Scriptures* 4 (2004). http://www.jhsonline.org/Articles/article_36.pdf

Schniedewind makes a good case for the potential benefit that sociolinguistics could have for studies of Biblical Hebrew. In §5.7 of the article, he lists the types of questions that a sociolinguistic approach could attempt to address, such as the effect of "the urbanization of the late Judean monarchy" on Hebrew or the impact that the Persian Empire's use of Aramaic as an administrative language could have had on Hebrew.

White, Hugh C., ed. *Semeia 41: Speech Act Theory and Biblical Criticism.* Decatur, GA: Society of Biblical Literature, 1987.

Semeia devoted an entire issue to speech-act theory with respect to biblical studies. Its nine articles include discussion of the theory, studies of particular texts, and a bibliography of additional resources on speech-act theory.

4
—
LANGUAGE UNIVERSALS, TYPOLOGY, AND MARKEDNESS

Daniel Wilson & Michael Aubrey

T his chapter introduces the concepts of language universals, linguistic typology, and markedness and demonstrates their relevance for research on the biblical languages. The study of how languages work in general has become an important means for evaluating linguistic hypotheses. By studying linguistic features across a broad range of languages, researchers can identify patterns that are typical and point out which patterns are actually extremely rare or unattested in all the languages they have studied. The search for common features in different languages manifests language universals. Comrie states, "The study of language universals aims to establish limits on variation within human language."[1] The related study of linguistic typology is concerned with categorizing the variations among languages and identifying any possible patterns. Research on language universals and linguistic typology is complementary, since the focus of both is the variation among languages.[2]

The concept of markedness is another general feature of language that has had considerable influence on linguistics because of its applicability in a wide range of linguistic subfields, including phonology, morphology,

---

1. Bernard Comrie, *Language Universals and Linguistic Typology* (Chicago: University of Chicago Press, 1981), 30–31.
2. Comrie, *Language Universals and Linguistic Typology*, 31.

semantics, syntax, pragmatics, and even linguistic typology. This concept is defined in detail below (see §4.2.2 Markedness Explained). In essence, markedness emphasizes how linguistic elements relate to each other. Usually this involves linguistic elements of the same kind (e.g., different tenses). Markedness is often related to features that indicate membership in a particular category. In the biological world, for example, one could say that mammals are "marked" as being warm-blooded (e.g., [+warm-blooded]; the presence or absence of a feature that characterizes a category is marked in linguistics as [+/-] that feature). Other biological entities, such as sharks and daisies, might be unmarked for the feature "warm-blooded" (e.g., [–warm-blooded]). Sharks, being cold-blooded, lack the feature, while daisies express no information about it one way or the other. Either way, both are *unmarked* for [+warm-blooded].

4.1 LANGUAGE UNIVERSALS AND TYPOLOGY

4.1.1 GENERATIVE UNIVERSAL GRAMMAR

In the framework of generative grammar, spearheaded by Noam Chomsky, the notion of language universals has to do with "universal grammar," a theory developed to explain how it is that children acquire language so efficiently. Chomsky argues that humans possess innate internal linguistic abilities and constraints that facilitate their rapid and effortless learning of language.[3] The central argument used to support this hypothesis is referred to as "the poverty of the stimulus."[4] This argument states that a child's limited and unstructured exposure to language is insufficient for the complex and limitless expressions that the child generates. Children produce grammatical sentences that they have never heard even after being raised in environments with broken, idiomatic, and incomplete communication. Therefore, the child must bring an innate set of principles, a "universal grammar," to bear on the limited amount of language input she has received. The child's universal grammar, together with the linguistic input received from other people, allows the child to extrapolate the

---

3. Chomsky's arguments were, in large part, a response to the popular view, espoused by behaviorist psychology in the first half of the twentieth century, that children acquire linguistic competence through stimulus-response patterns.

4. Noam Chomsky, *Reflections on Language* (London: Fontana, 1976).

correct patterns and rules that make up the adult grammar. The generative approach to the study of language universals is largely deductive—that is, abstract principles of universal grammar are derived through the close study of a particular language, from which parameters are proposed in order to explain the syntactic, semantic, and pragmatic diversity of the languages of the world.[5]

4.1.2 CROSSLINGUISTIC UNIVERSALS

In contrast to the deductive generative approach, many linguists approach the study of language universals inductively—that is, by analyzing and comparing data drawn from many languages and from many diverse language families. Where generative linguists begin with language-internal generalizations (universal grammar) and then use empirical constraints as well as crosslinguistic data to verify or falsify those generalizations, the inductive approach begins with a search for linguistic patterns across languages in pursuit of more precise categorization.

One of the main advantages of this crosslinguistic research is the ability to uncover different types of universals in language. Some universals can be framed in terms of frequency and probability. For example, 95 percent of languages show a preference for the grammatical subject of a clause to appear in front of the grammatical object (regardless of the position of the verb).[6] Other universals are called *implicational universals*. These are properties of languages that "must, or can only be, present if some other property is also present."[7] That is, if X exists in a language, then Y exists also. These types of universals are especially common with issues of word order. A quite striking instance of an implicational universal involves verbs and objects in relationship to prepositions/postpositions

---

5. For a helpful and accessible introduction to the most recent iteration of generative syntax (the minimalist program), see Andrew Radford, *Minimalist Syntax Revisited* (University of Essex, 2006), available online as an electronic course book (www.public.asu.edu/~gelderen/Radford2009.pdf). The electronic course book is a revision of Radford's *Minimalist Syntax: Exploring the Structure of English* (Cambridge: Cambridge University Press, 2004).

6. William Croft, *Typology and Universals*, 2nd ed. (Cambridge: Cambridge University Press, 2003), 52.

7. Comrie, *Language Universals and Linguistic Typology*, 17.

(adpositions).[8] Matthew Dryer provides the following information for the relationship between these elements.[9]

	Africa	Eurasia	Southeast Asia & Oceania	Australia & New Guinea	North America	South America	Total
VO and Prepositions	24	8	20	13	22	7	94
VO and Postpositions	6	2	0	1	3	5	17
OV and Prepositions	3	2	0	2	0	0	7
OV and Postpositions	20	26	12	45	26	28	157

The information in this chart essentially says that if a language has the word order *verb before object*, then in turn it is highly probable that the language will also have a preposition (i.e., adposition before noun). Similarly, if a language has the word order *object before verb*, then it is quite likely that the language will have postpositions (i.e., noun before adposition). Both of these are implicational universals: if one word order exists, then the implication is that the other word order exists. Since languages that have the verb-object order almost always also have the preposition-noun order, this becomes a significant guide for language research. Implicational universals like these are helpful for demonstrating the finite ways languages can vary and that there is a nonarbitrary organization to an individual language's structure. The value of this type of study for an analysis of the biblical languages is discussed below.

---

8. Most students of English are likely familiar with the term "preposition." In English the "pre-" refers to the word's location in front of the noun. Other languages in the world use postpositions, which appear after the noun. The term "adposition" encompasses both prepositions and postpositions.

9. Matthew S. Dryer, "Significant and Non-Significant Implicational Universals," *Linguistic Typology* 7 (2003): 108–28.

4.1.3 LINGUISTIC TYPOLOGY

The study of linguistic typology complements the search for language universals. Where the latter seeks to determine what all languages do and to describe the nature of how languages differ, the former attempts to organize all of that information in a way that is meaningful. No two languages are the same. Despite that, variation between languages is constrained. No two trees are identical, but there are defining features that nevertheless make an oak tree and Douglas fir both trees. The variation we find in language is of the same kind. It is regular and predictable and can be classified into types. When languages are compared based on the presence or absence of identical features—finding the "types" of languages that exist for a certain study—linguistic typology is being performed. Bernard Comrie summarizes the complementary relationship between these approaches:

> We can thus say that, over all, the study of language universals aims to establish limits on variation within human language. Typology is concerned directly with the study of this variation, and this makes it clearer why the two studies run so close together, since both are concerned with variation across languages, the only difference being that language universals research is concerned primarily with limits on this variation, whereas typological research is concerned more directly with possible variation.[10]

The discipline of linguistic typology assumes and utilizes language universals. Drawing on the discussion of implicational universals above, the conclusion is that, broadly speaking, there are two major language types, each following one of the two universals. There are VO-preposition languages, and there are OV-postposition languages. Of course, there are still twenty-four languages represented in the chart above that diverge from these two types. These are the platypuses of the linguistic world; they do not fit into the class of either mammal or bird, not quite. While rare, these sorts of divergences, where languages break from expected norms, are normal and expected in both the biological world and in linguistics (see

---

10. Comrie, *Language Universals and Linguistic Typology*, 33–34.

the discussion of important concepts in cognitive linguistics in chapter 5).
They represent important points of research for the field.

4.1.4 UNIVERSALS, TYPOLOGY, AND BIBLICAL LANGUAGES

This type of research is valuable for understanding the biblical languages
better. Ancient Greek and biblical Hebrew manifest certain patterns that
are similar to many contemporary languages. Historically, few scholars
have used the insights of typology and universals to inform their conclusions about Greek and Hebrew. This underutilization is due largely to the
different jargon used in biblical studies versus linguistics. The typological
studies that have been done by linguists are unintelligible to the average
Hebrew or Greek student. Nevertheless, a few scholars have learned the
technical language of both disciplines and demonstrated the explanatory
power of typological research.

One work that utilizes research in typology and universals is a recent
volume on the subject of time and aspect in the Hebrew verb. In *Time and
the Biblical Hebrew Verb*, John Cook draws from a typological study done
by linguist Leon Stassen.[11] Stassen observes what he calls the "Tensedness
Parameter." One aspect of this parameter reveals that languages can be predominantly tense based or aspect based in their verbal system. One implicational universal he discovered reveals that tense-based languages encode
their adjectival predicates (such as *John is tall*) in a way that resembles their
nominal strategy (how noun predicates are encoded). Aspect-prominent
languages, however, tend to encode their adjectival predicates according
to the verbal strategy (with verbs). In his study, Cook reflects on the stative adjective in biblical Hebrew and notices a gradual shift happening in
the development of Hebrew away from the verb-like stative adjective to a
more noun-like encoding of adjectival predicates. This change is ascribed
to the drift of Hebrew from a more aspect-based to a more tense-based language in the verbal system. In other words, biblical Hebrew is a snapshot
of a language whose verbal system is in a state of transition from aspect
prominence to tense prominence.[12] This drift is also reflected in other languages of the world, as recorded by Stassen's typological research.

---

11. Leon Stassen, *Intransitive Predication* (Oxford: Clarendon, 1997), 347–58.

12. John A. Cook, *Time and the Biblical Hebrew Verb* (Winona Lake, IN: Eisenbrauns, 2012),
223–33.

As Cook's work shows, using data from modern spoken languages of the world can reveal patterns that help our knowledge of so-called dead or unspoken languages, such as biblical Greek and Hebrew. If a language universal is true in a certain type of language, and biblical Hebrew, for example, falls into that category, it would be unexpected for that language universal not to hold true for biblical Hebrew.[13] Conversely, if a scholar were to make a suggestion at the grammatical, syntactic, or discourse level of biblical Greek, and that suggestion were unattested in all other languages similar to biblical Greek, there would be good reason to rethink that suggestion. In short, linguistic typology and language universals give us stronger probability in making claims about how biblical Hebrew and Greek work, and they prevent idiosyncratic suggestions from receiving undue influence.

4.2 MARKEDNESS

The notion of markedness has received a significant amount of attention in linguistic literature, resulting in an array of complex and sometimes disconnected definitions.[14] In its most general sense, however, markedness may be defined as "an analytic principle in linguistics whereby pairs of linguistic features, seen as oppositions, are given different values of positive (marked) and neutral or negative (unmarked)."[15] Put differently, the terms "marked" and "unmarked" are used to refer to the status or existence of particular linguistic features. Markedness relates to how much detail is communicated by a linguistic feature. For example, the English pronoun "they" indicates a plural group but gives no information about whether the group includes just men, just women, or a mix of both. The pronoun is *marked* for person (third) and number (plural) but *unmarked* for gender. By contrast, the Spanish pronoun "ellas" refers to a group of women and is *marked* for person (third), number (plural), and gender (feminine). The importance of this concept in linguistics is inestimable. Though it has its

---

13. Indeed, such a divergence would call for more study cross-linguistically.

14. Martin Haspelmath, "Against Markedness (and What to Replace It with)," *Journal of Linguistics* 42 (2006): 1–37. Haspelmath distinguishes twelve different senses for the notion of "markedness" in linguistic literature.

15. David Crystal, *A Dictionary of Linguistics and Phonetics*, 6th ed. (Malden, MA: Blackwell, 2008).

roots in phonology, markedness has been applied to almost every subdomain of linguistics. A brief explanation of the history of the concept will help make sense of present usage and why it is valuable in the study of biblical languages.

4.2.1 HISTORY OF MARKEDNESS

Markedness theory began in the Prague school of linguistics of the 1920s and '30s (see §5.3 Functionalism). The first scholars to develop and apply its principles were Nikolai Trubetzkoy and Roman Jakobson. Trubetzkoy is well known for applying markedness principles at the level of phonology, and Jakobson extended its application to the levels of grammar and semantics. Contemporary linguists such as Joseph Greenberg have extended the concept even further to the level of syntax and language typology.[16] What follows is an explanation of the role of markedness theory at each level of linguistic analysis and how it has been applied throughout history.

4.2.2 MARKEDNESS EXPLAINED

It is difficult to overstate the ubiquity of markedness theory in linguistics. The concept has been used to explain everything from the phonological difference between *p* and *b* to the semantic difference between *horse* and *mare* and even the meaningful difference between the various word orders found in different languages. Since the impact of this concept is so great, a broad-to-narrow, simple-to-complex explanation is needed. The hierarchy in (1) will provide guidance in examining the impact of markedness theory on all the subdomains of linguistics.

(1) Markedness hierarchy

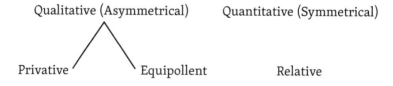

Qualitative (Asymmetrical) Quantitative (Symmetrical)

Privative Equipollent   Relative

---

16. Joseph H. Greenberg, "Some Universals of Grammar with Particular Reference to the Order of Meaningful Elements," in *Universals of Language*, ed. Joseph H. Greenberg (Cambridge, MA: MIT Press, 1963).

Under the qualitative heading, there are two approaches to marked-ness. The first is the relationship of privative oppositions. Edwin Battistella represents this view, saying:

> Markedness is probably most easily understood as a relation between a very specific linguistic sign (the marked term) and a sign that is unspecified for the grammatical or conceptual feature in question. In this sense, marked and unmarked elements are not strictly opposite.[17]

This kind of markedness is based on what is called privative opposition. The marked term has feature A, and the unmarked term either does not have feature A or says nothing about the presence of feature A. Privative oppositions can be represented by the contrast *A vs. not-A*. For example, the words "mare" and "horse" both refer to animals of the equine species. "Mare" is the marked term because it specifies that the animal is female. "Horse" is unmarked because it says nothing about the sex of the animal.

The second kind of qualitative markedness is based on equipollent oppositions. Equipollent oppositions can be represented by the contrast *A vs. B*, where *A=not-B* and *B=not-A*. The example *singular vs. plural* is an equipollent opposition. These oppositions are mutually exclusive with reference to the marked feature. If a noun is singular, then it cannot be plural. The marked element has feature A, and the unmarked element has feature B in equipollent opposition. Just as "mare" and "horse" are in privative opposition, the terms "mare" and "stallion" are in equipollent opposition because both are marked for gender.

An example will illustrate how qualitative markedness works.[18] When we want to ask generally about a person's age, we use the English sentence in 2a below:

(2)   a. How old are you?
      b. How young are you?

---

17. Edwin L. Battistella, *Markedness: The Evaluative Superstructure of Language* (New York: State University of New York Press, 1990), 2.

18. Example from Battistella, *Markedness*, 3.

On the one hand, when an English speaker is merely seeking general information about a person's age without any ulterior motive, one would expect them to use a question like the 2a example. The 2a question functions as the *default* or *unmarked* means of gaining information about age. On the other hand, if a speaker uses the form in the 2b question, they are drawing attention to the concept of youth for some reason. Perhaps they believe the person is much younger than they should be for their job. Or perhaps they know the person is over a certain age, but want to slyly compliment them by implying that they look younger than they should. In sum, the concept of age in question 2a is unmarked in the sense that it draws no attention to the age of the addressee (privative *A vs. not-A* opposition).

The second major type of markedness is *quantitative* markedness. This type of markedness is usually found in typological and grammatical research and concerns a scale of markedness qualities. Quantitative markedness is also called relative markedness. Those who use markedness this way typically describe a form as more or less marked relative to another similar form. Typically an implicational hierarchy of markedness is developed, displaying a scale of relative markedness, as in example (3).

(3)   singular < plural < dual < trial/paucal[19]

Some languages do not have the simple binary opposition singular/plural. This implicational hierarchy displays a language universal. Languages that contain a trial form necessarily contain a dual and plural form. Languages that contain a dual form necessarily contain a plural form. The converse is not necessarily true, however. The existence of a plural category does not necessitate the existence of a dual category.

Quantitative markedness is determined using a number of different criteria. Linguists such as William Croft,[20] Greenberg,[21] and Talmy Givón[22] have highlighted features such as formal complexity (complex = more

---

19. Frederick J. Newmeyer, *Language Form and Language Function* (Cambridge, MA: MIT Press, 1998), 198. See also Edna Andrews, *Markedness Theory* (Durham, NC: Duke University Press, 1990), 139.

20. William Croft, *Typology and Universals* (Cambridge: Cambridge University Press, 1990).

21. Joseph H. Greenberg, *Language Universals* (The Hague: Mouton, 1966).

22. Talmy Givón, *Syntax: A Functional-Typological Introduction*, vol. 2 (Amsterdam: John Benjamins, 1990).

marked) and frequency distribution (less frequent and more specific = more marked) to identify marked forms. Once again, this approach to markedness is usually restricted to language typology and universals. Battistella comments:

> In the view in which markedness is part of the theory of univer-
> sals, markedness is essentially a theory of correlations—a theory
> of evidence for hierarchy—and the theoretical result is the set of
> correlations. ... Typological markedness provides a set of criteria
> that can be applied regardless of whether a category is phonological,
> semantic, morphological, or syntactic, and regardless of whether
> different languages have the same categories.[23]

What remains is to show how markedness applies to each subdomain of linguistics and how it has been used in biblical language research. The complexity of the subject continues to foster debate over how scholars have applied markedness to the study of the biblical languages.

4.2.2.a Phonological Application

The origin of markedness theory is linked to the pursuit of the relationship between sound and meaning in language. Ferdinand de Saussure demonstrated that linguistic signs consist of both sound and meaning, the signifier and the signified (see §5.2.2.c Signifier and Signified). The Prague school was driven by the pursuit of how sounds function as vehicles for meaning. Such an investigation revealed that opposing sounds in the structure of a language enable the sounds to serve as the vehicles of meaning.

Trubetzkoy[24] and Jakobson[25] pioneered the idea that the distinguishing features of sounds could be classified into units smaller than the phoneme. Rather than reducing the sound system of a language into a host of oppositions of the phonemes, they categorized these phonemes into a more economical system. The phonemes could be reduced, and a comprehensive system could be developed that measures the presence or absence of

---

23. Battistella, *Markedness*, 53.

24. Nikolai Trubetzkoy, *Principles of Phonology*, trans. Christiane A. M. Baltaxe (Berkeley: University of California Press, 1969).

25. Roman Jakobson, *Six Lectures on Sound and Meaning*, trans. John Mepham (Cambridge, MA: MIT Press, 1978).

certain phonological properties (i.e., nasality, voicing, etc.). Entire vowel systems could be reduced to the presence or absence of a few phonological parameters. Battistella explains a benefit of this development, saying, "One important result of the analysis of phoneme systems into features was that sound systems were now analyzed as systems of relations rather than inventories of phonemes."[26]

The quantitative approach to markedness has been applied to phonological markedness in its distinguishing of these features. Phonemes like *p* and *b* are distinguished as follows:

(4) Bilabial plosive

	voiced	unvoiced
p	–	+
b	+	–

The phoneme p is unmarked for voicing, but b is marked.

4.2.2.b Semantic Application

To illustrate the application of the principles of markedness to semantics, consider the comparison between "horse" and "mare":

(5)

	female
horse	+/–
mare	+

The term "mare" is considered marked for the feature feminine gender, while the more generic term "horse" is unmarked for gender. This is an example of privative markedness. It is important to remember, however, that the use of the unmarked form does not connote the absence of the feature, but rather merely that the presence or absence of this feature is unspecified by the form. In other words, the term "horse" could denote either masculine or feminine, but the term "mare" can only denote feminine.

A good example of semantic equipollent markedness would be the comparison of "mare" and "stallion." There is a clear opposition on the basis of gender in these two terms represented in (6).

---

26. Battistella, *Markedness*, 13.

(6)

	male	female
mare	–	+
stallion	+	–

A qualitative approach to semantic markedness might look at the frequency of a word such as "mare" compared to "horse," as well as its specificity, and determine it to be more marked. Many linguists, however, hesitate to base a conclusion of markedness merely on frequency or specificity. They assert that frequency and specificity are the consequence, not the cause, of a word or phrase being marked.

4.2.2.c *Grammatical Application*

The grammatical application of markedness relates to the morphology of related terms. This kind of markedness is also called material markedness.[27] Person, gender, and number inflection are often cited as examples of grammatical markedness. In English pronouns there is a distinction between singular and plural pronouns with reference to number. "I" is first-person singular; "we" is first-person plural. "You," however, is unmarked for number; "you" is used in both singular and plural. A similar phenomenon happens with gender and English pronouns. The singular "he" and "she" are marked for gender, but the plural pronouns "we," "you," and "they" are unmarked for gender.

In the quantitative sense, the concept of relative markedness is featured at the grammatical level. As mentioned previously, in languages where number can be specified as singular, plural, or dual, there is a grade of relative markedness. Plural has the feature >1 (greater than one) but does not specify how many. Dual, on the other hand, also has the feature >1, but it has the added specification of "two." In this example, dual is more marked than plural, and plural is more marked than singular. Relative markedness takes into account that there are often more than two options in related forms. Binary oppositions are still possible in relative markedness,

---

27. Arnold M. Zwicky, "On Markedness in Morphology," *Die Sprache: Zeitschrift für Sprachwissenschaft Wien* 24, no. 2 (1978): 130.

however, through the identification of features. In the present example a chart like the following makes this clear:

(7)

	>1	specified
Singular	-	
Plural	+	-
Dual	+	+

This chart shows that the plural is marked relative to the singular in reference to number, and the dual is marked relative to the plural in reference to specificity.

4.2.2.d Syntactic/Pragmatic Application

The syntactic application of markedness is one of the most beneficial for biblical exegesis. Often markedness at the syntactic level is labeled pragmatic markedness. Pragmatics is the study of how form and function relate in a speech act (see §3.1 Pragmatics). When a word or phrase has "emphasis" or "prominence," what is meant (in a broad and unspecific sense) is that the word or phrase has pragmatic markedness. Compare the following sentences:

(8)
a. The bus hit the dog.
b. It was the **bus** that hit the dog.

Example 8a is a pragmatically unmarked sentence. Barring any special intonational inflection, the only information delivered by this sentence is the simple proposition it makes. Example 8b, however, emphasizes "bus." If this sentence were spoken, the word "bus" would receive the stress, and the information communicated would be that the bus hit the dog as opposed to some other vehicle. This sentence implies that the addressee of this sentence needed clarification about who perpetrated this tragedy. Example 8b is a syntactically/pragmatically marked sentence. This sentence has been marked for argument focus (see §5.3.3.b Topic and Comment). Example 8a, however, is pragmatically unmarked and says nothing about the perceptions of the addressee. This is an example of a privative opposition at the syntactic level.

4.2.3 MARKEDNESS AND THE BIBLICAL LANGUAGES

The diverse ways in which markedness has been used in the study of the biblical languages demonstrate the confusion about the terms discussed above. Both definitions of markedness—qualitative and quantitative—are employed by biblical scholars, and the privative/equipollent distinction is not always specified. Below are some areas in which markedness has been applied to the study of the biblical languages.

4.2.3.a Quantitative Approaches

In her essay published in *Narrative Syntax and the Hebrew Bible*, Ellen van Wolde includes a section titled "Hebrew Syntax and the Concept of Markedness."[28] She defines markedness as "a theoretical concept of qualitative oppositions that enable linguists to analyse the inherently asymmetric relationship by which linguistic elements function."[29] She argues for understanding the Hebrew *qatal* verb form, typically functioning as a third-person singular, as unmarked for person, gender, and number. The verb forms in second person are marked for gender in both singular and plural. The first-person verb forms are not marked for gender, but they are marked for number. Van Wolde concludes, then, that the third person is the least marked, the first person is more marked, and the second person is the most marked. The value of this relative hierarchy for van Wolde is that it "can explain their differences in influence exerted on the reader."[30]

In following sections, van Wolde shows how the concept of markedness can be applied at the discourse level, differentiating the narrative from embedded speech. At the end of the section, she states very plainly, "Markedness is not a member of a binary opposition, but a continuum of relatively more or less marked elements."[31] This is a very clear example of quantitative markedness applied at the grammatical level (even though she defines markedness as "asymmetric").

---

28. Ellen van Wolde, "Linguistic Motivation and Biblical Exegesis," *Narrative Syntax and the Hebrew Bible*, ed. Ellen van Wolde (Leiden: Brill, 1997), 21–50.

29. Van Wolde, "Linguistic Motivation," 25. While van Wolde references qualitative oppositions and asymmetric relationships, her attempt to place linguistic features in a relative hierarchy or continuum reflects a type of quantitative markedness.

30. Van Wolde, "Linguistic Motivation," 28.

31. Van Wolde, "Linguistic Motivation," 43.

Among Greek scholars, Stanley Porter has applied a quantitative approach to markedness. He says:

> Markedness has undergone much evaluation. What started as an attempt to mark certain phonological features, has broadened to include a variety of features that go toward indicating markedness. The result is that markedness is a concept that includes a complex of factors, depending upon the items being considered. Markedness in this scheme is not a matter of privative opposition regarding a single feature, but a cline of markedness values, from the least to the most heavily marked, but all formally based.[32]

This is a very clear description of quantitative markedness. When he defines the terms "marked" and "unmarked," however, he writes that they are

> labels given to various constructions to imply their relative semantic weights. The unmarked structure is often more frequently found, more diverse in form, less regular in structure, of less formal substance, less emphatic and of minimal essential meaning. The marked structure is often less frequent in appearance, more stable in form, more regular in structure, of greater formal substance, more emphatic, and of greater significance in meaning.[33]

This quantitative approach is used to weigh more or less semantically marked items. The problem, however, is that semantics is not the typical domain of quantitative markedness. With descriptions such as "more emphatic" in the definition, pragmatics is also included in Porter's quantitative cline. This is also not typically how quantitative markedness is used. Porter's rather idiosyncratic use of quantitative markedness, especially as it relates to verbal aspect, has caused substantial debate among those who study biblical Greek.[34]

---

32. Stanley Porter, *Idioms of the Greek New Testament*, 2nd ed. (Sheffield: Sheffield Academic, 1999), 55–56.

33. Porter, *Idioms of the Greek New Testament*, 311–12.

34. For example, Steven E. Runge challenges Stanley Porter's application of markedness to verbal aspect in biblical Greek in a recent issue of the *Bulletin for Biblical Research* (BBR). See Steven E. Runge, "Markedness: Contrasting Porter's Model with the Linguists Cited as

Finally, Gerhard Mussies has shown how markedness functions in Greek gender with substantive participles. He argues:

> The gender value of the masculine categories is the positive reference to a person, but this person may be male or female. Often the context gives a clue for us to decide whether woman (women) or man (men) is (are) spoken about, but not always so; in e.g. [Rev 22:11] ὁ δίκαιος δικαιοσύνην ποιησάτω ἔτι καὶ ὁ ἅγιος ἁγιασθήτω ἔτι[35] both sexes are meant indiscriminately. The masculine category is therefore unmarked as opposed to the feminine.[36]

Indeed, for substantival adjectives and participles for which grammatical gender is not lexically determined, Mussies proposes the following table:[37]

Marked		Unmarked
Referent is a person		Referent is a person or nonperson
Marked	Unmarked	
Referent is female	Reference is male	
Feminine gender	Masculine gender	Neuter gender

Mussies makes the case that for substantival adjectives and substantival participles, the chosen gender says something about the substantive's referent. The masculine and feminine genders are marked for personhood, but the neuter is not. The referent of a neuter participle might be a person or not. It is unmarked. Likewise, the feminine participle is marked for female biological gender with substantival participles and adjectives, but the masculine is not.

Support," *BBR* 26 (2016): 43–56. For Porter's response, see Stanley E. Porter, "What More Shall I Say? A Response to Steve Runge and Benjamin Merkle," *BBR* 26 (2016): 75–79.

35. *ho dikaios dikaiosynēn poiēsatō eti kai ho agios hagiasthētō eti* ("the righteous still do right, and the holy still be holy," ESV).

36. Gerhard Mussies, *The Morphology of Koine Greek as Used in the Apocalypse of St. John: A Study in Bilingualism* (Leiden: Brill, 1971), 123.

37. Adapted from Mussies, *Morphology of Koine Greek*, 124.

4.2.3.b Qualitative Approaches

Often the concept of markedness is applied to biblical Greek or Hebrew with the understanding that it designates a strictly binary opposition of marked and unmarked elements. One of the more frequent applications of qualitative markedness in the study of biblical Hebrew concerns unmarked and marked word order. Entire monographs and countless articles have been written that argue various theories about the default (unmarked) and marked word orders.[38] The debate hinges on the placement of the subject in relation to the verb. There are typically two options: subject-verb-object (SVO) or verb-subject-object (VSO).[39] As stated above, this discussion is in the subdomain of pragmatics, and the markedness at work is qualitative. Scholars are trying to understand what the marked word order is and, once defined, what the marking communicates. Markedness in the biblical languages has been predominantly used in the debate over word order. Unfortunately, markedness itself has been a loosely defined concept in much of the literature.

Because the literature defines markedness loosely, those practicing exegesis are hunting for the ever-popular "emphasis." "Marked," "emphatic," and "salient" are all terms that exegetes and commentators use carelessly. Certainly there are emphatic words and phrases in the biblical text—and these can be discerned through linguistic analysis—but a careful and appropriate application of markedness will identify the subdomain (grammatical, semantic, pragmatic, etc.) as well as the type (qualitative/quantitative, privative/equipollent) of markedness. Often the term "emphasis" is used for an element that is pragmatically marked for focus. When the word "emphasis" is used, though, the possibility exists that the reader of such a term could take it to mean that the word or phrase receiving the

---

38. The following works are representative of the word order debate in biblical Hebrew: Barry L. Bandstra, "Word Order and Emphasis in Biblical Hebrew Narrative: Syntactic Observations on Genesis 22 from a Discourse Perspective," in *Linguistics and Biblical Hebrew*, ed. Walter R. Bodine (Winona Lake, IN: Eisenbrauns, 1992), 108–23; Walter Bodine, ed., *Discourse Analysis of Biblical Literature: What It Is and What It Offers* (Atlanta: Scholars Press, 1995); Adina Moshavi, *Word Order in the Biblical Hebrew Finite Clause* (Winona Lake, IN: Eisenbrauns, 2010); Robert Holmstedt, "The Typological Classification of the Hebrew of Genesis: Subject-Verb or Verb-Subject?," *JHS* 11 (2011), article 14.

39. Proponents of VSO include Randall Buth, Bruce Waltke, Michael Patrick O'Connor, Takamitsu Muraoka, Adina Moshavi, Christo van der Merwe, Jan Joosten, and Joshua Westbury. Proponents of SVO include Robert Holmstedt, Geoffrey Khan, and Edit Doron.

emphasis is the most important element in the sentence. This may or may not be true. The same could be said for the word "salient." The solution to such a problem is an informed, unified understanding of markedness in its many forms. As readers engage with linguistic analyses of texts, they need to take into account the diverse ways markedness has been used. A valuable question to ask of any claims for a marked structure/constituent is: "Marked for what?" This question will help readers remember that there are many features that can be marked in an expression and keep them from labeling every unique structure as "emphatic."

4.3 RESOURCES FOR FURTHER STUDY

Battistella, Edwin L. *The Logic of Markedness.* New York: Oxford
    University Press, 1996.

> Battistella has written two books on markedness and has
> attempted to clarify the different approaches to the concept
> that have come out of different linguistic traditions, e.g., those
> indebted to Noam Chomsky versus those following the work of
> Roman Jakobson. Battistella's book assumes some familiarity
> with linguistics, but the first chapter provides a fairly readable
> overview of the subject.

Moshavi, Adina. *Word Order in the Biblical Hebrew Finite Clause.* Winona
    Lake, IN: Eisenbrauns, 2010.

> In her second chapter, Moshavi provides a discussion on
> markedness as it is brought to bear on the issue of word order
> variation in biblical Hebrew. She discusses, among other things,
> how the unmarked, or "basic," word order pattern is discerned as
> well as the various positions and arguments on each side of the
> word order debate (i.e., VSO vs. SVO) in biblical Hebrew.

Runge, Steven E. *Discourse Grammar of the Greek New Testament: A*
    Practical Introduction for Teaching and Exegesis. Peabody, MA:
    Hendrickson; Bellingham, WA: Lexham Press, 2010.

> In the introductory chapter, Runge provides a brief summary
> of markedness as it applies to discourse grammar and
> pragmatics. He then systematically demonstrates throughout

each subsequent chapter how markedness theory applies in distinguishing various grammatical devices in Greek that are marked for some pragmatic feature.

Runge, Steven E. "Markedness: Contrasting Porter's Model with the Linguists Cited as Support." *BBR* 26 (2016): 43–56; Porter, Stanley E. "What More Shall I Say? A Response to Steve Runge and Benjamin Merkle." *BBR* 26 (2016): 75–79.

The challenge of understanding and applying markedness is evident in these two journal articles. Runge reviewed the works of the linguists Porter often cites in connection with his ideas about markedness, but Runge did not find clear support for Porter's markedness claims in the linguistic literature. In his response, Porter insists that Runge is the one who has misunderstood the linguistic literature. However, Runge's article provides a helpful introduction to markedness theory and the different kinds of markedness that is largely compatible with the overview provided in this chapter.

5

MAJOR APPROACHES TO LINGUISTICS

Jeremy Thompson & Wendy Widder

The field of modern linguistics is relatively young, but its brief history is complex and multi-layered. People have been studying languages since at least as early as the second millennium BC. Writings from India and the ancient Near East give evidence of grammatical and phonetic analysis, and a first-millennium BC grammar of Sanskrit remains a definitive resource for modern students of the ancient language.[1] But although the field of modern linguistics continues the tradition of language study that began with these ancient works, its more immediate background is the nineteenth-century study of Indo-European languages, primarily conducted by scholars in Europe. This research was mainly comparative and historical, but it laid the groundwork for the developments to come in the twentieth century.[2]

In this chapter we introduce the major linguistic approaches that are relevant for the study of the biblical languages. The work on biblical languages in the nineteenth and early twentieth centuries derives mainly from the tradition of comparative philology. The origin of modern linguistics is typically linked to the work of Ferdinand de Saussure and structuralism.

---

1. Walter R. Bodine, "Linguistics and Biblical Studies," *AYBD* 4:327.
2. R. H. Robins, *A Short History of Linguistics*, 2nd ed. (London: Longman, 1979), 198. For a thorough overview of linguistic research in the nineteenth century, see Robins, *Short History*, 164–97.

The other major approaches covered in this chapter are functionalism, generative grammar, discourse analysis, and cognitive linguistics.

5.1 COMPARATIVE PHILOLOGY

Comparative philology, also called comparative or historical linguistics, was the dominant approach to language in the nineteenth century (see §1.4.1 Philology: The Traditional Approach to Languages). Comparative philology is the comparison of languages based on historical written sources in order to determine their relationships. This method proved useful in the study of biblical languages, especially biblical Hebrew with its lack of a significant amount of external evidence. While Bible scholars today rely much less on comparative and historical data, many grammars and lexicons for the biblical languages derive from this tradition of language study. Certain concepts of comparative philology—such as the focus on diachronic development (or changes over time)—are still relevant in contemporary linguistic debates about biblical Hebrew.[3]

With regard to biblical studies, the comparative philological approach has been far less common for Greek than for Hebrew.[4] This is largely due to the limited data for the ancient Hebrew language (see §6.1 Problems with the Data, which contrasts with the abundance of data for ancient Greek). Comparative philology has receded somewhat in recent work on biblical languages, as noted in the postscript to James Barr's *Comparative Philology and the Text of the Old Testament*.[5] However, many of the resources that interpreters of the Bible still use have comparative philology in the background. This is unsurprising since comparative philology, which Pieter Seuren traces back to a speech by Sir William Jones in 1786, played a major role in the study of languages from the early nineteenth to the early twentieth century, until the advent of structuralist linguistics.[6]

---

3. For example, see the essays contained in Cynthia L. Miller-Naudé and Ziony Zevit, eds., *Diachrony in Biblical Hebrew* (Winona Lake, IN: Eisenbrauns, 2012).

4. James Barr, *Comparative Philology and the Text of the Old Testament* (Winona Lake, IN: Eisenbrauns, 1987), 16–17. We should note, however, that modern historical linguistics continues some of the comparative and reconstructive work of comparative philology and that Greek is a significant source of data for research on the development of Indo-European languages.

5. Barr, *Comparative Philology*, 359.

6. For a full early history, see Pieter Seuren, *Western Linguistics: An Historical Introduction* (Malden, MA: Blackwell, 1998), 79–89.

5.1.1 DIACHRONY

Comparative philology looks at historical sources to determine relationships among languages. These sources are obviously written since there were no early methods for audio recording. The stages of the language over time are reconstructed and extrapolated from these written sources.[7] It is clear from this that comparative philology is diachronic in nature. Anyone familiar with the Brown-Driver-Briggs (BDB) lexicon of biblical Hebrew is familiar with comparative philological information. The following is an image of the initial section in the BDB entry for the root יד׳ (yd‘) from the electronic edition of BDB in Logos Bible Software.[8]

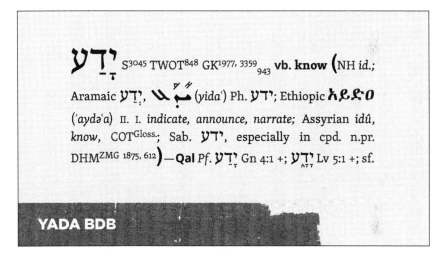

YADA BDB

Here the lexicon user finds historical relationships with languages such as Phoenician, Ethiopic, and Assyrian. As Barr notes, this word is generally taken to mean "know," and when this meaning is clear, this historical information is not called upon. The information about historical relationships is more often put to use to elucidate the meanings of rare usages. For this particular word, Barr notes at least five possible meanings distinct from to "know" based on comparative philological arguments, several of which he regards as more likely than others.[9]

---

7. Margaret Winters, "Languages Across Time," in *Cognitive Exploration of Language and Linguistics*, ed. R. Dirven and M. Verspoor (Philadelphia: John Benjamins, 2004), 208.

8. Francis Brown et al., *Enhanced Brown-Driver-Briggs Hebrew and English Lexicon* (Oak Harbor, WA: Logos Research Systems, 2000).

9. Barr, *Comparative Philology*, 27–33.

5.1.2 LANGUAGE FAMILIES

One of the other emphases of comparative philology is the delineation of language families. For example, comparative philologists are interested in reconstructing languages like Proto-Germanic as the ancestor of the Germanic languages and grouping all of the Germanic languages together under it, or even more ambitiously, Proto-Indo-European as the ancestor of languages spoken from India to Western Europe.[10] In most biblical Hebrew reference grammars, there is a section situating biblical Hebrew among the Semitic languages, which form a subdivision of the Afro-Asiatic languages. The breakdown of the Semitic languages typically looks something like the following:[11]

1. Semitic Languages
   a. East Semitic
      i. Eblaite
      ii. Akkadian
         1. Old Akkadian
         2. Assyrian
         3. Babylonian
   b. West Semitic
      i. Northwest Semitic
         1. Amorite
         2. Ugaritic
         3. Canaanite
            a. Phoenician
            b. Hebrew
            c. Moabite
            d. Ammonite
            e. Edomite
         4. Aramaic

---

10. Winters, "Languages Across Time," 204.

11. For other examples categorizing Hebrew within the family of Semitic languages, see Bruce K. Waltke and M. O'Connor, *An Introduction to Biblical Hebrew Syntax* (Winona Lake, IN: Eisenbrauns, 1990), 5–6; Christo H. J. van der Merwe, Jackie A. Naudé, and Jan H. Kroeze, *A Biblical Hebrew Reference Grammar* (Sheffield: Sheffield Academic Press, 1999), 15–16; Paul Joüon and T. Muraoka, *A Grammar of Biblical Hebrew*, rev. ed. (Roma: Pontificio istituto biblico, 2006), 2–8; John Huehnergard, "Languages: Introductory Survey," *AYBD* 4:155–62.

ii. Southwest Semitic
1. Arabian
a. North Arabic dialects
b. Classical Arabic
2. Ethiopian
3. South Arabian

The diachronic orientation of comparative philology is apparent here also. This kind of information is not normally used in the process of interpretation; we are simply noting it to demonstrate some of the interests of comparative philology before moving on to the importance of this method for biblical languages.

5.1.3 IMPORTANCE FOR BIBLICAL LANGUAGES

We noted at the beginning of this section that comparative philological analysis has receded to some degree; however, we should make clear that the method is not problematic in all its forms. Barr's examination of the subject was not aimed at doing away with comparative philological methods; rather he wanted to provide a more principled way to use them in light of many of the excesses of his time. For example, in his introduction he writes:

> The limited scope of the Old Testament provides a reason in favour of the philological approach. It is a comparatively small body of literature; there is little direct external evidence for the Hebrew of biblical times, and the post-biblical language has some striking differences. Not surprisingly the Old Testament contains many rare or unique expressions, which are difficult because they are unexampled elsewhere in Hebrew. Is it not then natural to turn to the large resources of the cognate languages, such as Arabic? These may suggest words which in their form could be cognate with a Hebrew form and which by their known meaning could suggest a suitable sense for it.[12]

---

12. Barr, *Comparative Philology*, 10.

Further, in the postscript:

> Looking back over nearly twenty years, the author can hardly fail to
> be satisfied with the effect that this book had. For it can scarcely be
> doubted that it succeeded in its central aim, which was to introduce
> an element of systematic and critical reflection into the prolifera-
> tion of novel identification of Hebrew words, supposedly based on
> the methods of comparative philology. *That such identifications could
> be right, that the method could work successfully, remains true, and I
> myself never doubted it.*[13]

In the book, Barr cites a number of comparative philological treatments
that he finds convincing and lays out a method for how to evaluate others.
With this in mind, what were the issues with comparative philology that
led to the adoption of other methods? Barr identifies several problems:
"The number of such identifications suggested, their constantly increasing
proliferation, and the frequent contradictions between one such solution
and another could not but lead to a deep scepticism in the end."[14] In terms
of broader trends in linguistics, however, the adoption of other methods
may have also had to do with the shift in focus to the study of one language
on its own terms. In his suggestions to students at the end of the book, he
states the following:

> An increased emphasis should be laid upon the statement of mean-
> ing in one language only. A Hebrew word has its meaning only
> in Hebrew, an Arabic word only in Arabic. We have to overcome
> the heritage of that supposedly comparative approach (actually
> anti-comparative in its effects) which defines a Hebrew word by
> thinking about what 'it means' in another language. The resources
> used in philological treatments (for example, the meaning of an
> Arabic word) are meanings in that language, while the results to
> be reached are meanings in Hebrew. Meaning in Hebrew is inde-
> pendent of meaning in Arabic, and depends on choices within the
> Hebrew lexical stock of a given time.[15]

---

13. Barr, *Comparative Philology*, 359; emphasis added.
14. Barr, *Comparative Philology*, 359.
15. Barr, *Comparative Philology*, 292.

This view is consonant with the earlier move within the field of linguistics as a whole to structuralist linguistics, where a language itself at one time should be the object of study.

Comparative philology studies historical written sources to identify relationships among languages. The method is valuable for elucidating the meanings of rare words, and Barr has made a number of important proposals about how to go about comparative philological analysis in a principled manner. However, despite proposals for a more principled approach, comparative philology has fallen out of use to some degree in research on the biblical languages due to a variety of factors, not the least of which was the advent of other types of linguistics, such as structuralism, with its primarily synchronic focus (that is, a focus on the language system as a whole, not its historical development). Many aspects of comparative philology, including categorizing languages by family and reconstructing diachronic changes in a language or language family, are now areas of research in historical linguistics.

5.1.4 RESOURCES FOR FURTHER STUDY

Groom, Susan A. "Chapter 4: Comparative Philology." Pages 45–71 in *Linguistic Analysis of Biblical Hebrew*. Waynesboro, GA: Paternoster, 2003

> Groom provides a detailed discussion of the presuppositions and principles of comparative philology with respect to biblical Hebrew study. She also provides an overview of Barr's concerns and guidelines for applying comparative philology to biblical texts.

Robertson, A. T. "Chapter 1.4: The New Grammatical Equipment for N.T. Study." Pages 8–30 in *A Grammar of the Greek New Testament in Light of Historical Research*. 3rd ed. New York: Hodder & Stoughton, 1919.

> In the first chapter of *A Grammar of the Greek New Testament in Light of Historical Research*, Robertson considers the contribution of comparative philology to the study of New Testament Greek.

Silva, Moisés. *God, Language and Scripture: Reading the Bible in the Light of General Linguistics*. Foundations of Contemporary Interpretation 4. Grand Rapids: Zondervan, 1990.

> Silva's book, an accessible introduction to linguistics in general, overviews a theology of language, the history of linguistics, and features of the biblical languages.

5.2 STRUCTURAL LINGUISTICS

5.2.1 FOUNDATION FOR MODERN LINGUISTICS

Most linguists mark the advent of structuralism as the beginning of modern linguistics. The same linguists, however, disagree over the degree to which modern linguistics has now departed from the structuralist approach. In what follows, we will give a brief overview of the history of structuralism and provide some indication of the degree to which structuralist approaches may still be in use. Structuralism conceives of meaning, at least partly, in terms of a set of contrasts;[16] therefore, it will be fitting, after the brief overview, to delve more deeply into structuralism by considering three of its important distinctions: synchrony versus diachrony, *langue* versus *parole*, and signifier versus signified.

Linguists generally agree that structuralist linguistics began with the work of the Swiss linguist Ferdinand de Saussure.[17] The landmark work in this regard was Saussure's *Course in General Linguistics*, published early in the twentieth century. The beginnings of structuralism are obscured due to uncertainty over which ideas in the *Course in General Linguistics* were actually Saussure's. He did not write the book; rather, it was compiled from his lectures by his students after his death. Thus, after a lengthy consideration of the book in which he criticizes some of its key ideas, Seuren concludes:

---

16. In the case of syntagmatic relationships, Saussure states: "In its place in a syntagma, any unit acquires its value simply in opposition to what precedes, or to what follows, or to both" (Ferdinand de Saussure, *Course in General Linguistics*, trans. Roy Harris [Chicago: Open Court, 1986], 121). Associative relations can be either based on opposition or similarity (ibid., 123-24).

17. For a sketch of Saussure's life and major ideas, see Peter H. Matthews, *Linguistics: A Very Short Introduction* (Oxford: Oxford University Press, 2002), 85-86.

It is important to realize that the criticisms we have do not apply to de Saussure as a person. First of all, we do not have his own text but only a text distilled from lecture notes. Then, we have reason to believe that de Saussure would not have approved the publication of the *Cours*, and if this was because he himself saw its inadequacies we can only respect him for not wanting to see it published. What we do see with great clarity is a man struggling to get certain ideas right, trying to find the right concepts for a proper structural linguistic analysis, and design an adequate terminology. He did not succeed as he himself knew, but he has helped others to make better progress.[18]

Indeed, Saussure's ideas were taken up by a variety of scholars with both a European school and American school of structural linguistics developing, each with their own interests. Seuren identifies Jan Baudouin de Courtenay and Saussure as the foundational figures in the European branch and Leonard Bloomfield and Edward Sapir in the American. Further, he states that the European variety was more introspective and the American more behavioristic. Despite these differences, he claims the one common thread was a modular view of language that set linguistics as a field of its own apart from the rest of psychology.[19]

The influence of an explicitly structuralist approach in linguistics began to wane to some degree with the advent of generative grammar and subsequently cognitive linguistics.[20] Each of these more recent schools of linguistics still works with some structuralist distinctions, though also departing in a number of important ways. For example, Saussure focused on the word as the primary unit of analysis,[21] whereas Chomsky focused

---

18. Seuren, *Western Linguistics*, 156. The French title for Saussure's work is *Cours de linguistique générale*.

19. Seuren, *Western Linguistics*, 143–44.

20. Though it is fading to some degree in the field of linguistics itself, structuralism has also had lasting effects in the movement referred to as poststructuralism. This movement included such well-known figures as Barthes, Derrida, and Foucault. For a brief introduction to the movement and its roots in the work of Saussure, see Catherine Belsey, *Poststructuralism: A Very Short Introduction* (Oxford: Oxford University Press, 2002).

21. Seuren, *Western Linguistics*, 155–56.

on syntax.[22] Saussure focused on meaning in terms of relations between linguistic units, whereas a cognitive approach to language views meaning as encyclopedic.[23] In other words, there is not as neat a separation between word knowledge and knowledge of the world in a cognitive approach

Yet despite the criticisms of generative and cognitive linguists, structuralism has re-emerged to some degree in the work on semantics of scholars like Anna Wierzbicka and Ray Jackendoff, whom Geeraerts classifies as neostructuralist.[24] Geeraerts goes so far as to claim that there are important potential points of contact between neostructuralist linguistics and cognitive linguistics.[25] To provide one example, Geeraerts explicitly identifies the English WordNet project[26] as neostructuralist.[27] Structuralism's interest in oppositions (e.g., love/hate) resulted in an interest in synonymy and antonymy, among other lexical relationships. WordNet emerged out of a different background of modern research in psycholinguistics on matters such as semantic priming and spreading activation.[28] In that research, relationships like synonymy and antonymy have been demonstrated to have some degree of psychological reality. Synonymy and the hyperonym-hyponym relationship provide the major organizational principles in WordNet. Thus, even though WordNet has a different starting point, it ended up with some of the same interests as structuralism.

---

22. For example, Chomsky's foundational work was his *Aspects of the Theory of Syntax* (Cambridge, MA: MIT Press, 1965).

23. See Vyvyan Evans and Melanie Green, *Cognitive Linguistics: An Introduction* (Edinburgh: Edinburgh University Press, 2006), 206-44.

24. For a full account of neostructuralist lexical semantics, see Dirk Geeraerts, *Theories of Lexical Semantics* (Oxford: Oxford University Press, 2010), 124-78.

25. For what follows on neostructuralism and WordNet, see Geeraerts, *Lexical Semantics*, 124-26, 158-60; and Jeremy Thompson, "The Bible Sense Lexicon: WordNet Theory Adapted for Biblical Languages" (paper presented at the Annual Meeting of the Society of Biblical Literature, Baltimore, MD, 2013), http://jeremythompson.ws/docs/BSLLexicographyThompsonSBL2013.pdf.

26. For more information on WordNet, see Princeton University, "About WordNet," *WordNet: A Lexical Database for English*, 2016, http://wordnet.princeton.edu/.

27. Geeraerts, *Lexical Semantics*, 125.

28. Christiane Fellbaum, "Introduction," in *WordNet: An Electronic Lexical Database*, ed. Christiane Fellbaum (Cambridge: MIT Press, 1998), 1-19.

5.2.2 IMPORTANT CONCEPTS

5.2.2.a Synchrony vs. Diachrony

The shift from diachronic study of language to synchronic study has been one of structuralism's lasting effects, though more recent research on matters such as grammaticalization has brought diachrony back into focus to some degree.[29] Saussure is explicit in stating what he means by synchronic and diachronic linguistics. He defines the terms as follows:

> *Synchronic linguistics* will be concerned with logical and psychological connexions between coexisting items constituting a system, as perceived by the same collective consciousness.
>
> *Diachronic linguistics* on the other hand will be concerned with connexions between sequences of items not perceived by the same collective consciousness, which replace one another without themselves constituting a system.[30]

Two aspects of these definitions are important. First, the distinction between synchrony and diachrony has to do with time. Synchronic study examines a language within a delimited period of time during which it was used by people with a shared "collective consciousness"; diachronic study examines a language over an extended period of time during which it was used by different sets of people who did not share the "same collective consciousness." Second, Saussure states that synchronic study views language as a system, whereas diachronic study views language as a sequence. In synchronic study, this system is made up of logical and psychological connections between coexisting items.

An example of the synchronic focus on a system of logical and psychological connections is Saussure's discussion of what he calls syntagmatic relations and associative relations, the latter of which are also often referred to as paradigmatic relations.[31] We provide our own examples here since Saussure's are not based on English. Syntagmatic relations are based on co-occurrence. For example, there is a syntagmatic relation between

---

29. For a fuller treatment of grammaticalization, see Evans and Green, *Cognitive Linguistics*, 707–34.

30. Saussure, *Course*, 98.

31. Saussure, *Course*, 121–23.

"of" and "course" because they frequently co-occur in the phrase "of course." The phrase "of course" also has a syntagmatic relation with the word "not" since we often say "of course not." According to Saussure, associative relations, on the other hand, are based on associations in the memory" or "in an individual's brain."[32] Saussure can be forgiven for being relatively vague about this, considering the state of knowledge of psychology and the brain at the time; however, the types of relations he has in mind are those between words like "teach," "learn," "instruct," "student," "school," etc. As hinted at above, the residual effect of the concepts of syntagmatic and associative relations can still be found in approaches to lexical semantics that focus on relationships like synonymy and antonymy.

5.2.2.b Langue and Parole

A second major distinction in structuralism is between "langue" and "parole." One could also perhaps include the term "langage." Seuren explains this set of three terms as they are used by Saussure as follows:

> De Saussure struggles with the threefold terminology of langage, langue, and parole. Langage, which has no equivalent in English, covers all manifestations of language: physical, physiological, psychological, social. It is best taken as the cover term for both langue, the type-level language system, and parole, the token-level physical use made of the language system, best translated as 'speech'.[33]

Langue is the language system that is abstracted away from actual use of language, whereas parole refers to language in use. This is in some ways parallel to the later distinction that would be made by Chomsky between language competence and language performance, though langue is not perfectly parallel to competence in the Chomskyan sense.[34]

Given Saussure's definition of synchronic linguistics in the last section, it is unsurprising to learn that he believed langue, the more systematic

---

32. Saussure, Course, 121–22.

33. Seuren, Western Linguistics, 148.

34. Chomsky, Aspects, 4. Lyons suggests that both Saussure and Chomsky focus on the language system, but Saussure's approach is more social psychological, and Chomsky's more generally psychological. See John Lyons, Language and Linguistics (Cambridge: Cambridge University Press, 1981), 10.

part of *langage*, is the proper object of linguistic study. Though modern linguists may not work within the same categories, it is interesting to note that one major distinction between the schools of generative and cognitive linguistics is the degree to which they focus on either an abstract idealization away from language, more characteristic of the Chomskyan generative school,[35] or on the data of actual language use, more characteristic of cognitive linguists.[36]

5.2.2.c Signifier and Signified

The final distinction introduced by Saussure is that between *signifier* and *signified*, to which we might also add the term *sign*, since a sign is the result of an association between a signifier and a signified. Saussure's reflections on signs led to the development of the field of semiology or semiotics, which is closely related to linguistics;[37] however, the distinctions he made often cause some confusion since in ordinary language usage we are accustomed to thinking about words being used to make reference to objects in the real world. Yet recall from the previous section that Saussure is interested in the abstract idealization of language and not language in use. Therefore, in Saussure, a sign is a purely mental entity.[38] An oversimplified example may help: the sign CAT is an association between the sounds used to make up the word "cat" in a person's mind (i.e., not the physical sounds produced when the words are spoken) and the mental representation a person has of a cat.[39]

One of the other aspects of signs that is important in Saussure is that signs are arbitrary. Early philosophers did not always believe this; however, in modern linguistics, this is generally accepted . For example, there is nothing about the sounds that make up the word "table" that make it

---

35. Chomsky, *Aspects*, 3–4.

36. Evans and Green, *Cognitive Linguistics*, 108–47.

37. For example, Cruse includes a section in the introductory chapter of his *Meaning in Language* entitled "Language as a Sign System: Some Basic Notions of Semiotics" (Alan Cruse, *Meaning in Language: An Introduction to Semantics and Pragmatics*, 3rd ed. [Oxford: Oxford University Press, 2011], 10–12).

38. Seuren, *Western Linguistics*, 152.

39. If this seems like a difficult concept to grasp, keep in mind that one of the criticisms of Saussure's account of meaning would be a failure to give an account of reference. See Seuren, *Western Lingiustics*, 155.

ideal to represent a piece of furniture that has a flat surface people often eat on and that often has four legs. Pinker notes that the closest we can get to nonarbitrary signs are onomatopoeia and certain kinds of words that cluster around certain combinations of letters like "gl- for the dimension of light: *glare, glass, glaze, gleam, glimmer, glimpse, glint, glisten, glitter, gloaming, gloss, glow*."[40] But it is agreed that this kind of "sound symbolism" is very limited.

5.2.3 IMPORTANCE FOR BIBLICAL LANGUAGES

Structuralism did have its effects on the grammatical study of biblical languages; however, since Saussure viewed the word as the primary unit of linguistic analysis, it is easiest to see the effects of structuralism in the area of lexicography. Four recent lexicons of biblical languages are influenced by a structuralist framework, whether or not they explicitly recognize this influence: *A Greek-English Lexicon of the New Testament: Based on Semantic Domains, The Dictionary of Classical Hebrew*, the *Semantic Dictionary of Biblical Hebrew*, and the *Bible Sense Lexicon*.[41] We will discuss the first, third, and fourth of these in more detail. Concerning *The Dictionary of Classical Hebrew*, van Hecke concludes that "structuralism is clearly the 'modern linguistics' in which the dictionary has its theoretical basis, even if the editors do not explicitly acknowledge it."[42]

With their arrangement at least partly based on ontological domains, the other three lexicons are influenced by structuralism to some degree, though their explicitly stated frameworks may be different. For example, de Blois seeks to bring in much more of the cognitive perspective in the *Semantic Dictionary of Biblical Hebrew*.[43] The *Bible Sense Lexicon* finds its roots

---

40. Steven Pinker, *The Stuff of Thought: Language as a Window into Human Nature* (New York: Viking, 2007), 304.

41. Johannes P. Louw and Eugene A. Nida, eds., *Greek-English Lexicon of the New Testament: Based on Semantic Domains*, 2 vols. (New York: United Bible Societies, 1989); David J. A. Clines, ed., *The Dictionary of Classical Hebrew*, 8 vols. (Sheffield: Sheffield Academic Press, 1993-2011); Reinier de Blois, ed., *Semantic Dictionary of Biblical Hebrew* (New York: United Bible Societies, 2000-2012), http://www.sdbh.org/; Jeremy Thompson, *Bible Sense Lexicon: Dataset Documentation* (Bellingham, WA: Faithlife Corporation, 2015).

42. Pierre van Hecke, *From Linguistics to Hermeneutics: A Functional and Cognitive Approach to Job 12-14* (Leiden: Brill, 2011), 290.

43. Reinier de Blois, "Lexicography and Cognitive Linguistics: Hebrew Metaphors from a Cognitive Perspective" (paper presented at the Annual Meeting of the Society of Biblical

in WordNet, which, as mentioned above, emerges out of psycholinguistics research. Yet despite the different provenances of these lexicons, the resulting arrangements at least partly hark back to Saussure's conception of paradigmatic relations. As Geeraerts makes clear, the organization of words into lexical and semantic fields can be traced back within structuralism to Jost Trier.[44] There have obviously been developments. For example, de Blois attempts to make clearer the important distinction between lexical and contextual domains.[45] Further, none of those who worked on these lexicons are likely to state that meaning is purely determined by a set of contrasts; however, not to note the influence of structuralism on these resources would also be an oversight.

5.2.4 RESOURCES FOR FURTHER STUDY

Matthews, Peter. *A Short History of Structural Linguistics*. Cambridge: Cambridge University Press, 2001.

> Matthews provides a concise historical survey of structural linguistics, charting its development from the 1870s to the present day.

Seuren, Pieter. *Western Linguistics: An Historical Introduction*. Malden, MA: Blackwell, 1998.

> For a more comprehensive discussion of the development of structuralism, particularly with respect to how it relates to other linguistic theories, the reader should refer to Seuren's *Western Linguistics*.

Van der Merwe, Christo H. J., et al. "Chapter 1.3: A Short Review of the Grammatical Treatment of Biblical Hebrew." Pages 18–21 in *A Biblical Hebrew Reference Grammar*. Sheffield: Sheffield Academic Press, 1999.

> Van der Merwe et al. provide a very brief discussion of the influence of structural linguistics on modern Hebrew grammars,

---

Literature, Toronto, ON, 2002). http://www.sdbh.org/documentation/Paper_SBL_2002.pdf.

44. Geeraerts, *Lexical Semantics*, 53–70.

45. Reinier de Blois, "Towards a New Dictionary of Biblical Hebrew Based on Semantic Domains" (paper presented at the Annual Meeting of the Society of Biblical Literature, Nashville, TN, 2000). http://www.sdbh.org/documentation/Paper_SBL_2000.pdf.

with particular reference to Joüon and Muraoka's *A Grammar
of Biblical Hebrew* and Waltke and O'Connor's *An Introduction to
Biblical Hebrew Syntax.*

5.3 FUNCTIONALISM

Functionalism takes as its starting point that the end function of language
is communication, and it works backward toward understanding language
as a whole. This approach is debated. For example, Chomsky rejects both
the premise that the primary purpose of language is communication and
the idea that knowing a system's function can aid in understanding the
system as a whole.[46] On the other hand, other linguists see no reason why
formal and functional perspectives cannot both play important roles in
language analysis. Pinker, who in many ways popularizes Chomsky's views
on Universal Grammar, goes so far in his preface to *The Language Instinct* as
to state, "If my personal synthesis seems to embrace both sides of debates
like 'formalism versus functionalism' ... perhaps it was because there never
was an issue there to begin with."[47] In other words, both form and function
can provide important insights into language as a whole.

This introduction to functionalism will consist of four parts. First, we
trace functionalism's relationships with other schools of linguistics. Second,
we discuss the variety within functionalism itself. Third, we review several important concepts within functionalism, such as markedness, topic-
comment, and typology and universals (see chap. 4). Finally, we discuss some
of the impact that functionalism has had on the study of biblical languages.

5.3.1 RELATIONSHIP TO OTHER LINGUISTIC APPROACHES

We will see that functionalism's relationship to the Chomskyan school of
generative grammar is mixed (see §5.4 Generative Grammar). The two
schools of linguistic thought to which functionalism is most closely aligned

---

46. Chomsky believes that language is primarily a vehicle for thought and suggests that
function is interesting only from an evolutionary perspective and not from the perspective
of the individual language user. See Noam Chomsky, *On Language* (New York: New Press,
2007), 86–88.

47. Steven Pinker, *The Language Instinct: How the Mind Creates Language* (New York:
William Morrow, 1994), xiv.

are structuralism and cognitive linguistics (see §5.6 Cognitive Linguistics). More specifically, functionalism grew out of structuralism and shares similar goals with cognitive linguistics. Many linguists trace the beginnings of functional linguistics to the development of the Prague school.

Seuren claims that Saussure's *Course in General Linguistics*, a foundational text for structuralism, had a significant effect on the Prague school. Two particular aspects of structuralism that influenced the Prague school were its psychological view of meaning and the view that language is an autonomous system that can be studied in its own right. A psychological view of meaning was apparent in the work of Anton Marty, to whom Seuren traces the beginnings of the Prague school and to whom he attributes the view that "everything semantic is psychological, not logical."[48] The structuralist emphasis on language as a system can be seen clearly in approaches like Systemic Functional Linguistics. For example, Suzanne Eggins devotes an entire chapter to the systematic nature of language in her introduction to Systemic Functional Linguistics.[49]

More recently, scholars have recognized a close connection between functionalism and the modern school of cognitive linguistics. For example, Brigitte Nerlich and David Clarke state,

> Natural allies of Cognitive Linguistics by contrast are functionalists and contextualists of all persuasions from the Prague School onward: Functional Grammar (Dik), Systemic-Functional Grammar (Halliday), functional-typological theories (Givón) ...[50]

They further cite Ronald Langacker as follows: "The movement called *Cognitive Linguistics* belongs to the functionalist tradition."[51] In sum, functionalism developed with strong influences from structuralism and has affinities with cognitive linguistics while maintaining a somewhat mixed relationship with the school of generative grammar.

---

48. Seuren, *Western Linguistics*, 157.

49. Suzanne Eggins, *An Introduction to Systemic Functional Linguistics*, 2nd ed. (London: Continuum, 2004), 188–205.

50. Brigitte Nerlich and David Clarke, "Cognitive Linguistics and the History of Linguistics," in *The Oxford Handbook of Cognitive Linguistics*, ed. D. Geeraerts and H. Cuyckens (Oxford: Oxford University Press, 2007), 590.

51. Nerlich and Clarke, "Cognitive Linguistics and the History of Linguistics," 590.

5.3.2 VARIETY WITHIN FUNCTIONALISM

Already some variety within functionalism could be seen in the different focus areas of the Prague school. Scholars in the Prague school focused on matters as distinct as topic–comment and phonology. Work on topic–comment was conducted by Vilém Mathesius and much of the work on phonology was done by Jakobson and Trubetzkoy.[52] In more recent years, however, the variety has increased to such an extent that three particular functionalist approaches have merited large-scale comparison and contrast: Functional Grammar, Systemic Functional Grammar, and Role and Reference Grammar.[53]

5.3.2.a Functional Grammar

The linguist primarily associated with Functional Grammar is Simon Dik. Dik's major work on Functional Grammar was published in two parts after his death with each book having the main title *The Theory of Functional Grammar* and differing in subtitle.[54] In the introductory chapter of the first of these works, he articulates the goals of a functionalist approach to language in contrast to a formalist approach. According to Dik, a formalist approach is interested in specifying the rules used to construct linguistic utterances "independently of the meanings and uses of the constructions described."[55] Functionalism, likewise, is interested in determining the rules for forming linguistic constructions; however, the functionalist must go one step further. Not only must functionalists decipher "the rules which govern the constitution of linguistic expressions (semantic, syntactic, morphological, and phonological rules)," but also they must determine "the rules which govern the patterns of verbal interaction in which these linguistic expressions are used (pragmatic rules)."[56] In other words, the functionalist linguist must connect form with function.

---

52. Seuren, *Western Linguistics*, 158–59.

53. Matthew Anstey and J. Lachlan Mackenzie, "Introduction," in *Crucial Readings in Functional Grammar*, ed. Matthew Anstey and J. Lachlan Mackenzie (Berlin: Mouton de Gruyter, 2005), vii.

54. More specifically, the first part was published in a second edition while the second part was published for the first time after his death. See Anstey and Mackenzie, "Introduction," vii.

55. Simon C. Dik, *The Theory of Functional Grammar, Part 1: The Structure of the Clause*, ed. K. Hengeveld (Berlin: Mouton de Gruyter, 1997), 2–3.

56. Dik, *Functional Grammar*, 3–4.

5.3.2.b Systemic Functional Grammar

In *The Linguistics Encyclopedia*, Kirsten Malmkjaer primarily focuses on the work of Michael Halliday in her entry for Functional Grammar, though Halliday's particular approach is technically referred to as Systemic Functional Grammar or Systemic Functional Linguistics.[57] However, she does begin the article by contrasting Halliday's approach with Dik's, which provides a starting point for us to understand Systemic Functional Grammar since we can compare it with Functional Grammar. Dik's approach is oriented toward communicative competence (broken down into grammatical competence and pragmatic competence) and, in some ways, shares in Chomsky's cognitive psychological outlook, whereas Halliday's approach is more oriented toward social psychology or sociolinguistics.[58] As an approach in its own right, Eggins states that there are two primary goals of Systemic Functional Linguistics, namely "it seeks to develop both a theory about language as social process *and* an analytical methodology which permits the detailed and systematic description of language patterns."[59] Therefore Systemic Functional Linguistics seeks to explain "what language is, how it works, its relation with context" and to provide a "set of techniques for analysing different aspects of the language system (e.g., analyses of transitivity, mood, theme, the clause complex)."[60]

5.3.2.c Role and Reference Grammar

Role and Reference Grammar (RRG) shares some similarities with other types of functional grammar. For example, Robert Van Valin states in his summary of RRG:

> With respect to cognitive issues, RRG adopts the criterion of psychological adequacy formulated in Dik (1991), which states that a theory should be 'compatible with the results of psycholinguistic

---

57. Kirsten Malmkjaer, "Functional Grammar," in *The Linguistics Encyclopedia*, ed. K. Malmkjaer (London: Routledge, 2003).

58. Malmkjaer, "Functional Grammar," 190.

59. Eggins, *Systemic Functional Linguistics*, 21.

60. Eggins, *Systemic Functional Linguistics*, 21.

research on the acquisition, processing, production, interpretation and memorization of linguistic expressions.'[61]

Yet he also states what motivated the development of RRG in general, which distinguishes it from other types of functional grammar as follows:

Role and Reference Grammar ... grew out of an attempt to answer two basic questions: (i) what would linguistic theory look like if it were based on the analysis of languages with diverse structures such as Lakhota, Tagalog, Dyirbal and Barai, rather than on the analysis of English?, and (ii) how can the interaction of syntax, semantics and pragmatics in different grammatical systems best be explained?[62]

From this we can gather that typological concerns play a much more important role in RRG than in other functional approaches. This typological orientation results in a different kind of formalization. RRG has shown promise for analyzing biblical language; therefore, those interested in learning more about this approach may wish to access the useful summaries and introductions to RRG that Van Valin has made available online.[63] For those who would also like to gain some experience in employing RRG, Emma Pavey's *The Structure of Language* provides a significant number of useful exercises.[64]

---

61. Robert D. Van Valin Jr., "A Brief Overview of Role and Reference Grammar," §1 (unpublished paper, Department of Linguistics & Center for Cognitive Science, State University of New York at Buffalo, 2002) http://www.acsu.buffalo.edu/~vanvalin/rrg/RRGpaper.pdf.

62. Robert D. Van Valin Jr., "A Summary of Role and Reference Grammar," §1 (unpublished paper, University at Buffalo, The State University of New York, 2008), http://www.acsu.buffalo.edu/~vanvalin/rrg/RRGsummary.pdf.

63. Van Valin's website with resources related to RRG can be found at http://www.acsu.buffalo.edu/~vanvalin/rrg.html.

64. Emma Pavey, *The Structure of Language: An Introduction to Grammatical Analysis* (Cambridge: Cambridge University Press, 2010).

5.3.3 IMPORTANT CONCEPTS IN FUNCTIONALISM

Three of the important concepts that we will discuss in relation to functionalism are markedness, topic and comment, and linguistic typology and language universals.[65]

5.3.3.a *Markedness*

In simplest terms, work on markedness begins with the assumption that linguistic units can either be unmarked or marked (see §4.2 Markedness). A linguistic unit that is unmarked is "most typical/usual" and marked means "atypical, unusual."[66] For example, in English, we typically use a Subject-Verb-Object word order as in "John hit the ball." This example sentence follows unmarked word order. On the other hand, if someone said "It was the ball that John hit," this would be considered marked word order since it is less typical. This second sentence might indicate that the speaker means that John hit the *ball* as opposed to something else.

Work on markedness goes beyond syntactical issues, such as word order, to include issues related to phonology and morphology as well. Sometimes a speaker can even mark a linguistic unit simply by violating the normal way of referring to something. An interesting biblical example occurs when the author of Genesis 1 refers to "the greater light" and "the lesser light" (v. 16). This could be considered marked usage since these entities are generally referred to as simply "the sun" and "the moon." In this case, the marked usage may be because the author is trying to avoid using the Hebrew words for "sun" and "moon," since these are also the names of Canaanite deities.[67]

5.3.3.b *Topic and Comment*

Related to markedness, functionalists are also interested in the concept of "topic and comment," an aspect of information structure. The functionalist interest in "topic and comment (or focus), theme and rheme, given and new" can be traced back to the beginnings of functionalism in the Prague

---

65. Aside from "topic and comment," these concepts were introduced in chapter 4 on "Language Universals, Typology, and Markedness."

66. Eggins, *Systemic Functional Linguistics*, 317.

67. Ronald Hendel, *The Book of Genesis: A Biography* (Princeton: Princeton University Press, 2013), 149.

school with the work of Mathesius on his "functional sentence perspective." According to Seuren, this work on topic and comment began with Mathesius and has continued until the present day—"in the mid-1980s the Prague developments in this respect have merged with work done in various centers in the world ...."[68] In fact, a whole area of research has developed around these concepts referred to as information structure. It would be impossible to do justice to the complexities of this area of research here. As Nomi Erteschik-Shir notes, there are at least two different binary approaches to information structure in addition to her own model.[69] Thus, we will mention only the most basic distinctions and allow readers to delve further into the complexities if they so desire.

In general, a "topic" is taken to refer to what a sentence is about (i.e., the given information in a sentence), whereas a "comment" is new information being provided about a topic. Erteschik-Shir notes that topic and comment "can be marked intonationally, syntactically (by word order), and morphologically."[70] As an example of how topic and comment work, Erteschik-Shir provides the following question-answer pairs in which the topic is marked in italics and the focus is in all capitals:

(1)   a   Q: What did John do?
          A: *He* WASHED THE DISHES.
      b   Q: What did John wash?
          A: *He* washed THE DISHES.[71]

In each case, John is the topic of the answer because he is mentioned in the question. Two analogous ways of saying this would be that John is the given information in the answers or that John is what the answers are about. The comment answers the respective questions of "what." In the first case, the what-question refers to John's activity; therefore, the comment, or new information, is that he "washed the dishes." In the second example, the what-question refers to the object of John's activity of washing, so the comment is simply "the dishes." These are relatively simple

---

68. Seuren, *Western Linguistics*, 158.

69. Nomi Erteschik-Shir, *Information Structure: The Syntax Discourse Interface* (Oxford: Oxford University Press, 2007), 42–43.

70. Erteschik-Shir, *Information Structure*, 43.

71. Erteschik-Shir, *Information Structure*, 1.

examples, and matters very quickly become complicated. Readers interested in delving further into information structure should begin with the works of Erteschik-Shir and Knud Lambrecht.[72]

5.3.3.c Typology and Language Universals

Finally, as seen in the discussion of Role and Reference Grammar above, typology and language universals also play an important role in functionalism. This is in contrast to the school of generative grammar, which has often been criticized for its tendency to focus on English to the exclusion of the wide majority of the world's languages.[73] According to Croft, there are three kinds of work in linguistic typology, namely typological classification, typological generalization, and typological theorizing (see §4.1 Language Universals and Typology). Typological classification involves a language being taken "to belong to a single type, and a typology of languages is a definition of the types and an enumeration or classification of languages into those types."[74] Typological generalization works on the data discovered in classification and is "the study of the patterns that occur systematically across languages. ... The patterns found in typological generalization are language universals."[75] The most common kind of language universal is an implicational universal of the kind "if a language has x, then the language also has y." For example, one proposed universal is, "If a language has dominant SOV order and the genitive follows the governing noun, then the adjective likewise follows the noun."[76] Typological theorizing involves "constructing explanations" over typological generalizations. This results in an approach to the study of language that has been referred

---

72. Erteschik-Shir, *Information Structure*; Knud Lambrecht, *Information Structure and Sentence Form: Topic, Focus and the Mental Representations of Discourse Referents* (Cambridge: Cambridge University Press, 1996).

73. Note, however, that generative grammar attempts to arrive at language universals or Universal Grammar via the in-depth study of the structure of one language (English) and rejects the relevance of cross-linguistic universals.

74. William Croft, *Typology and Universals*, 2nd ed. (Cambridge: Cambridge University Press, 2003), 1–2.

75. Croft, *Typology and Universals*, 1–2.

76. This is universal number five, which can be found in "The Universals Archive." To get a feel for the different types of linguistic universals that functional linguists use in their theorizing, you can examine their broad array of universals here: http://typo.uni-konstanz.de/archive/intro/.

to as the functional-typological approach, which can be traced back to Joseph Greenberg and is associated with scholars such as Bernard Comrie.[77]

5.3.4 IMPORTANCE FOR BIBLICAL LANGUAGES

For research on biblical Hebrew, the influence of functionalism can be found in the works of scholars such as van der Merwe and Nicolai Winther-Nielsen. For an overview of functionalist developments within the study of biblical Hebrew it would be impossible to do better than the summary in van der Merwe's article entitled "Some Recent Trends in Biblical Hebrew Linguistics."[78] In the footnotes to the section of the article devoted to functional approaches, he cites more than forty references related to the study of biblical Hebrew in which functionalist approaches played a major role.[79] As one example of a specific functionalist framework being employed, Winther-Nielsen has done a significant amount of work related to the application of RRG to biblical Hebrew.[80] With regard to biblical Greek, the influence of functionalism can be seen in approaches like Runge's discourse grammar.[81] One of Runge's foremost principles, that "choice implies meaning," plays a prominent role in Halliday's Systemic Functional Grammar. The work of Stephen Levinsohn also reflects functionalist influences as in his *Discourse Features of the New Testament*, which bears the subtitle *A Coursebook on the Information Structure of New Testament Greek*.[82]

5.3.5 RESOURCES FOR FURTHER STUDY

Pavey, Emma. *The Structure of Language: An Introduction to Grammatical Analysis*. Cambridge: Cambridge University Press, 2010.

---

77. Croft, *Typology and Universals*, 2.

78. Christo H. J. van der Merwe, "Some Recent Trends in Biblical Hebrew Linguistics: A Few Pointers Towards a More Comprehensive Model of Language Use," *Hebrew Studies* 44 (2003): 7–24.

79. Van der Merwe, "Some Recent Trends in Biblical Hebrew Linguistics," 17–20.

80. For example, see Nicolai Winther-Nielsen, "Biblical Hebrew Parsing on Display: The Role-Lexical Module (RLM) as a Tool for Role and Reference Grammar," *Hiphil Novum* 6 (2009): 1–51.

81. Steven E. Runge, *Discourse Grammar of the Greek New Testament: A Practical Introduction for Teaching and Exegesis* (Bellingham, WA: Lexham Press, 2010), 5–7. With reference to this principle in Halliday's approach, see Eggins, *Systemic Functional Linguistics*, 188–90.

82. Stephen Levinsohn, *Discourse Features of New Testament Greek: A Coursebook on the Information Structure of New Testament Greek*, 2nd ed. (Dallas: SIL, 2000).

Pavey provides an accessible and practical introduction to RRG. She assumes no prior knowledge of linguistic terminology and includes over 100 exercises designed to reinforce each major concept that is discussed.

Runge, Steven E. "Chapter 9: Information Structure." Pages 181–205 in *Discourse Grammar of the Greek New Testament: A Practical Guide for Teaching and Exegesis*. Bellingham, WA: Lexham Press, 2010.

Runge's chapter on information structure describes the various functions of word order variation in the Greek New Testament. He presupposes no prior familiarity with the linguistic concepts involved and provides numerous examples from the New Testament.

Van Hecke, Pierre. *From Linguistics to Hermeneutics: A Functional and Cognitive Approach to Job 12–14*. Leiden: Brill, 2011.

Van Hecke includes an overview of the relationship between Functional and Cognitive Linguistics and how these complementary linguistic fields can shed light on issues of biblical interpretation, with particular reference to Job 12–14.

5.4 GENERATIVE GRAMMAR

The most influential movement in linguistics during the twentieth century was generative grammar, variously called "Transformational Grammar" (TG), "Standard Theory," "Extended Standard Theory" (also the Lexicalist Hypothesis), "Trace Theory," "Government and Binding" (later "Principles and Parameters"), and the "Minimalist Program."[83] The theory of generative grammar has developed and even diverged into differing viewpoints over the years, but it dominated the linguistic landscape for the latter half of the twentieth century and continues to be important today.

---

83. Lyle Campbell, "The History of Linguistics," in *The Handbook of Linguistics*, ed. Mark Aronoff and Janie Rees-Miller (Oxford: Wiley Blackwell, 2002), 102.

5.4.1 NOAM CHOMSKY

Noam Chomsky, one of the most influential American linguists of the twentieth century, is the originator of generative grammar. Chomsky spent his career as a professor at MIT, where he wrote prolifically in the field of linguistics. He also published extensively on war, politics, and mass media, and in 1994 was "among the ten most-cited writers in all of the humanities [and social sciences] (behind only Marx, Lenin, Shakespeare, the Bible, Aristotle, Plato, and Freud) and the only living member of the top ten."[84]

The driving question behind Chomsky's linguistic research was how every human being is able to learn a first language with ease and then also able to create an infinite number of grammatically correct sentences that have never before been uttered. Also, speakers who never formally study the rules of their own language are able to identify grammatically correct and incorrect statements. Chomsky's goal was to explain this innate competence and versatility of native speakers in every language. This goal determined the primary level of linguistic analysis for generative grammar: namely, the syntax of the sentence. Reflecting this emphasis, Chomsky published *Syntactic Structures* in 1957, effectively beginning the subfield of linguistics known as generative grammar, defined as "a formal system ... which makes explicit the finite mechanisms available to the brain to produce infinite sentences in ways that have empirical consequences and can be tested as in the natural sciences."[85]

5.4.2 RELATIONSHIP TO OTHER LINGUISTIC APPROACHES

Chomsky's research developed in response to structuralist ideas of language as a self-contained, autonomous system, independent of its users.[86] Instead Chomsky held that language was one of many systems in the mind.

> Just as the human body consists of various parts each with its own function and developmental history (liver, kidneys, eyes, etc.), so the human mind consists of components which, though interacting,

---

84. Pinker, *The Language Instinct*, 23.

85. Campbell, "The History of Linguistics," 100.

86. John R. Taylor, *Linguistic Categorization*, 3rd ed. (Oxford: Oxford University Press, 2003), 15.

nevertheless develop and operate independently. One such component is the language faculty.[87]

In spite of this major difference between structuralism and generative grammar, there are similarities in the structuralist distinction between *langue* and *parole* and the generativist distinction between the "competence" and "performance" of a native speaker. Competence is "the internalized ability acquired as a child to produce grammatical, that is, acceptable or well-formed, sentences"[88] in one's native language, while "performance" is the way the language is actually used.

Chomsky's approach to linguistics was also a reaction against behaviorist views of language, "which held that language is a set of learned responses to stimuli."[89] According to the generativist view, the variety, creativity, and productivity of spoken language are not a kind of reflex but rather reflect an innate human system of knowledge.

5.4.3 IMPORTANT CONCEPTS

Generative grammar has several important and interrelated concepts: Universal Grammar, deep structure and surface structure, and transformations. Together these concepts comprise the basic tenets of the original theory of generative grammar. Variations of the theory may nuance and apply these concepts differently, but for our purposes, this general introduction will suffice.

5.4.3.a Universal Grammar

Every language shares characteristics with others. For example, every language has a way to ask and answer questions, to make requests and assertions, and so on. All languages combine sounds to make words and then group words into phrases, clauses, and sentences. While vocabulary and syntax may differ, "there is nothing that can be expressed in one language

---

87. Taylor, *Linguistic Categorization*, 15.

88. Walter R. Bodine, "How Linguists Study Syntax," in *Linguistics and Biblical Hebrew*, ed. Walter R. Bodine (Winona Lake, IN: Eisenbrauns, 1992), 99.

89. Victoria Fromkin, Robert Rodman, and Nina M. Hyams, *An Introduction to Language*, 9th ed. (Boston: Wadsworth, Cengage Learning, 2011), 290.

that cannot be expressed in any other."[90] Even the word "language" or the expression "natural human language" reveals a "belief that at the abstract level beneath the surface variation, languages are remarkably similar in form and function and conform to certain universal principles."[91]

Generative grammar proposes that underneath all these similarities—these "language universals"—is a Universal Grammar, a set of rules that can explain what appear to be universal properties of language and also account for a wide range of differences among languages. This Universal Grammar also addresses the native speaker's innate competence and versatility (see §4.1.1 Generative Universal Grammar).

5.4.3.b Deep Structure and Surface Structure

A tenet of Universal Grammar is that every sentence has a "deep structure" and a "surface structure". Consider the following pair of sentences:

> The girl is reading.
> Is the girl reading?

We intuitively know that these sentences are related. One is a declarative statement and the other is an interrogative, but they both involve a girl reading. Their meanings only differ in that one makes an assertion and the other asks a question. The signal of this difference is the word order of the sentences. That is, they exhibit different surface structures.[92] Generativists explain the relationship between these two sentences by positing a common underlying structure, the deep structure, which has undergone syntactic changes to create the two surface structures.

5.4.3.c Transformations

The syntactic changes that occur in a deep structure to create corresponding surface structures are called "transformations". This is the reason generative grammar is also known as "Transformational Grammar" or even "Transformational-Generative Grammar." According to the theory of generative grammar, a finite set of rules dictates the transformations that a

---

90. Adrian Akmajian et al., *Linguistics: An Introduction to Language and Communication*, 5th ed. (Cambridge: MIT Press, 2001), 8.

91. Akmajian, *Linguistics*, 8.

92. Illustration adapted from Fromkin et al., *An Introduction to Language*, 115.

deep structure can undergo. Native speakers intuitively know these rules, so they can easily create an infinite number of new, grammatically correct sentences.

The idea of transformations is rooted in a universal feature of language in which sentences are composed of phrases in a particular order. No language allows its words and phrases to occur in a random order. Further, the order of the phrases operates in a hierarchical system.[93] The illustration below shows how this hierarchy works.

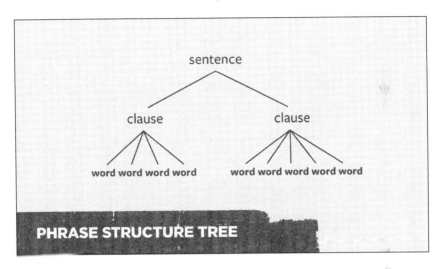

PHRASE STRUCTURE TREE

This hierarchy, illustrated in what is called a "tree structure" (or a "phrase structure tree" or a "constituent structure tree"), is based on the relationships among constituents, words or phrases that function as single units. Determining the constituents in a sentence or clause is as simple as asking a few questions. These questions are "who?," "where?," and "what?" Consider the sentence "The quick brown fox jumped over the lazy dog." Who jumped over the lazy dog? The quick brown *fox*. What did the quick brown fox do? *Jumped*. Where did the quick brown fox jump? *Over* the lazy dog. These questions and answers identify three constituents: "the quick brown fox," "jumped," and "over the lazy dog." A second way to identify

---

93. Generativists differ in their approaches to the relationships among phrases in a sentence, and some prefer to think in terms of "dependency" rather than "hierarchy." Further, the idea of hierarchy in syntax is not limited to the theory of generative grammar.

constituents is to try replacing each with a pronoun or another word. If they can be replaced, then the constituents have been correctly identified:[94]

He (the quick brown fox) jumped over the lazy dog.
The quick brown fox *did* (jumped [over the lazy dog]).
The quick brown fox jumped *there* (over the lazy dog).

In a tree structure, the constituents remain grouped together:

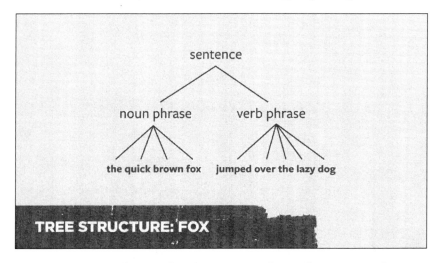

TREE STRUCTURE: FOX

Some sentences have ambiguous syntax—that is, there is more than one way to read it. Such ambiguity can be the basis for humorous misreadings. Consider the sentence "I shot a bear in my pajamas," where the ambiguous syntax allows that either I or the bear wore my pajamas. Compare the two tree structures below to see how each represents the syntactic hierarchy:[95]

---

94. Illustration adapted from Peter James Silzer and Thomas John Finley, *How Biblical Languages Work: A Student's Guide to Learning Hebrew and Greek* (Grand Rapids: Kregel, 2004), 122.

95. These tree structures represent simplified versions of the hierarchy that generativists would use.

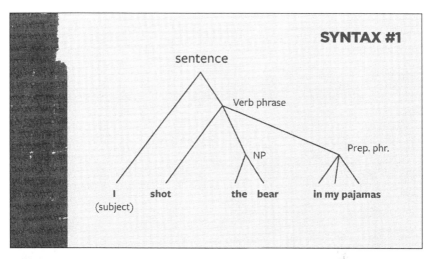

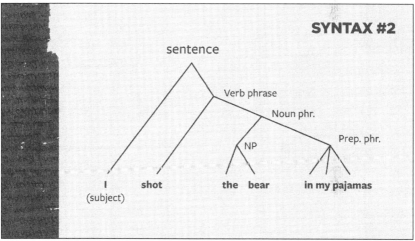

This illustration simply shows how tree structures and hierarchies work. There are no "transformations" in it. To illustrate a transformation, we return to the pair of related sentences above:

The girl is reading.
Is the girl reading?

English is an SVO language—that is, the order of constituents in its sentences is subject-verb-object. We see this in the first sentence, "The girl (S) is reading (V) [a book (O)]."[96] More technically, the verb in this sentence

---

96. The object is not required but is added here in brackets for illustration.

has two parts: an "auxiliary" ("is") and a verb ("reading").[97] Its tree structure looks like this:[98]

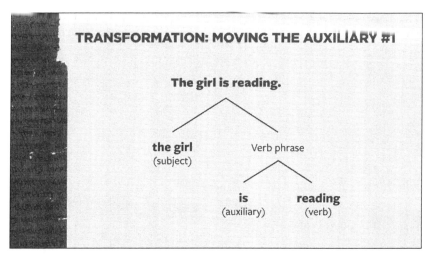

The interrogative sentence represents a variation on this pattern
and is more specifically called a "yes-no question." A native speaker of
English knows intuitively how to turn the declarative first sentence into
the "yes-no" interrogative second sentence. Generativists say it occurs
when syntactic movement occurs according to a "transformational rule."
The transformational rule of "yes-no" questions requires an "auxiliary" slot
before the subject in the tree structure. The tree structure looks like this:

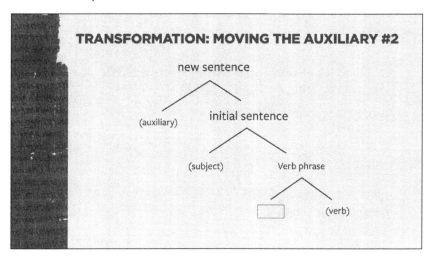

97. Such "auxiliary" words are more commonly called "helping verbs" in English grammar.
98. For the sake of simplicity, we omit the object "the book" in the tree illustrations.

The transformation of the declarative sentence into a yes-no question occurs when the auxiliary "is" moves from its slot in the verb phrase to the "auxiliary" slot before the subject. The new tree structure looks like this (notice the now empty auxiliary slot under the verb phrase):

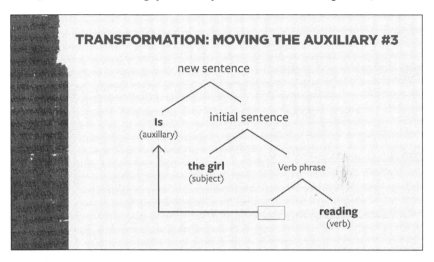

These syntactic trees illustrate the process of transformation in generative grammar. While Chomsky introduced the theory of generative grammar, his ideas about transformations were not new. His teacher, Zellig Harris, had previously incorporated transformational relations between sentences with different syntactic structure. However, Chomsky proposed a set of transformational rules that went beyond the work of his teacher and was also in line with "the older European tradition" of language instruction.[99]

5.4.4 IMPORTANCE FOR BIBLICAL LANGUAGES

The dominance of generative grammar in the field of linguistics for several decades means that many biblical scholars who have incorporated linguistics into their scholarship have used its methodology. For example, Richard Young uses transformational rules explicitly throughout his intermediate Greek grammar, though he uses non-generative theories as well.[100] David

99. Robins, *A Short History of Linguistics*, 227.

100. Richard A. Young, *Intermediate New Testament Greek: A Linguistic and Exegetical Approach* (Nashville, TN: Broadman & Holman, 1994).

Alan Black, in his chapter on Greek syntax, includes a brief discussion of generative grammar (he uses the label "transformational–generative grammar") in which he talks about how the theory can be applied to New Testament Greek.[101] Bruce Waltke and Michael O'Connor consider differences between deep and surface structures in their *Introduction to Biblical Hebrew Syntax*,[102] and Adele Berlin contrasts the same throughout her analysis of parallelism in biblical Hebrew.[103] Further, the notions of deep and surface structure have been applied beyond the sentence level of generative grammar and are used by those who focus on discourse and refer to such things as the "deep structure of a narrative."[104] Even those who may be unfamiliar with generative linguistic theory have drawn on its ideas, especially the notions of deep and surface structure.[105]

5.4.5 RESOURCES FOR FURTHER STUDY

Black, David Alan. *Linguistics for Students of New Testament Greek: A Survey of Basic Concepts and Applications*. 2nd ed. Grand Rapids: Baker, 1995.

Black provides a brief discussion of generative grammar as it is applied to New Testament Greek syntax.

---

101. David Alan Black, *Linguistics for Students of New Testament Greek: A Survey of Basic Concepts and Applications*, 2nd ed. (Grand Rapids: Baker, 1995), 114–18. Elsewhere he uses the terminology "deep" and "surface structure" apart from the generative framework (see, e.g., p. 18).

102. Waltke and O'Connor, *An Introduction to Biblical Hebrew Syntax*, 141. Also note their brief introduction to the concepts of deep and surface structure on p. 61.

103. Adele Berlin, *The Dynamics of Biblical Parallelism*, rev. and exp. ed. (Grand Rapids: Eerdmans, 2008), 132.

104. Jean-Marc Heimerdinger, *Topic, Focus and Foreground in Ancient Hebrew Narratives* (Sheffield: Sheffield Academic Press, 1999), 54. See similar usage in David Allan Dawson, *Text-Linguistics and Biblical Hebrew* (Sheffield: Sheffield Academic Press, 1994).

105. Many of these applications occur in cultural studies, where the "deep structure" is something like worldview and "surface structure" roughly equates to behavior. See, e.g., Ben Peays, "Fantasy Funerals and Other Designer Ways of Going Out in Style," in *Everyday Theology: How to Read Cultural Texts and Interpret Trends*, ed. Kevin J. Vanhoozer et al. (Grand Rapids: Baker, 2007), 210. For other uses, see, e.g., David Buttrick, "Interpretation and Preaching," in *The Renewal of Sunday Worship*, ed. Robert E. Webber (Nashville, TN: Star Song, 1993), 329; and Adrian Thatcher, "Living Together before Marriage: The Theological and Pastoral Opportunities," in *Celebrating Christian Marriage*, ed. Adrian Thatcher (Edinburgh: T & T Clark, 2001), 66.

DeCaen, Vincent. "A Unified Analysis of Verbal and Verbless Clauses within Government-Binding Theory." Pages 109–31 in *The Verbless Clause in Biblical Hebrew: Linguistic Approaches*, edited by Cynthia L. Miller-Naudé. Winona Lake, IN: Eisenbrauns, 1999.

DeCaen has applied the generative notion of transformational grammar, as represented by the Government–Binding Theory, to a syntactic analysis of the verbless clause in biblical Hebrew.

5.5 DISCOURSE ANALYSIS

Discourse analysis approaches language at higher levels than the sentence. It is interested in units of several sentences or paragraphs and it even extends to the level of genre. Scholars who apply discourse analysis to written texts (and not to speech) may also use the label "text linguistics" or even "discourse linguistics."[106]

Discourse analysis is a term that "has become nearly synonymous with contextual studies of almost any kind."[107] Discourse analysis encompasses writing, speech, conversation, and any other kind of communicative event (e.g., movies), making the term too broad to be very helpful. Many different disciplines engage in "discourse analysis," including sociology, anthropology, and communication arts. Broadly speaking, these studies involve "questions of style, appropriateness, cohesiveness, rhetorical force, topic/subtopic structure, differences between written and spoken discourse, as well as grammatical properties."[108]

Some biblical scholars use the discourse labels loosely and interchangeably, calling their work discourse analysis, text-linguistics, discourse grammar, discourse linguistics, and so on. But other scholars mean very specific things by their use of the terms and may not think everything done "in

---

106. "Discourse analysis" is a rather vague and overused label. In Europe, the term "text linguistics" is used for a discourse approach focused on written texts, and "conversation analysis" is used to designate a focus on spoken discourse. "Discourse linguistics" is something of a hybrid label, apparently indicating text-based analysis similar to "text linguistics" but retaining the association with "discourse" (see Robert Bergen, ed., *Biblical Hebrew and Discourse Linguistics* [Dallas: SIL, 1994]). The term "discourse grammar" is also used to specify a discourse approach to language (see Runge, *Discourse Grammar of the Greek New Testament*).

107. Peter J. MacDonald, "Discourse Analysis and Biblical Interpretation," in *Linguistics and Biblical Hebrew*, ed. Walter R. Bodine (Winona Lake, IN: Eisenbrauns, 1992), 154.

108. Fromkin et al., *An Introduction to Language*, 167.

their name" qualifies as discourse analysis.[109] Nonetheless, in our broad overview of the discourse approach to language, we will not distinguish between these terms.

5.5.1 RELATIONSHIP TO PREVIOUS APPROACHES

The focus of generative grammar was the sentence, but not the meaning of the sentence—just its syntax. Chomsky famously illustrated the difference between syntax and semantics in his sentence "Colorless green ideas sleep furiously," which is grammatically correct but nonsensical.[110] The limitations of such an approach became apparent when scholars could not account for "syntactic phenomena such as variations of word order, tenses, and pronoun usage" without recourse to semantics.[111] Meaning and function above the sentence level are integral to the ways humans use language.

Discourse linguistics recognized that the formal and structural approaches of structuralism and generative grammar could not account for certain grammatical phenomena and how they affected meaning. However, some of the categories of functionalism provided ways to explain features of language at the multi-sentence/paragraph level and at the "extra-sentential (from the linguistic and wider context of the utterance)" level.[112] Functional categories such as topic, focus, and markedness are key concepts in discourse linguistics (see §5.3 Functionalism).

5.5.2 IMPORTANT ASSUMPTIONS AND CONCEPTS

Robert Bergen identifies five basic assumptions about language that are fundamental to the discourse perspective.[113] First, every language is a code known to the writer/speaker and the reader/listener. They both understand a set of symbols to have certain meanings, or their communication

---

109. Linguist and biblical Hebrew scholar Michael O'Connor contends that "discourse linguistics has attracted a certain amount of abuse." He cites just one example and concludes the label "serves only to distance the work from ordinary biblical studies and applies a thin veneer of science to the whole" (Michael O'Connor, "Discourse Linguistics and the Study of Biblical Hebrew," in *Congress Volume Basel 2001*, ed. A. Lemaire [Leiden: Brill, 2002], 38–39n79).

110. Noam Chomsky, *Syntactic Structures*, 2nd ed. (The Hague: Mouton de Gruyter, 2002), 15.

111. MacDonald, "Discourse Analysis and Biblical Interpretation," 153.

112. MacDonald, "Discourse Analysis and Biblical Interpretation," 153.

113. Robert D. Bergen, "Text as a Guide to Authorial Intention: An Introduction to Discourse Criticism," *JETS* 30.3 (1987): 327–36.

would be unintelligible. For example, English speakers understand the word "chair" to mean something that a person can sit on. If someone said, "I basted the chair," the listener would not know what this statement means because it violates what the symbol "chair" means. However, a shared code is not only a matter of vocabulary. For example, consider the expression "September 11." An American English speaker knows that very often this does not simply refer to a day of the year. It refers to an event and it is weighted with significance. The concept of language as a shared code creates an obvious problem for study of the biblical languages: namely, we neither know the full code nor can we ask anyone who does. One of the tasks of discourse analysis, in conjunction with the findings of other areas of biblical scholarship, is to recover as much of the language codes that we can but to recognize that we will always be limited in our knowledge.

A second assumption is that "most of the communication process occurs at the subliminal level of human consciousness."[114] Such things as length of sentences and paragraphs, the order of words, and the kind of information are all subliminal. For example, a relatively short book that uses very simple sentences does not need to specify that it is for children. By contrast, a long book with varied prose is clearly for advanced readers, whether or not it explicitly says so.

A third, related assumption is that these subliminal factors contain essential information about the speaker/author's intent. In the example above, the two authors intended to write for different audiences. Consider another example. If a father arrives home from work and his wife says, "Guess what *your* son did?," she probably intends something very different than if she said, "Guess what *our* son did?" The referent of "your son" and "our son" is the same, but the choice of pronoun is significant to the intent of her statement.

A fourth assumption is that a language code is genre-specific, that is, the code differs according to genre. The listener/reader expects certain signals of the code to reveal the writer's intention. For example, when a work begins with the phrase "Once upon a time," the reader expects to read a fairy tale. Or when a reader sees a list of ingredients with specific portions, the expectation is that a list of cooking directives will follow.

---

114. Bergen, "Text as a Guide," 328.

The [fifth and] final assumption is that although language codes are specific to each language, there is also a shared set of principles among the world's languages. These include that (1) texts are multi-tiered in organization (phonemes, morphemes, etc.) and (2) "each successively higher level of textual organization influences all of the lower levels of which it is composed"[115] (i.e., language is organized from the top down; e.g., the genre of "American evangelical sermon" has an expected length, format, language, etc.). Further, (3) authors do not intend every part of a text to carry equal significance and (4) the language code allows them to indicate significance, (5) which they do. To indicate degrees of significance in a text, an author can vary the order of information, spend more time on one topic than another, use unusual language, or omit expected information. These can all signal to native speakers/readers, who know what is "normal" in their language, when the author considers a section of writing to be more significant. Again, the difficulty of studying the biblical languages is that the data is limited. However, discourse analysts work to discover what they can of biblical language "norms."

Given all these assumptions, discourse-oriented scholars analyze texts to determine their structure—that is, their beginning, middle, and end, along with all the paragraphs in between. They assume that the text is both coherent (semantically held together) and cohesive (syntactically held together). They establish what material qualifies as background information and what is in the foreground. They isolate how authors develop themes, highlight topics, and work within specific genres. By these and other means, they attempt to understand what an author intended to communicate through a text.

5.5.3 IMPORTANCE FOR BIBLICAL LANGUAGES

Discourse analysis is a growing field of interest among biblical scholars. Extensive work has already been done in biblical Hebrew, and scholars of New Testament Greek are beginning to produce more in this area of study. In early OT discourse scholarship, the work of Robert Longacre dominated the field. Focusing on the function of the Hebrew verb in narrative discourse, he produced a full-length book studying the discourse

---

115. Bergen, "Text as a Guide," 330.

features of the Joseph story in Genesis.[116] In a later notable study, Jean-Marc Heimerdinger critiqued the limited scope of Longacre's methodology and integrated the broader research of narrative studies into his analysis of discourse features in biblical Hebrew.[117]

Another important advance in biblical Hebrew that has come from discourse analysis is the awareness of deference language, explained by O'Connor: "The various societies reflected in the Bible are class-based and show strong gender differentiation, and resulting social distinctions are often coded deep in the language."[118] The OT shows this coding in interactions between social superiors, typically called "my lord" (אֲדֹנִי ʾădônay), and their inferiors, who typically call themselves "your servant" (עַבְדְּךָ ʿabdĕkā). The inferior uses such language to "deflect attention from himself and to avoid encroaching on his superior or threatening his superior's social status, his 'face.'"[119]

Discourse studies in New Testament Greek began in earnest during the 1990s with three edited volumes by Stanley Porter and D. A. Carson.[120] The first volume dealt with a broad range of linguistic topics, including discourse analysis, and the second two specifically focused on discourse analysis. Additionally, linguist Stephen Levinsohn's book, *Discourse Features of New Testament Greek: A Coursebook on the Information Structure of New Testament Greek*,[121] provided translators with tools they needed to analyze the New Testament text beyond the sentence level. Building on the work of Levinsohn and others, Steven Runge produced a discourse grammar for New Testament Greek aimed at students of the language who are

---

116. Robert E. Longacre, *Joseph: A Study in Divine Providence: A Text Theoretical and Textlinguistic Analysis of Genesis 37 and 39–48*, 2nd ed. (Winona Lake, IN: Eisenbrauns, 2003).

117. Heimerdinger, *Topic, Focus and Foreground in Ancient Hebrew Narratives*.

118. O'Connor, "Discourse Linguistics," 23.

119. O'Connor, "Discourse Linguistics," 23.

120. Stanley E. Porter and D. A. Carson, eds., *Biblical Greek Language and Linguistics: Open Questions in Current Research* (Sheffield: Sheffield Academic Press, 1993); *Discourse Analysis and Other Topics in Biblical Greek* (Sheffield: Sheffield Academic Press, 1995); *Linguistics and the New Testament: Critical Junctures* (Sheffield: Sheffield Academic Press, 1999). See also Stanley E. Porter and Jeffrey T. Reed, eds., *Discourse Analysis and the New Testament: Approaches and Results* (Sheffield: Sheffield Academic Press, 1999).

121. Levinsohn, *Discourse Features of New Testament Greek*.

nonspecialists. He attempts to "bridge the chasm that has too long existed between traditional and linguistic approaches."[122]

5.5.4 RESOURCES FOR FURTHER STUDY

Bergen, Robert D. "Text as a Guide to Authorial Intention: An Introduction to Discourse Criticism." *JETS* 30.3 (1987): 327–36.

> Bergen is interested in how the advances of discourse studies can help exegetes understand what the biblical authors meant. He provides an excellent summary of basic concepts in discourse linguistics and some examples of how they are evident in the Bible.

Bodine, Walter R., ed. *Linguistics and Biblical Hebrew.* Winona Lake, IN: Eisenbrauns, 1992.

> Bodine's overview of how linguistics has intersected with biblical Hebrew includes a pair of chapters on discourse analysis and a pair on comparative linguistics. The first chapter of each pair introduces the particular method and the second is an example of the method's usage in research on biblical Hebrew.

Dooley, Robert A., and Stephen H. Levinsohn. *Analyzing Discourse: A Manual of Basic Concepts.* Dallas: SIL, 2001.

> Dooley and Levinsohn's practical handbook introduces and illustrates basic concepts in discourse linguistics. They wrote the manual for linguists working on living languages, but many of the concepts are also applicable to biblical studies.

Runge, Steven E. *Discourse Grammar of the Greek New Testament: A Practical Introduction for Teaching and Exegesis.* Bellingham, WA: Lexham Press, 2010.

> Runge's discourse grammar builds on the work of Stephen Levinsohn, making it available to a wider audience of Greek students who are nonspecialists.

---

122. Runge, *Discourse Grammar of the Greek New Testament*, 18.

5.6 COGNITIVE LINGUISTICS

Cognitive linguistics emerged in the 1970s. It is not a single linguistic theory, unlike many fields of linguistics. Instead it is "a conglomerate of more or less extensive, more or less active centers of linguistic research that are closely knit together by a shared perspective."[123] Geeraerts identifies twelve fundamental centers of cognitive linguistic research, including cognitive grammar, prototype theory, conceptual metaphor, and frame semantics. We will only deal specifically with a few aspects of cognitive linguistics.

The "shared perspective" of cognitive linguists, regardless of their particular interest, revolves around a basic principle and four tenets. The basic principle is that language is all about meaning. Understandably then, semantics has been the focus of much of the research of cognitive linguists, although there is a good amount of work being done in other areas as well. The first of four basic tenets is that meaning is perspectival and language "embodies" these different perspectives. For example, compare these two apparently contradictory statements: "The bike is behind the house" and "The bike is in front of the house." Geeraerts explains how each embodies a different perspective on the same situation: If you are standing in the backyard facing the house,

> In the first expression, the perspective is determined by the way you look. the object that is situated in the direction of your gaze is in front of you, but if there is an obstacle along that direction, the thing is behind that obstacle. In this case, you're looking in the direction of your bicycle from the back garden, but the house blocks the view, and so the bike is behind the house.
>
> In the second expression, however, the point of view is that of the house: a house has a canonical direction, with a front that is similar to the face of a person. The way a house is facing, then, is determined by its front, and the second expression takes the point of view of the house rather than the speaker, as if the house were a person looking in a certain direction.[124]

---

123. Dirk Geeraerts, "Introduction: A Rough Guide to Cognitive Linguistics," in *Cognitive Linguistics: Basic Readings*, ed. D. Geeraerts (The Hague: Mouton de Gruyter, 2006), 2.

124. Geeraerts, "Introduction," 4.

The second tenet of cognitive linguistics is that meaning is dynamic and flexible. Language adapts as our experiences and environments change. The third tenet is that meaning is encyclopedic and nonautonomous. That is, it is neither a separate structure (Saussure) nor an independent component in the mind (Chomsky). Meaning entails our knowledge of the world and reflects what we experience. Finally, meaning is based on usage and experience, not abstract structures.[125] Grammatical patterns such as "subject-verb-object" are useful in theory, but "they are always part of actual utterances and actual conversations." Cognitive linguistics is a "usage-based model of grammar."[126]

5.6.1 RELATIONSHIP TO OTHER LINGUISTIC APPROACHES

It may be clear already from these four tenets how cognitive linguistics is related to previous linguistic approaches. Structuralism viewed language as an autonomous entity governed by a set of rules, and generative grammar similarly said language was governed by a set of innate rules. Cognitive linguistics contends that language is not an autonomous cognitive faculty, but instead operates in conjunction with life experiences and other cognitive abilities.[127] Knowledge of language must derive from language use, not abstract, theoretical structures.

When generativists Charles Fillmore and George Lakoff tried to apply the syntax-oriented generative framework to semantics, it did not work. The inadequacy of generative grammar for semantic study, combined with advances in study of human cognition, led to a reconsideration of earlier ideas about the connection between language and thought (see §5.6.2.a Sapir-Whorf Hypothesis below) and eventually resulted in the field of cognitive linguistics, which asserts that language "offers a window into cognitive function, providing insights into the nature, structure and organisation of thoughts and ideas."[128]

---

125. Geeraerts, "Introduction," 5–6.

126. Geeraerts, "Introduction," 6.

127. William Croft and D. Alan Cruse, *Cognitive Linguistics* (Cambridge: Cambridge University Press, 2004), 1.

128. Evans and Green, *Cognitive Linguistics*, 5.

5.6.2 IMPORTANT CONCEPTS

Cognitive linguistics has at least twelve fundamental areas of research. In this introductory volume, we will focus our attention on one key area of research (i.e., prototype theory) and one important concept used widely in linguistics (i.e., frames). We begin by discussing a hypothesis that predates cognitive linguistics by several decades but laid some groundwork for it.

5.6.2.a Sapir-Whorf Hypothesis

Cognitive linguistics did not emerge as a discipline until the second half of the twentieth century, but some of its core ideas developed out of the work of early twentieth-century American linguists Edward Sapir and Benjamin Lee Whorf. Sapir did extensive fieldwork among Native Americans, and Whorf, his student, developed his teacher's insights into a linguistic hypothesis that came to be known as the "Whorf Hypothesis" or the "Sapir-Whorf Hypothesis." Whorf proposed that the structure of a language determines or limits the way its speakers view the world.[129] For example, in some studies of biblical languages, scholars have suggested that Greek was a better language than Hebrew for NT revelation because it has a past, present, and future tense. D. A. Carson describes this erroneous thinking: "New Testament writers needed to be able to look back to what God had revealed in the *past*, grasp what God was going to do in the *present*, and anticipate what God was going to do in the *future*. But did not the covenant community in Isaiah's day have similar needs? Were the ancient Hebrews unable to distinguish past, present, and future because their language has only two aspects?"[130] Later linguists largely rejected this theory because it posits that language constricts a person's worldview, but the notion that language and cognitive processes are somehow related is foundational to cognitive linguistics.[131]

---

129. Fromkin et al., *Introduction to Language*, 311.

130. D. A. Carson, *Exegetical Fallacies*, 2nd ed. (Grand Rapids: Baker, 1996), 45.

131. Modern linguistic research has unequivocally demonstrated that language does not determine, constrain, or limit thought as the Sapir-Whorf hypothesis claimed (Fromkin et al., *Introduction to Language*, 312–13), and cognitive linguistics is not resurrecting this sort of linguistic determinism. However, cognitive linguistics is interested in the same problem, namely, the intersection of language, cognition, and culture. See §3.2.2.a Language, Culture, and Thought.

5.6.2.b Prototype Theory

One fundamental area of cognitive linguistic research is prototype theory, which originated in the research of cognitive psychologist Eleanor Rosch during the mid-1970s. A prototype is the best example of a given linguistic category. For example, in cognitive semantics, the category "bird" may have a robin as its prototype for people from the American Midwest.[132] Prototypes are also used in other areas of linguistics, such as grammar. For example, many verbs are transitive, that is, they have a subject that acts in some way on an object (e.g., "hit" is a transitive verb: "He hit the ball"). But linguists consider some verbs *more* transitive than others, that is, they are better prototypes for the category "transitivity." A prototypically transitive verb involves "a volitionally acting [subject] performing a concrete, dynamic action which has a perceptible and lasting effect on a specific [object]."[133] For example, "teach" can be a transitive verb, as in, "I teach children," but it is less transitive than verbs like "hit" or "break," which are more concrete and dynamic and exhibit a more perceptible effect on the object. A prototype serves as a point of reference, or even a core meaning, for a category and enables people to navigate the category's "not-so-clear instances" with relative ease.[134]

Prototype theory has four basic concepts about mental categories. First, every mental category has an exemplar that depicts the category's relevant features (e.g., "robin" for the category "bird"). Second, there are good and bad (or marginal) members in every category (e.g., "robin" and "penguin"). Third, every category has features that are important but not necessarily essential (e.g., "birds fly"). Finally, the boundaries of a category are blurry, so something may actually be a member of more than one category at a time (e.g., an 18-year-old can be considered both an "adult" and a "youth" or "teen").

---

132. Prototypes are not absolutes. They vary according to people's experiences. Thus, people living in the Amazon region would likely have a different exemplar than "robin" for their mental category "bird."

133. Åshild Næss, *Prototypical Transitivity* (Amsterdam: John Benjamins, 2007), 15.

134. Taylor, *Linguistic Categorization*, 45.

5.6.2.c Frames

A fundamental idea in cognitive linguistics is that the meaning of a word is better described in terms of an encyclopedia entry than a dictionary entry.[135] The meaning of a word entails a range of semantic or cognitive domains. George Lakoff illustrates with the word "mother." There are at least five domains for the word "mother":

> (a) the genetic domain. A mother is a female who contributes genetic material to a child; (b) the birth domain. A mother is a female who gives birth to the child; (c) the nurturance domain. A mother is a female adult who nurtures and raises a child; (d) the genealogical domain. A mother is the closest female ancestor; (e) the marital domain. The mother is the wife of the father.[136]

This collection of domains makes up what cognitive linguists call a "frame," "the knowledge network linking the multiple domains associated with a given linguistic form."[137] This "mother frame" is more than a random set of domains. Together these domains create the context for our understanding of the word "mother" and the entire frame "embodies deeply held beliefs about the status and role of the family in society."[138] However, not every usage of a word activates all the domains in a given frame. Consider the word "mother." Not every mother is a birth mother (i.e., the genetic and birth domains). Not every mother is married (i.e., the marital domain). Not every mother is the primary caregiver (i.e., the nurturance domain). But the conceptual structure of the frame helps us organize and categorize reality.[139]

5.6.3 IMPORTANCE FOR BIBLICAL LANGUAGES

The most widely used aspect of cognitive linguistics in biblical studies is cognitive semantics, although some scholars are beginning to publish in

---

135. Evans and Green, *Cognitive Linguistics*, 215–22.

136. Taylor, *Linguistic Categorization*, 89–90. Taylor is rephrasing and condensing George Lakoff, who uses the word "model" instead of "domain" (*Women, Fire, and Dangerous Things: What Categories Reveal about the Mind* [Chicago: The University of Chicago Press, 1987], 74–75).

137. Taylor, *Linguistic Categorization*, 90.

138. Taylor, *Linguistic Categorization*, 91.

139. Croft and Cruse, *Cognitive Linguistics*, 8.

other areas, including cognitive grammar and cognitive syntax.[140] One of the areas of particular interest in cognitive semantics is the study of metaphor. Metaphors and other figurative language occur extensively in the Bible, and it is an ongoing challenge to effectively and accurately translate such language.

The concepts of domains and frames are foundational to understanding how metaphors work, because while every metaphor has a network of ideas behind it, it only draws on particular ideas in a given use. To interpret it otherwise is to misinterpret it. For example, when Jesus says, "I am the door," we should not try to interpret what kind of material the door is, or whether it is paneled, or what its hinges might look like. The metaphor in the context Jesus used it (John 10:9) refers to a door*way*—the entrance to the pasture, another metaphor.

Metaphors become more complex when we try to translate them from one language into another because figurative language is culturally specific. For example, consider the familiar metaphor in Psalm 23, "the Lord is my shepherd." The ancient audience of Psalm 23 had a frame for "shepherd" that matched that of the author, so they would have understood which aspects the metaphor highlighted. The pastoral imagery reflected their life experiences. However, we are culturally far removed from such an environment, and correct understanding of the metaphor requires that we understand the ancient culture. Further, Bible translators may discover that words for "shepherd" in other languages entail (and omit) domains that were not part of the original frame. If these differences skew the meaning of the metaphor, the translator has to decide whether to translate "literally" or to capture the meaning of the metaphor instead.

5.6.4 RESOURCES FOR FURTHER STUDY

Taylor, John R. *Linguistic Categorization.* 3rd ed. Oxford: Oxford University Press, 2003.

> Taylor's book is a classic and readable introduction to the important concept of prototypes. He also addresses how

---

140. See Ellen van Wolde, *Reframing Biblical Studies: When Language and Text Meet Culture, Cognition, and Context* (Winona Lake, IN: Eisenbrauns, 2009), 8.

cognitive linguistics applies to polysemy, metaphor, morphology, syntax, and phonology.

van Wolde, Ellen. *Reframing Biblical Studies: When Language and Text Meet Culture, Cognition, and Context*. Winona Lake, IN: Eisenbrauns, 2009.

Van Wolde provides a detailed discussion of cognitive linguistics (with particular focus on Langacker's Cognitive Grammar) and then applies this framework to a variety of case studies in biblical Hebrew.

6

LINGUISTIC ISSUES IN BIBLICAL HEBREW

Wendy Widder

T he application of modern linguistics to biblical Hebrew has greatly advanced our knowledge of the language. However, there remain several challenges for scholars attempting to do linguistic analysis with the language of the Old Testament. In this chapter, we consider some of the most significant issues facing linguists and biblical scholars working with biblical Hebrew.

6.1 PROBLEMS WITH THE DATA

The field of modern linguistics developed as a way to analyze living languages—that is, languages that are presently spoken and are continually developing. Since written language is a derivation of spoken language, it provides linguistic data that is secondary to spoken data. These foundations of linguistic study present the biblical Hebrew linguist with at least three challenges in their analyses of the language of the Old Testament.

The first difficulty of studying biblical Hebrew using linguistic methodology is that our knowledge of the language is confined to what we have in the Old Testament, which was composed and compiled over a thousand-year period of time.[1] Even including epigraphic materials written in

---

1. This represents the consensus view. Other scholars think the Old Testament was composed in its entirety during the Persian period. See §6.5 The Chronology and Typology Debate below.

ancient Hebrew does not significantly increase the corpus.[2] When one considers how much the English language has changed since just the time of Shakespeare, it is clear that the potential for changes over the long period of time in which the OT was composed creates one of the core challenges of studying "biblical Hebrew." The scribes who preserved the final versions of the OT appear to have updated vocabulary and other grammatical aspects of older material. However, this has produced a text that some contend was never truly a "language" in its own right.[3]

A second problem with the linguistic data of the Old Testament is its selectivity. Although the OT is a diverse book, it is still very limited in its interests. For example, we know very little about how the Israelites cooked, but they undoubtedly had an array of techniques and vessels for different kinds of food preparation.[4] Archaeological discoveries have helped us piece together our knowledge about many things in the ancient world, but the lack of descriptive detail in the OT about matters of everyday life limits our knowledge. On the other hand, the OT tells us a great deal about ritual procedures in the tabernacle and dietary restrictions for the Israelites. The OT concentrates on particular things, and while it also obliquely includes information about many other things, it is hardly a comprehensive resource on the vocabulary and grammar of the ancient Israelites.

This brings us to a third difficulty with the linguistic data of the Old Testament. Biblical Hebrew is a dead language; that is, no one living speaks it as a first language.[5] Linguists who work to understand and describe modern languages do so in cooperation with native speakers of the

---

2. These artifacts include the Siloam inscription, the Lachish letters, the Arad ostraca, and others. They have added some to our understanding of the language, but they are small in number and limited in scope.

3. For example, Edward Ullendorff argues that biblical Hebrew "is clearly no more than a linguistic fragment," based on the three challenges addressed in this section. See Edward Ullendorff, "Is Biblical Hebrew a Language?" *Bulletin of the School of Oriental and African Studies* 34 (1971): 241–55.

4. Philip J. King and Lawrence E. Stager include a nice summary of what we do know about food preparation and meals in Israel based on archaeological finds and the biblical text (Philip J. King and Lawrence E. Stager, *Life in Biblical Israel* [Louisville: Westminster John Knox, 2001], 64–68).

5. One of the current models for teaching/learning the biblical languages is immersion, that is, speaking the language in daily life. However, even if people learn biblical Hebrew to the point of fluency (given its vocabulary limitations), it will still not be their first language; that is, they can never be native speakers.

languages. This enables them to ask questions when they do not understand the data or when they lack data. "What do you call *this*?" or "How would you say …?" are questions that anyone can answer about their first language, whether or not they know the formal rules of its grammar. When linguists studying biblical Hebrew encounter difficulties, they have no one with an intuitive grasp of the language to ask. Thus, their answers can only ever be hypothetical.

These limitations on the study of biblical Hebrew present real challenges for linguists. However, they are not so great as to negate the value of linguistics for biblical Hebrew. Linguist Cynthia Miller-Naudé has cautioned against overstating the challenges: "It is important not to overstate the difficulties of lexicographic analysis of ancient texts, nor the poverty of the lexicographical remains."[6] She continues by describing the work of computational linguists who have judged the Bible to be "adequate as a computer corpus, both in terms of size and of vocabulary coverage."[7] There will be much we cannot say about biblical Hebrew, but that should not prevent us from saying what we can.

6.2 VERBAL SYSTEM

The verbal system in biblical Hebrew is a highly nuanced system that scholars are still trying to fully understand.[8] The lack of consensus on

---

6. Cynthia L. Miller-Naudé, "Methodological Issues in Reconstructing Language Systems from Epigraphic Fragments," in *The Future of Biblical Archaeology: Reassessing Methodologies and Assumptions; The Proceedings of a Symposium August 12–14, 2001 at Trinity International University*, ed. James K. Hoffmeier and Alan Millard (Grand Rapids: Eerdmans, 2004), 286.

7. Miller-Naudé, "Methodological Issues," 286–87.

8. The task of explaining the biblical Hebrew verbal system has been taken up in countless monographs, essays, and grammars. Even a brief review of this research is beyond the scope of this section, but a helpful survey of the research up to 2014 is found in John A. Cook, "Current Issues in the Study of the Biblical Hebrew Verbal System," *KUSATU* 17 (2014): 79–108. Important recent monographs on the subject include: Alexander W. Andrason, *El sistema verbal hebreo en su contexto semítico: una visión dinámica* (Estella: Editorial Verbo Divino, 2013); Ohad Cohen, *The Verbal Tense System in Late Biblical Hebrew Prose* (Winona Lake, IN: Eisenbrauns, 2013); John A. Cook, *Time and the Biblical Hebrew Verb: The Expression of Tense, Aspect, and Modality in Biblical Hebrew* (Winona Lake, IN: Eisenbrauns, 2012); Jan Joosten, *The Verbal System of Biblical Hebrew: A New Synthesis Elaborated on the Basis of Classical Prose* (Jerusalem: Simor Ltd., 2012); Elizabeth Robar, *The Verb and the Paragraph in Biblical Hebrew: A Cognitive-Linguistic Approach* (Leiden: Brill, 2014). Older, but still valuable, studies of the verbal system include: Randall Buth, "The Hebrew Verb in Current Discussions," *Journal of Translation and Textlinguistics* 5 (1992): 91–105; Leslie McFall, *The Enigma of the Hebrew Verbal System: Solutions from Ewald to the Present Day* (Sheffield: Almond Press, 1982); Alviero Niccacci,

the meaning of particular verb forms makes linguistic analysis an ongoing problem. In this section we discuss key concepts for understanding verbs, introduce the structure of the biblical Hebrew verbal system, and summarize the ongoing debate over tense, aspect, and modality in biblical Hebrew.

The biblical Hebrew verbal system includes seven major stems, or "binyanim" (the plural of the Hebrew word בִּנְיָן [binyān], "building"), that are related to one another in an integrated fashion. The seven major patterns are traditionally called qal, niphal, piel, pual, hitpael, hiphil, and hophal, following the lead of the medieval Hebrew grammarians, who also originally applied the term "binyanim" to these patterns. These binyanim encode the kind of verbal information that English reflects in compound verbal phrases. For example, the causation in the English sentence "Jack caused the ball to roll down the hill" would be expressed with the hiphil stem in Hebrew. But the Hebrew verbal system also encodes more subtly nuanced variations of verbal action than the English verbal system. On the one hand, this is the beauty of the system—a rich mode of expression capable of defining fine nuances of meaning. On the other hand, this is a stumbling block for linguistic analysis because we are not always able to grasp the nuances and see the differences presented by the system.

6.2.1 KEY CONCEPTS

There are three key concepts about verbs that are helpful to understand before we discuss the seven verb stems: voice, type of movement or activity, and valency.

6.2.1.a Voice

"Voice" defines the relationship of the subject to the verb or predicate. Biblical Hebrew distinguishes active, passive, middle, and reflexive voice. Different verbal stems are generally associated with different nuances of voice.[9] The distinction between syntactic roles (like subject and object) and semantic roles (like agent and patient) can help illustrate the concept of voice. The agent is responsible for a situation, usually an action. The patient is the

---

The Syntax of the Verb in Classical Hebrew Prose, trans. W. G. E. Watson (Sheffield: JSOT Press, 1990).

9. For example, the qal stem is active, but the niphal can be passive, middle, or reflexive depending on context.

recipient of the action. In the active voice, the agent is the subject and the patient is the object (e.g., "Bob [agent] typed the paper [patient]"). In passive voice, the patient is the subject and the agent may be named or unnamed (e.g., "The paper [patient] was typed"). In middle voice and reflexive voice, the subject can be both agent and patient. Middle voice can also be used when there is no external agent responsible for the action (e.g., "The paper [patient] yellowed over time"). In reflexive voice, the agent is also the subject and acts upon itself (e.g., Bob dressed [himself]).

ACTIVE	agent is subject; patient is object
MIDDLE	agent is both subject and object
PASSIVE	patient is subject; agent is named or unnamed
REFLEXIVE	agent is subject and object, and acts on itself

GRAMMATICAL VOICES

6.2.1.b Type of Movement

Every verb describes a type of movement or activity or a state. Those that describe an activity are "fientive" (or "dynamic"), while verbs that describe a state are "stative." Another element of activity that must be considered is transitivity. Transitivity refers to whether or not the verb takes an object, and if so, how many. A verb can be intransitive (taking zero objects), transitive (taking one object), or ditransitive (taking two objects). Consider the following English examples:

(1) a. *The boy was sleepy.*
         In English, this stative sentence is represented by an adjective ("sleepy") and a linking verb ("was"). In biblical Hebrew, this sentence would be represented by a single stative verb meaning "to be sleepy."

b.   *The boy crawled out of bed.*
The verb "crawled" is fientive, indicating a dynamic situation. It is also intransitive because it does not take an object.
c.   *The boy rubbed his eyes.*
The verb "rubbed" is fientive, indicating a dynamic situ
ation. It is also transitive, taking only one object, "eyes."
d.   *The boy gave his dog a bone.*
The verb "gave" is fientive and transitive. It is ditransitive
transitive, taking the objects "dog" and "bone."

6.2.1.c Valency

A third important concept about verbs is valency, which refers to the
number of noun phrases governed by the verb. An intransitive verb will
have a valency of one (the subject), and a transitive verb may have a valency
of two (the subject and a single object) or three (the subject and two objects).
In example 1 above, the valency of the first example (1a) is one ("boy"); the
second (1b) is one ("boy"); the third (1c) is two ("boy," "eyes"); the fourth
(1d) is three ("boy," "dog," "bone").

6.2.2 THE SEVEN VERBAL STEMS

Biblical Hebrew has seven primary stems: qal (G), niphal (N), piel (D), pual
(Dp), hitpael (Dt or HtD), hiphil (H), and hophal (Hp). These stems generally relate to one another in terms of the concepts described above: voice,
type of movement or activity, and valency. While all grammars of biblical Hebrew describe the various stems, the workings of the verbal stem
system as a whole are only partially understood. The stems are distinguished primarily by morphology with general observations regarding the
functions of each stem deriving from syntax and semantics. Much uncertainty remains regarding how the stems function as a system because different stems appear to serve the same functions. The following summary
of the seven verbal stems is derived primarily from the grammar of Waltke
and O'Connor, though similar descriptions can be found in most biblical
Hebrew reference grammars.[10]

---

10. Bruce K. Waltke and Michael Patrick O'Connor, *An Introduction to Biblical Hebrew
Syntax* (Winona Lake, IN: Eisenbrauns, 1990), 341–452 [*IBHS*]. Compare Paul Joüon and
Takamitsu Muraoka, *A Grammar of Biblical Hebrew*, rev. English ed. (Roma: Pontificio istituto

6.2.2.a Qal

The qal, or G-stem ("G" from German "Grundstamm") is the most commonly used and the most basic verbal stem. It has no consonantal affixes, and it does not include notions of causation. The voice of the primary subject is active. The qal can be fientive or stative, transitive or intransitive, and it can have a valency of one or two.

6.2.2.b Niphal

The niphal, or N-stem, also lacks causation, and its form includes a prefix (either an "n" or an "h"). The niphal often functions in relationship to the qal by forming its reflexive forms as well as its passive forms; however, some niphal verbs are related semantically to verbs in the piel or hiphil.[11] The niphal is one area of the verbal system where significant issues remain unresolved.[12]

6.2.2.c Piel

The piel stem, or D-stem ("D" from German "Duppelstamm"), is characterized by a doubled middle root letter. The piel exhibits such a variety of usages and meanings so as to almost defy explanation for an otherwise "morphologically unified" verbal stem.[13] With some verbs that occur in both qal and piel forms, there appears to be some type of semantic relationship, but the nature of the relationship varies. Traditionally, the piel was thought to intensify the basic meaning of the qal.[14] A common example offered as evidence of the intensifying nature of the piel is the verb שׁבר

---

biblico, 2006), 113–216 [JM]; Christo H.J. van der Merwe, Jackie A. Naudé, and Jan H. Kroeze, *A Biblical Hebrew Reference Grammar* (Sheffield: Sheffield Academic Press, 1999), 73–88 [*BHRG*]; Wilhelm Gesenius, *Gesenius' Hebrew Grammar*, ed. E. Kautzsch and A. E. Cowley, 2nd English ed. (Oxford: Clarendon Press, 1910), 114–220 [GKC].

11. According to van der Merwe, Naudé, and Kroeze, 60% of verbs that have a niphal form are related to the qal form of the verb, but 10% are related to the piel form, another 10% are related to the hiphil, and 10% do not appear to have a semantic relationship with any active stem (*BHRG*, 78).

12. Recently, Richard Benton addressed some of the issues related to understanding the niphil using the concepts of aspect and voice; see Richard C. Benton, "Aspect and the Biblical Hebrew Niphal and Hitpael" (Ph.D. diss., University of Wisconsin-Madison, 2009).

13. *IBHS*, 397.

14. GKC §52.f.

(*šbr*), defined to mean "break" in the qal but "shatter" in the piel.[15] Gesenius gives the example of the verb שאל (*š ʾl*), which he takes to mean "ask" in the qal but "beg" in the piel.[16] A survey of the biblical usage of שאל, however, reveals the difficulty with attempting to explain the piel as an intensification of the qal. The piel of שאל only occurs twice in the Old Testament (2 Sam 20:18; Ps 109:10), but the meaning of "beg" only makes sense for one of the occurrences (Ps 109:10). On the other hand, שאל appears in the qal over 150 times, and, in some cases, the idea of begging or asking earnestly makes good sense in context, even though the verb is in the qal stem (e.g., 1 Kgs 19:4; Jonah 4:8).

The piel can also have a causative (or factitive) sense, as in, "And it shattered [שִׁבֵּר; *šibbēr*] every tree of the field" (Exod 9:25). The hail caused the trees of the field to shatter. With this meaning, the piel "indicates the cause that places an object in the condition to which the Qal form (with a stative meaning) of the same stem refers."[17] With the example of Exod 9:25, the piel indicates the cause that led to the trees being in the state or condition of being broken. Scholars continue to discuss the nature of the piel, but its multifaceted nuances present a challenge for linguistic studies.

6.2.2.d Pual

The pual (Dp) is the passive voice counterpart of the active voice piel. Thus, the patient of a piel verb would be the subject of a corresponding pual (e.g., "every tree in the field was shattered"; compare Exod 9:25). As the counterpart of the piel, its meanings tend to correspond to those of the piel.

6.2.2.e Hitpael

The hitpael (Dt or HtD) is the reflexive of the piel. Like the piel (and pual), the second root letter is doubled, but the hitpael is also characterized by an infixed *tav* (ת; "t"). The patient in the piel becomes the subject of the hitpael, and then "transforms itself/is transformed into the effected state signified by the root."[18] For example, in Exod 19:22, the priests are the ones

15. *IBHS*, 397
16. GKC §52.f.
17. *BHRG*, 80.
18. *IBHS*, 429.

being made holy (i.e., they are the patient), but they are the subject of the verse: "And also the priests who will be drawing near to Yahweh should make themselves holy [יִתְקַדָּשׁוּ; *yitqaddāšû*]." Like the niphal, the hitpael can express the middle and the passive. It can also express the iterative, that is, repeated action. The precise function of the hitpael stem is another elusive aspect of the verbal system, especially its relationship with the passive binyanim.

6.2.2.f Hiphil

In the perfect, the hiphil (H) is characterized by the prefix הִ. The hiphil stem vowel—a long /i/—is evident in many of the forms (e.g., הִקְטִיל; *hiqṭîl*). The hiphil is typically defined as the causative stem of the Hebrew verbal system, but this categorization makes it difficult to distinguish it from the piel which can also sometimes have a causative sense. Waltke and O'Connor follow Ernst Jenni in explaining the causative piel as bringing about a change of state while the hiphil relates to causing an action or event.[19]

Generally, the hiphil expresses a causative action related to the verb's meaning in the qal. For example, the verb נחל (*nḥl*) means "inherit." Note the contrast in the sense of the verb between Num 26:55 and Deut 31:7:

Num 26:55	Deut 31:7
יִנְחָלוּ	וְאַתָּה תַּנְחִילֶנָּה אוֹתָם
yinḥālû	*wĕ'attâ tanḥîlennâ 'ôtām*
they *will inherit*	and you *will cause* them *to inherit* it

Both passages refer to the people of Israel taking possession of the land of Canaan—the promised land. In Num 26:55, God is giving Moses instructions related to the future event of Israel inheriting the land. In Deut 31:7, Moses is referring to Joshua's role in bringing about that future event.

6.2.2.g Hophal

The hophal (Hp) is the passive of the hiphil. For example, if a sentence in the hiphil states, "you will cause them to inherit the land," then an alternate

---

19. *IBHS*, 433–35.

way of expressing that in the hophal would be "they will be caused to inherit the land by you." In the hophal, the subject of the sentence is the patient—the one receiving the action.

6.2.2.h Summary

While modern linguistic studies recognize the systemic nature of the bin-yanim,[20] there remain several unresolved issues in our understanding of the verbal system. The first of these is the piel, as discussed above. A second issue relates to the function of the niphal in the system and its relationship to the qal. It is extremely likely based on the comparative Semitic evidence and the traces in biblical Hebrew that an earlier stage of the language had a specific qal passive stem (Gp). This complicates the relationship described above for the G- and N-stems because the N was defined as the simple passive of G. A third issue is the overlap of functions between the binyanim as seen in the discussion of the relationship of H and D. Such overlap is evident elsewhere in the system and contributes to the linguistic difficulties associated with biblical Hebrew.

6.2.3 TENSE, ASPECT, AND MODALITY

One of the most vexing issues in biblical Hebrew linguistics is the way the verbal system encodes tense, aspect, and modality. These three verbal categories are common across the languages of the world, but a complete understanding of them in biblical Hebrew remains elusive. In this section we will define the categories and discuss them with respect to biblical Hebrew.

Tense is a verbal category that indicates when an activity or situation happened in relationship to when an utterance is made. The three most basic tenses are past (e.g., "I wrote the essay"), present (e.g., "I write the essay"), and future (e.g., "I will write the essay"), but "verbal systems are rarely, if ever, so simply structured."[21] Aspect conveys the "contour of a situation in time," that is, the nature of the activity or situation.[22] For example,

---

20. In traditional studies, the "system" was understood and described in terms of the qal as the basic stem and everything else as derived from it. This, obviously, blurs the systemic relationships and treats each stem in an atomistic fashion.

21. Cook, *Time and the Biblical Hebrew Verb*, 1.

22. Waltke and O'Connor, *An Introduction to Biblical Hebrew Syntax*, 347.

in English, we refer to a verb as being "progressive" when the situation is ongoing (e.g., "I am/was writing," or "I will be writing"). This kind of verb is also called imperfective, that is, it reflects an action or situation that has not been completed. By contrast, a verb can also be perfective, as in "I write" or "I wrote," which both convey a complete situation. Modality indicates the statement's relationship to reality. Another way to describe modality is that it reflects how the speaker perceives his or her words. For example, the indicative mood expresses something that the speaker believes to be certain, while the subjunctive mood indicates uncertainty, as in a wish, desire, or impossibility.[23]

The difficulty of tense, aspect, and modality in biblical Hebrew is three-fold. First, the two dominant forms of the verb can express a wide variety of tenses and aspects, defying a singular classification. Both the *qatal* (also "perfect" or "suffix conjugation") and *yiqtol* (also "imperfect" or "prefix conjugation") forms *may* express simple past ("God created"), present ("he says"), and future ("they will believe").[24] Additionally, both forms serve various uses. This variety makes "the determination of a general meaning for each of these forms appear impossible" and, further, it makes it difficult to make distinctions between how the forms are used.[25]

Second, two secondary forms of the verb include a prefixed *waw* ("and"), but they do not simply add "and" to the meaning of the verbs. Instead, the prefixed *waw* on the *qatal* (*weqatal*) and *yiqtol* (*wayyiqtol*) appears to convert the tense of the verbs from past to future and future to past, respectively.[26] Niccacci comments on how unhelpful it was that grammars of biblical Hebrew allowed that the *wayyiqtol* "could be translated by virtually all

---

23. Linguistic discussions of modality typically discuss indicative and subjunctive according to the concepts of realis (known) and irrealis (unknown), rather than certainty or uncertainty.

24. The *qatal* form has commonly been called the "perfect," and the *yiqtol* the "imperfect."

25. Cook, *Time and the Biblical Hebrew Verb*, 79.

26. The forms with prefixed *waw* are often called *waw*-consecutive or *waw*-conversive, though these labels reflect older understandings of the forms either "converting" a verb's tense (e.g., future tense to past tense) or marking "consecutive" action. The current consensus is that the *wayyiqtol* developed from combining the *waw* conjunction with the "short prefix-tense" (or jussive) form of the verb (see Blau, *Phonology and Morphology of Biblical Hebrew*, 195–97). The forms are now typically labeled simply as *wayyiqtol* or *weqatal*.

the finite tenses of modern languages."[27] Linguist R. Binnick summarizes the difficulty:

> If the waw adds no temporal (tense or aspect) meaning then the difference between verbs with waw and verbs without waw cannot be a semantic one. But apparently it is, for the forms with the waw are generally seen as 'reversing' the values the 'tenses' normally have. To reconcile the two, we must assume that the forms without the waw and those with it do not in fact differ in semantics, but the only way this is possible is if the 'tense' forms do not differ from one another in meaning to begin with.[28]

Finally, the division between the verbal moods in biblical Hebrew is not always clear. Most Hebrew verbs are in the indicative mood, and biblical Hebrew can also morphologically indicate other moods, namely, the imperative and cohortative. There is also evidence that in earlier stages of the language, Hebrew verbal morphology indicated the subjunctive mood. The difficulty with modality in the biblical Hebrew verbal system arises from the fact that the morphology does not always indicate the mood, and both yiqtol and weqatal forms can be used to express non-indicative moods.

Prior to the nineteenth century, the prevailing theory in Hebrew language study was that the verbal system reflects three tenses. The qatal form expresses past tense, the participle expresses present tense, and the yiqtol expresses future tense. When a waw is prefixed to the forms of the qatal (i.e., the weqatal form) and the yiqtol (i.e., the wayyiqtol form), the respective tenses are "converted" from past to future or future to past. This theory is often called the "waw-conversive theory" and reflects the perspective of medieval Jewish grammarians. Since the nineteenth century, Hebrew scholars have hypothesized that the biblical Hebrew verbal system encodes aspect (i.e., perfect and imperfect) and may or may not indicate tense.[29] These difficulties with the Hebrew verbal system pres-

---

27. Niccacci, *The Syntax of the Verb*, 9.

28. Robert I. Binnick, *Time and the Verb: A Guide to Tense and Aspect* (Oxford: Oxford University Press, 1991), 441. Cited in Cook, *Time and the Biblical Hebrew Verb*, 81–82.

29. For a detailed review of the research from the nineteenth century to the early twenty-first century, see Cook, *Time and the Biblical Hebrew Verb*, 77–175.

ent an ongoing problem to linguists and biblical scholars, who continue to debate the nature of the system and propose solutions to its challenges.[30]

6.3 SEMANTICS AND LEXICOGRAPHY

A subdiscipline of semantics is lexicography, the science and art of creating dictionaries (i.e., lexicons or lexica). A dictionary is an inventory or catalog of a language's "lexemes," that is, the language's words. Typically, lexicons also provide basic information about a given word's patterns of usage, such as how to make a word plural or how the meaning of a verb changes when it is followed by different adverbs or prepositions (see, e.g., "go" in a dictionary of English: go about, go against, go along, go around, etc.). Lexicography is an important work in the field of biblical studies since it provides us with the tools we need to understand Hebrew and Greek, even if we are not able to study the languages for ourselves.

But creating lexicons is a complex process, and it is an ongoing challenge in any language to maintain a lexicon that accurately represents the language's words and their meanings. This challenge occurs partly because language is constantly changing. However, it is also because "meaning" is broad and multifaceted (see §2.3 Semantics). Furthermore, a usable dictionary cannot include all the lexical and grammatical information a word entails. Lexicographers must make choices, and these choices often reflect different philosophies of language and meaning.

Since biblical Hebrew is a dead language and its catalog of words and meanings is not changing, it might seem that creating a dictionary for the language should be easier. However, biblical Hebrew lexicography is complicated by the language's distance from us historically and culturally. The difficulties with the data previously discussed apply here as well: We have a limited, selective corpus and no native speakers to consult.

There are several basic decisions biblical Hebrew lexicographers make at the beginning of their project. First, they must define their corpus. Obviously, it includes the Old Testament, but there are other ancient Hebrew writings that they could include as well. For example, they could

---

30. For a recent contribution to the debate, see Alexander W. Andrason, "The Complexity of Verbal Semantics—An Intricate Relationship Between *Qatal* and *Wayyiqtol*," *JHS* 16 (2016): art. 4, doi:10.5508/jhs.2016.v16.a4.

include the Hebrew from the Dead Sea Scrolls or ancient inscriptions, such as the inscription from the Siloam Tunnel, a project of King Hezekiah's men (2 Kgs 20:20). Including Hebrew from extra-biblical texts of the same time period might provide a greater context for understanding biblical Hebrew. Related to this is the issue of data from comparative languages (see §5.1 Comparative Philology). To what extent—if at all—will a lexicon factor in the meanings of words from Aramaic, Arabic, and other Semitic languages into its assessment of a word's meaning? Many words in biblical Hebrew occur infrequently, making it difficult to get a strong sense of their semantic range. The presence of related words in cognate languages may help clarify the meaning of a rare Hebrew word. Other decisions involve the presentation of the data in the lexicon. Will entries be listed by root (e.g., BDB), word (e.g., *HALOT*), or even concept (compare Louw and Nida's dictionary organized by semantic domains in NT Greek)? How much morphological and philological data will be included?[31] The answers to such questions distinguish the different lexicons of biblical Hebrew from each other.

In the following sections we will discuss several important dictionaries of biblical Hebrew and describe how they differ in their approaches. Each has its benefits and weaknesses, and this discussion will demonstrate the need for continued work in the art and science of biblical Hebrew lexicography. We will also briefly consider some recent approaches to lexicography and biblical Hebrew.

6.3.1 TRADITIONAL LEXICONS

Two of the most important traditional dictionaries for Biblical Hebrew are the *Hebrew and English Lexicon of the Old Testament* by Brown, Driver, and Briggs (BDB)[32] and *The Hebrew and Aramaic Lexicon of the Old Testament* by Koehler and Baumgartner (known as KB3 or *HALOT*, an English translation of the German HALAT, *Hebräisches und Aramäisches Handwörterbuch über*

---

31. Michael O'Connor, "Semitic Lexicography: European Dictionaries of Biblical Hebrew in the Twentieth Century," in *Israel Oriental Studies XX. Semitic Linguistics: The State of the Art at the Turn of the Twenty-first Century*, ed. Shlomo Izre'el (Winona Lake, IN: Eisenbrauns, 2002), 173–212.

32. F. Brown, S. R. Driver, and C. A. Briggs, eds., *A Hebrew and English Lexicon of the Old Testament, with an Appendix Containing the Biblical Aramaic* (Oxford: Clarendon, 1906).

das Alte Testament).[33] Both of these projects grew out of medieval work in Arabic lexicography. Since both Hebrew and Arabic are Semitic languages, each has a three-letter root system. This basic shared feature made it easy for early lexicographers to compare the two languages, a practice which came to be known as comparative philology. This method grew as scholars also compared Hebrew to Aramaic and Mishnaic Hebrew. As nineteenth- and twentieth-century archaeology uncovered more textual evidence from the ancient Near East, lexicographers of biblical Hebrew extended their comparative work to include Akkadian, Phoenician, Moabite, and Ugaritic. Some comparative work also included the lexicon of Egyptian, a non-Semitic Afro-Asiatic language.

6.3.1.a BDB

The commonly-used BDB lexicon grew out of a dictionary project by Hebrew scholar Wilhelm Gesenius (1786–1842), who is generally regarded as the father of modern lexicography for biblical Hebrew.[34] BDB aims to examine words in their Old Testament context, compare them with similar languages, and "thus fix their proper meanings in Hebrew."[35] What the editors of BDB called "proper meanings," lexicographers today call "glosses." Glosses are essential for making a basic translation, but they are best considered translation equivalents and not definitions.

BDB lists its entries according to root, which can make it a challenge for biblical Hebrew beginners to find what they are looking for. The dictionary

---

33. Ludwig Koehler, Walter Baumgartner, and Johann Jakob Stamm, eds., *The Hebrew and Aramaic Lexicon of the Old Testament*, trans. M. E. J. Richardson, electronic ed. (Leiden: Brill, 1994–2000).

34. W. C. van Wyk, "The Present State of OT Lexicography," in *Lexicography and Translation*, ed. J. P. Louw (Cape Town: Bible Society of South Africa, 1985), 83. Gesenius produced a number of works on Hebrew lexicography between 1810 and 1842. BDB is based on an English translation of Wilhelm Gesenius, *Lexicon Manuale Hebraicum et Chaldaicum in Veteris Testamenti Libros* (Leipzig, 1833). In the preface to his 1857 translation of Gesenius' *Lexicon Manuale*, Tregelles lists some of Gesenius' lexicographical publications (*Gesenius' Hebrew and Chaldee Lexicon to the Old Testament Scriptures*, trans. Samuel Prideaux Tregelles [London: Samuel Bagster and Sons, 1857], iii–iv. Gesenius' Hebrew-German dictionary has also been updated and published in six volumes (*Hebräisches und aramäisches Handwörterbuch über das Alte Testament*, ed. Rudolf Meyer and Herbert Donner, 18th ed. [Berlin: Springer, 1987–2010]), and recently in a one-volume edition (2013).

35. Brown et al., *A Hebrew and English Lexicon of the Old Testament*, vi.

does include comparative philological data, but since it predates the discoveries of Ugarit and the Dead Sea Scrolls, much of the data is outdated.

6.3.1.b HALOT

Unlike BDB, *HALOT* lists its entries according to word instead of root, making the dictionary more navigable for most users. However, *HALOT* adheres to the same method as BDB—namely, comparative philology, or what the editors call "genetical sequence":

> The safe principle of modern semantics is to look first for the original meaning of a word … and from this to derive the word's more abstract and even more spiritual meanings. As a rule today one tries to draw a genetical sequence of the meanings a word is apt to assume.[36]

Since the publication of *HALOT* dates to the second half of the twentieth century, significantly later than BDB, its comparative data includes more recent textual data of the Semitic languages, including some of the material from the Dead Sea Scrolls and Ugarit.

A weakness of both dictionaries is their use of glosses, which cannot provide a word's full semantic range and nuance. Scholar James Barr warns that glosses "are not themselves meanings nor do they tell us the meanings; the meanings reside in the actual Hebrew usage, and for real semantic analysis the glosses have no greater value than that of indicators or labels for a meaning which resides in the Hebrew itself."[37] A second problem of glosses is that many students approach them with a "pick and choose" philosophy. If one meaning results in a preferred translation, it wins. Worse, a student may import more than one of the glosses into a text, as if the author was not sure what he was saying. A third difficulty of glosses is that a lexicon may use the same gloss for several words without indicating how the words differ in meaning. For example, *HALOT* glosses both ירה-hiphil and יסר-qal as "to instruct," but does not provide a clear sense of how the meanings might vary.

---

36. Koehler et al., *The Hebrew and Aramaic Lexicon of the Old Testament*, lxx.

37. James Barr, "Hebrew Lexicography," in *Studies in Semitic Lexicography*, ed. P. Fronzaroli (Florence: Instituto di Linguistica, Università di Firenze, 1973), 120.

A second weakness of these and other traditional dictionaries is that they largely overlook the role of syntax in creating meaning. Christo van der Merwe says they show a "haphazard treatment of syntactic information" and it is impossible to know whether different syntax results in different meanings.[38]

These traditional dictionaries and the comparative philological method have great value, but more work is needed. Since "a word has meaning only within its own language and its own period of usage,"[39] knowing what related words in other languages mean does not help us understand how a particular author uses words or how the structure of a language is organized. Because of their methodologies, BDB and *HALOT* cannot offer what biblical Hebrew linguist Reinier de Blois calls a "*structural* semantic analysis," that is, "a detailed study of the way different concepts in the world behind a language are perceived by the speakers of that language and how these concepts are transferred into semantic forms."[40]

6.3.2 NEWER METHODS FOR LEXICOGRAPHY

The limitations of the comparative philological method drove scholars to find other ways to analyze and describe the lexicon of biblical Hebrew using scientific–linguistic methods. The first significant effort in this direction was the massive *Dictionary of Classical Hebrew*, and a second significant effort still in progress is the *Semantic Dictionary of Biblical Hebrew*. We discuss each in more detail below.

6.3.2.a *Dictionary of Classical Hebrew*

In 1988 a team of scholars began a different sort of biblical Hebrew dictionary project for publication with Sheffield Academic Press.[41] Edited by David J. A. Clines, the eight-volume *Dictionary of Classical Hebrew* (*DCH*) differs from BDB and *HALOT* in its claim to use "modern linguistics" as the

---

38. Christo van der Merwe, "Towards a Principled Model for Biblical Hebrew Lexicology," *Journal of Northwest Semitic Languages* 30 (2004): 123.

39. James Barr, "Hebrew Lexicography: Informal Thoughts," in *Linguistics and Biblical Hebrew*, ed. Walter R. Bodine (Winona Lake, IN: Eisenbrauns, 1992), 141.

40. Reinier de Blois, "Towards a New Dictionary of Biblical Hebrew Based on Semantic Domains" (PhD diss., Free University Amsterdam, 2000), 12.

41. David J. A. Clines, ed., *The Dictionary of Classical Hebrew*, 8 vols. (Sheffield: Sheffield Academic Press, 1993–2011), 1:12.

philosophy underlying its approach to the meaning of words. Their assertion that "the meaning of a word is its use in the language"[42] contrasts with
the comparative philological method behind BDB and *HALOT*. Practically
speaking, the differences between the *DCH* and the traditional lexicons
are in scope, content, and format.

First, the scope of the project goes beyond biblical Hebrew and instead
encompasses "Classical Hebrew," defined as the language of any Hebrew
writing available through 200 AD. This means the lexical entries of *DCH*
include the vocabulary of the Old Testament, the Dead Sea Scrolls, Ben
Sira, and all Hebrew inscriptions during the same period.

The content and format of the lexical entries also differ from that of
traditional dictionaries. Unlike BDB and *HALOT*, the *DCH* does not include
any comparative data from other Semitic languages, nor does it provide
extensive glosses or attempts at definitions. Rather, it offers a simple translation equivalent for each entry and then lists all usages of words in their
syntactic constructions. By contrast, traditional lexicons group occurrences according to similar meaning or usage. Each entry in the *DCH* also
identifies the number of occurrences in each source (OT, Dead Sea Scrolls,
etc.) and the part of speech. The content and format of entries leave the task
of defining the word up to the user based on the contexts of usage. Overall,
this approach makes the *DCH* more like a concordance than a lexicon.

Several reviewers have questioned the claim that the *DCH* uses modern
linguistics. Muraoka, for example, says that the *DCH* "lacks methodological
precision"[43] and that "the impact of modern linguistics on the production of
the *DCH* is in fact marginal."[44] O'Connor evaluates the editor's thinking as
"distant ... from that of linguists."[45] One particular weakness is the leveling
of the language: that is, the dictionary does not account for changes in language over a thousand years, and it does not weigh the value of its sources.
Critics contend this approach distorts the evidence.[46] A second problem is

42. Clines, *The Dictionary of Classical Hebrew*, 1:14.

43. Takamitsu Muraoka, "A New Dictionary of Classical Hebrew," *Abr-Nahrain Supplement* 4 (1995): 90. Another review is Francis I. Andersen, "Review Article and Responses: *The Dictionary of Classical Hebrew*. Vol. 1 א," *Australian Biblical Review* 43 (1995): 50–75.

44. Muraoka, "A New Dictionary," 94.

45. O'Connor, "Semitic Lexicography," 198.

46. O'Connor, "Semitic Lexicography," 195.

that it does not help the user organize and process an immense amount of data; rather, it functions more like a database of Classical Hebrew. While such a project has its function, it is not really a lexicon in the proper sense.

6.3.2.b Semantic Domains and Cognitive Linguistics

Another newer approach to biblical Hebrew lexicography involves using semantic domains. Louw and Nida pioneered this approach with their *Greek-English Lexicon of the New Testament Based on Semantic Domains*, where they grouped words by semantic fields, or domains.[47] Each entry contains a group of words with certain common features. By organizing the lexicon this way, Louw and Nida could begin to identify the semantic structure of New Testament Greek, rather than simply glossing each individual word as traditional dictionaries had done. When biblical Hebrew scholar Reinier de Blois tried to apply the methodology and semantic domains of Louw and Nida to a lexicon of biblical Hebrew, he discovered two fundamental problems with the approach. First, the *Greek-English Lexicon* relied on componential analysis for its semantic analysis, a method many scholars deem inadequate for describing a word's meaning (see §2.3.2.a Componential Analysis). De Blois decided to work within the framework of cognitive linguistics instead. Secondly, he could not simply transfer the set of domains from Greek to biblical Hebrew since the research of cognitive linguists indicates that "every language has its own system of experience, beliefs, and practices. Every language has its own world view, thought patterns, etc."[48] A semantic dictionary of biblical Hebrew would require a different organization of ideas and domains that reflected the particulars of biblical Hebrew. De Blois's project, the *Semantic Dictionary of Biblical Hebrew* (SDBH), is an online tool[49] and a work in progress, but it represents a step forward in understanding the semantic structure of biblical Hebrew.

---

47. Johannes P. Louw and Eugene A. Nida, *Greek-English Lexicon of the New Testament: Based on Semantic Domains*, 2 vols., 2nd ed. (New York: United Bible Societies, 1989).

48. Reinier de Blois, "Semantic Domains for Biblical Hebrew," in *Bible and Computer: The Stellenbosch Aibi-6 Conference; Proceedings of the Association Internationale Bible et Informatique 'from Alpha to Byte'* (Leiden: Brill, 2002), 221.

49. Available online at http://www.sdbh.org/.

6.4 WORD ORDER

Scholars generally believe that every language follows certain rules for the order of its words and phrases (see §2.4 Syntax). Although some languages may show greater variation in the order of sentence constituents, no language exhibits genuinely "free" word order.[50] Further, the order of words in a sentence can be meaningful. However, determining when and how the order is meaningful is a matter of debate. Word order with respect to biblical Hebrew has been of particular interest since the 1980s and 1990s, and discussion continues over how to understand variation in the order of sentence constituents.

Languages fall into one of six word-order types, based on where they most commonly situate the subject (S), verb (V), and object (O) of a clause: SVO, SOV, VSO, OVS, VOS, OSV. No language exhibits a single order all the time, but each does seem to exhibit a "basic order," that is, the "order that occurs in stylistically neutral, independent, indicative clauses."[51]

Biblical Hebrew is most commonly classified as a VSO language. This means that the "statistically dominant and unmarked word-order" of narrative is verb-subject-object. In clauses that do not have verbs (i.e., the verbless or nominal clause), the preferred word order is subject-predicate. Some scholars disagree with the view that biblical Hebrew is a VSO language and argue instead that it is a SVO language.[52] This basic difference affects when scholars see variation in word order and how they interpret it.

Since the mainstream view of word order in biblical Hebrew is VSO, we will assume this order in the rest of our discussion. When a verbal clause begins with anything other than the verb, scholars have long assumed that the first word represented the "most emphatic or prominent part of the sentence,"[53] though this was not a hard and fast rule. However, they were

---

50. Anna Siewierska, *Word Order Rules* (London: Routledge, 1988), 1.

51. Siewierska, *Word Order Rules*, 8. Siewierska's full definition of the "basic order" is that it "occurs in stylistically neutral, independent, indicative clauses with full noun phrase (NP) participants, where the subject is definite, agentive and human, the object is a definite semantic patient, and the verb represents an action, not a state or an event."

52. E.g., Robert D. Holmstedt, "Word Order and Information Structure in Ruth and Jonah: A Generative-Typological Analysis," *Journal of Semitic Studies* 54.1 (2009): 111–39.

53. Steven E. Runge, *Discourse Grammar of the Greek New Testament: A Practical Introduction for Teaching and Exegesis* (Peabody, MA: Hendrickson; Bellingham, WA: Lexham Press, 2010), 182.

not very clear about what the emphasis meant or why an author might use it. An important work by Muraoka in 1985 addressed this intuition in a more systematic and focused way.[54] In 1994 Knud Lambrecht published a ground-breaking study that provided scholars with the necessary framework for thinking through word order in any given language.[55] Many biblical Hebrew scholars have developed and applied Lambrecht's framework to the language of the Old Testament, including Jean-Marc Heimerdinger,[56] who considered word order in narrative, and Nicholas Lunn,[57] who worked in poetry. Recently, Adina Moshavi has written an important book on word order in finite clauses.[58]

Scholars share the underlying assumption that the choices writers and speakers make are meaningful, but they continue to disagree over which word order typifies biblical Hebrew and what the significance is of different arrangements of words in a variety of genres.

6.5 THE CHRONOLOGY AND TYPOLOGY DEBATE

Another challenge to the linguistic analysis of the Old Testament is the nature of the Hebrew language that it reflects. Many scholars think that biblical Hebrew is a single language system that changed over the thousand-year period during which the OT was written. Variations evident in the language resulted from the development of the language over time. The approach of these scholars to biblical Hebrew is primarily diachronic. However, other scholars contend that the entire OT was written in a fairly short span of time during the post-exilic Persian period. Variations in the language, in their view, are largely a reflection of different social situations or the pragmatic purposes of the scribes who wrote the books. In other words, linguistic variations can be attributed to sociolinguistic factors

---

54. Takamitsu Muraoka, *Emphatic Words and Structures in Biblical Hebrew* (Jerusalem: Magnes; Leiden: Brill, 1985).

55. Knud Lambrecht, *Information Structure and Sentence Form: Topic, Focus, and the Mental Representations of Discourse Referents* (Cambridge: Cambridge University Press, 1994).

56. Jean-Marc Heimerdinger, *Topic, Focus and Foreground in Ancient Hebrew Narrative* (Sheffield: Sheffield Academic Press, 1999).

57. Nicholas P. Lunn, *Word-Order Variation in Biblical Hebrew Poetry: Differentiating Pragmatics and Poetics* (Milton Keynes, UK: Paternoster, 2006).

58. Adina Moshavi, *Word Order in the Biblical Hebrew Finite Clause: A Syntactic and Pragmatic Analysis of Preposing* (Winona Lake, IN: Eisenbrauns, 2010).

such as dialect or register (see §3.2 Sociolinguistics). This perspective approaches the language synchronically. Such a fundamental difference in approaches to the language makes linguistic consensus impossible.

Establishing a chronology of the language in the OT is infamously difficult because we lack firm dates for the composition of the biblical books. Most of the OT books do not explicitly identify their authors or the time of their composition. Scholars who think the Bible was written over a long period of time have tried to determine a chronology of the books based on the data that is available. A starting place for this process is comparing the features of the Hebrew language found in books that were obviously written later with those used in books believed to be earlier. Books that record post-exilic events cannot date before the end of exile in 538 BC and the dedication of the second temple in 515 BC, whereas books recording earlier events are generally presumed to have been written earlier. The later books include Chronicles, Ezra, Nehemiah, Esther, and Daniel. Since the Hebrew in these books shows variation from the Hebrew in other parts of the OT, some scholars refer to it as Late Biblical Hebrew (LBH) or post-exilic Hebrew, in contrast to the Early Biblical Hebrew (EBH) in many other books, also called pre-exilic or sometimes Standard Biblical Hebrew (SBH).[59] Other texts seem to form a link between these primary stages of the language (e.g., the Priestly source of the Pentateuch and the book of Ezekiel).[60] By identifying distinct features of these two main stages—or "types"—of the Hebrew language and then classifying books according to which stage of the language they reflect, scholars have produced a rough chronology of the OT books.

Scholars distinguish between the two stages in several ways. Two of the most common ways are "Aramaisms" and "loan words." The extent to which the Hebrew shows Aramaic influence suggests that the text in question is later, when Aramaic was the dominant language of the ancient Near East. Loan words are words borrowed from another language (such as "taco" in

---

59. On the varying terminology used to segment biblical Hebrew, see Ian Young, "Introduction: The Origin of the Problem," in *Biblical Hebrew: Studies in Chronology and Typology*, ed. Ian Young (London: T&T Clark, 2003), 3-4.

60. Jacobus A. Naudé, "The Transitions of Biblical Hebrew in the Perspective of Language Change and Diffusion," in *Biblical Hebrew: Studies in Chronology and Typology*, ed. Ian Young (London: T&T Clark, 2003), 190.

English, borrowed from Spanish), and when words from ancient languages such as from Greece or Persia appear in a Hebrew text, it may imply a later time when writers and speakers had greater contact with those other cultures. A third way of distinguishing between stages of biblical Hebrew is through historical linguistics, the process of reconstructing the stages of language development by tracing known patterns of language change and by comparing the stages of one language with similar stages in another language. The evidence from ancient Hebrew inscriptions and cognate languages allows scholars to hypothesize patterns of development and thus the chronology of biblical Hebrew.

The test case for the process of distinguishing between EBH and LBH is a comparison of Chronicles with Samuel and Kings. Chronicles appears to be post-exilic (see, e.g., 2 Chr 36:20–23), though it records pre-exilic events. "Thus the linguistic opposition between Samuel-Kings on the one hand, and Chronicles on the other ... gives us a firm grasp of the differences between pre-exilic and post-exilic Hebrew."[61]

However, not all scholars are convinced that these methods of diachronic analysis are sound. They agree that the language of the Old Testament shows a great degree of variety, but they argue that chronology does not have to be the explanation for these "types." They contend that typology, the idea that different types of Hebrew represent different stages in the historical development of the language, does not limit when a certain variation can be used: "It is possible for typologically older and younger sorts of language to coexist in the same chronological period."[62] In this synchronic assessment of biblical Hebrew, the Old Testament was composed during the Persian period and the variations in language can be accounted for by dialect differences between the northern and southern kingdoms, by different genres with different concerns and subject matter (register), and by scribes who wrote in both archaic and contemporary forms of Hebrew.

---

61. Young, "Introduction," 2. Note that Young is expressing the perspective of Avi Hurvitz, not his own.

62. Young, "Introduction," 2.

Few scholars fall neatly in one of these two positions. Rather, most recognize that a multi-faceted approach is necessary to explain the variations in biblical Hebrew.

6.6 RESOURCES FOR FURTHER STUDY

Barr, James. "Hebrew Lexicography: Informal Thoughts." Pages 137–51 in *Linguistics and Biblical Hebrew*. Edited by Walter R. Bodine. Winona Lake, IN: Eisenbrauns, 1992.

> James Barr has written extensively on how to understand the vocabulary of biblical Hebrew. His article in Bodine's volume is a good overview of the state of the discipline as well as his perspective on how to do lexicography well.

Cook, John A. *Time and the Biblical Hebrew Verb: The Expression of Tense, Aspect, and Modality in Biblical Hebrew*. Winona Lake, IN: Eisenbrauns, 2012.

> Cook provides a comprehensive work on tense and aspect in the Hebrew verb. His book is a good starting point for those interested in serious study of the subject.

Lunn, Nicholas P. *Word-Order Variation in Biblical Hebrew Poetry: Differentiating Pragmatics and Poetics*. Milton Keynes, UK: Paternoster, 2006.

> Lunn's study of word order, specifically related to biblical Hebrew poetry, is a useful resource for the broader question of word order in Hebrew. He stands in a line of Hebrew scholars who have incorporated the research of Knud Lambrecht, who provided a framework for thinking through word order in any given language.[63]

Moshavi, Adina. *Word Order in the Biblical Hebrew Finite Clause: A Syntactic and Pragmatic Analysis of Preposing*. Winona Lake, IN: Eisenbrauns, 2010.

> Moshavi applies insights on word order from linguistics to the question of word order in biblical Hebrew finite clauses. The

---

63. Lambrecht, *Information Structure and Sentence Form*.

book is filled with detailed discussions of many linguistic topics relevant to the issue of word order such as markedness, focusing, and topicalization. Moshavi identifies VSO (Verb–Subject–Object) as biblical Hebrew's default word order.

Naudé, Jacobus. "A Perspective on the Chronological Framework of Biblical Hebrew." *Journal of Northwest Semitic Languages* 30 (2004): 87–102.

Naudé's article on the chronological framework of biblical Hebrew provides an excellent overview of the chronology and typology debate, and his insights into language change and diffusion offer a helpful correction to tendencies to see the various stages of Hebrew as static entities.

Robar, Elizabeth. *The Verb and the Paragraph in Biblical Hebrew: A Cognitive-Linguistic Approach*. Leiden: Brill, 2014.

Robar's monograph is one of the most recent book-length studies on the biblical Hebrew verbal system. She uses concepts from cognitive linguistics, discourse analysis, markedness theory, pragmatics, and more, to create a new theoretical framework to explain the workings of the verbal system. She offers specific conclusions backed by detailed arguments, but her conclusions on the functions and meanings of various verb forms differ significantly from those of other scholars like Cook and Joosten.

Runge, Steven E. *Discourse Grammar of the Greek New Testament: A Practical Introduction for Teaching and Exegesis*. Peabody, MA: Hendrickson; Bellingham, WA: Lexham Press, 2010.

Runge provides an accessible and practical treatment of how word order affects exegesis (though his focus is biblical Greek). His manual is a good starting place, especially for students and pastors interpreting the Greek New Testament, but the insights into how careful language study can aid exegesis are relevant for students of biblical Hebrew as well.

Van der Merwe, Christo H. J. "Towards a Principled Model for Biblical Hebrew Lexicology." *Journal of Northwest Semitic Languages* 30 (2004): 119–37.

Christo van der Merwe critiques traditional approaches to lexicography and discusses how advances in cognitive semantics can help provide a better way of dealing with the biblical Hebrew lexicon.

Waltke, Bruce K., and Michael O'Connor. *An Introduction to Biblical Hebrew Syntax*. Winona Lake, IN: Eisenbrauns, 1990.

In their introduction to biblical Hebrew syntax, Waltke and O'Connor discuss the verbal system at length. They devote an entire chapter to verbal systems generally and then how biblical Hebrew fits within these general concepts. Another chapter focuses on issues related to the system of binyanim (i.e., "stems") in Hebrew.

Young, Ian, ed. *Biblical Hebrew: Studies in Chronology and Typology*. London: T&T Clark, 2003.

Young's edited volume includes articles by scholars who argue for dating the biblical books based on historical stages of biblical Hebrew and by those who contend that the different types of language are not restricted to specific timeframes. It is an excellent entry point into the broader discussion of chronology and typology.

Zevit, Ziony. Review of *Biblical Hebrew: Studies in Chronology and Typology*. *Review of Biblical Literature* 6 (2004): 1–15. http://www.bookreviews.org/pdf/4084_3967.pdf.

Zevit's thorough review of Young's volume provides an overview of the issues, summaries of most chapters, a critique of the arguments, and suggestions for moving the chronology/typology discussion forward.

7
—
LINGUISTIC ISSUES IN BIBLICAL GREEK

Michael Aubrey

T he use of linguistics for the study of biblical Greek has moved in fits and spurts over the past few decades, with progress in our understanding of biblical Greek moving in a similar manner. Today, we are faced with many of the same problems biblical scholars addressed a century ago, and we also encounter new ideas and challenges as the field of linguistics has developed over the past several decades. In this chapter, we examine some of the most important developments and issues currently facing linguists and biblical scholars working with biblical Greek.

7.1 PROBLEMS WITH THE DATA

The goal of the vast majority of linguistic theories and frameworks is to analyze spoken language. Most frameworks have not been designed with "dead" languages in mind.[1] Written language and text is derivative compared to spoken language. The research questions posed by contemporary linguistic theory are primarily focused on the production of language—its ability to produce an infinite number of sentences and meanings from finite means. But in biblical Greek, all of the relevant sentences already exist. We cannot elicit more example sentences from native speakers. For that reason, we are forced to develop creative means for evaluating the

---

1. That is, languages that are no longer spoken and are only known through written texts.

boundaries of Greek grammar. These boundaries exist in two realms. One involves the actual boundaries of the grammaticality of the language: Is a given sentence a grammatical sentence? For this question, we are primarily limited to statistical observations. If a particular construction appears consistently with high frequency across a variety of authors—particularly authors who are known historically to be native speakers—we can, with reasonable certainty, assume that the construction is a grammatical one. Conversely, if a given construction appears only rarely and is primarily limited to authors who were not native speakers, for whom Greek was a second or perhaps even third language, it is entirely possible that the construction is ungrammatical.[2] Both of these approaches can only be viewed as estimations of the grammatical nature of biblical Greek.

Beyond mere grammaticality, larger issues involve the question of interpretation. As non-native speakers/readers of Greek texts, we often conceive of a variety of possible interpretations of the NT and Septuagint texts. However, we must wonder how often it happens that one or more proposed interpretation would be viewed as completely improbable or even impossible to the writer or his audience. In these cases, there is often value in referring to the ancient interpreters of the text who were themselves native speakers. This is not to say that we should always defer to the Greek fathers and their exegetical conclusions. Rather, we should take notice when the Greek fathers appear to be completely unaware that a particular interpretation even exists. Moisés Silva, in his commentary on Philippians, puts it this way:

> Strange as it may sound, Chrysostom, along with other Greek fathers, can be particularly helpful when he does *not* offer an opinion on an exegetical problem. As a native Greek speaker, his innate sense of the language—but not necessarily his conscious reflection on it—provides an important bridge between the modern

---

2. Of course, there are two important caveats that must be made here. First, to claim that something is ungrammatical cannot be decisively demonstrated. One cannot prove a negative. Secondly, the grammaticality of a given sentence does not mean that it has no meaning or that its meaning is incoherent. The comprehensibility of language and the grammaticality of language are clearly related, but one does not inherently require the other. This is particularly true of the study of the Septuagint, where we are dealing with a Greek translation of a Hebrew text.

commentator and the Pauline writings (with the qualification that Paul's Greek was of course not identical to Chrysostom's). Educated speakers are notoriously unreliable in analyzing their own language. If Chrysostom weighs two competing interpretations, his conclusion should be valued as an important opinion and no more. If, on the other hand, he fails to address a linguistic problem because he does not appear to perceive a possible ambiguity, his silence is of the greatest value in helping us determine how Paul's first readers were likely to have interpreted the text.[3]

Thus, we can see that despite the orientation of linguistic theory as a whole toward contemporary languages rather than ancient languages, there is hope. Linguists and grammarians focused on ancient languages face more hurdles and challenges, but most of these issues can be overcome with creativity and determination.

There are additional problems with the data, however. As strange as it might sound, while the paucity of data is perhaps the primary difficulty in the analysis of biblical Hebrew, the exact opposite situation creates problems for analyzing biblical Greek. The corpus of texts available for the study of ancient Greek is in the tens of millions of words. Even if we constrain our focus to texts of the Hellenistic and Roman periods, roughly 300 BC to AD 300, we are still looking at millions of words of text. The sheer size of the corpus tends to completely overwhelm lexicographers and grammarians.

The discovery of the documentary papyri at the turn of the twentieth century has only exacerbated the problem. Thus, while there was a surge in interest in the inclusion of the papyri in the study of biblical Greek at the beginning of the twentieth century, scholarship simply did not have the manpower to integrate the new discoveries adequately. For example, Moulton and Milligan's *Vocabulary of the Greek Testament*[4] was a grand attempt at the integration of the papyri into the lexicographical work of the era, but it never went beyond being a supplement to other lexicons. To this day, even the papyriological references in the most modern lexicons

---

3. Moisés Silva, *Philippians*, 2nd ed. (Grand Rapids: Baker Academic, 2005), 27.

4. James H. Moulton and George Milligan, *The Vocabulary of the Greek Testament* (London: Hodder & Stoughton, 1930).

(such as BDAG) do little to go beyond the work of Moulton and Milligan. This is representative of the pattern: Many large grammatical or lexicographical projects begin, but few are ever finished. The scholars working on them either pass away, or their research interests change.[5]

However, the digitization of texts, particularly with morphological and syntactic annotation, has brought changes. What might have taken a lifetime or more one hundred years ago can now be accomplished in far less time with fewer people. A freshly produced, comprehensive reference grammar for biblical or Koine Greek has not been seen for forty years or more.[6] Nevertheless, these databases have made it possible for anyone to access vast amounts of grammatical evidence and draw their own conclusions in a manner that will only spur on continued research in biblical Greek grammar and lexicography. Moreover, the community of scholars interested in linguistics and biblical Greek is active, with an ever-growing body of specialized monographs and articles being published that will provide a strong foundation for any future reference grammar that might be produced.

7.2 VERBAL SYSTEM

The Greek verbal system has been a central focus of linguistic study for well over 150 years. It is highly complex in its morphological structure and involves the marking of several semantic distinctions that English makes quite differently. The contrasts between English and Greek, the former

---

5. James H. Moulton passed away in 1917 before he was able to complete either his grammar or his lexicographical work. Only the first volume of Moulton's *A Grammar of New Testament Greek* was published in his lifetime (1906, 1908). Conversely, Adolf Deissmann, another leading papyri researcher, had promised a lexicon but eventually turned to other scholarly pursuits. A contemporary example would be the never produced *Syntactical Concordance of the Greek New Testament*, a project promised by the Gramcord Institute and headed by D. A. Carson that also never saw the light of day. Its creators instead turned to other subjects such as hermeneutics, theology, and commentary writing.

6. Nigel Turner completed the volume on syntax of *A Grammar of New Testament Greek* in 1963, and prepared the volume on style that appeared in 1976 (James H. Moulton, Wilbert F. Howard, and Nigel Turner, *A Grammar of New Testament Greek*, 4 vols. [Edinburgh: T. & T. Clark, 1908, 1929, 1963, 1976]). Some have questioned both the quality and originality of Turner's work, however; see especially Horsley's review of the volume on syntax (G. H. R Horsley, *New Documents Illustrating Early Christianity*, Linguistic Essays 5 [Grand Rapids: Eerdmans, 2005], 49–66). If the charges are accurate, then we have not seen a full reference grammar of Greek since A. T. Robertson's *A Grammar of the Greek New Testament in the Light of Historical Research*, 4th ed. (London: Hodder & Stoughton, 1923).

with its system of auxiliary (helping) verbs and the latter with well-developed inflectional morphology, have made learning and comprehension difficult for English speakers. In what follows, we will survey several issues connected to the verbal system that have created problems for analysis and that continue to be discussed and debated in current grammatical literature. In doing so, we will work through the primary inflectional categories of the verb: voice, tense, aspect, and mood. We will also examine how the verb functions as a bridge between the lexicon and syntax.

7.2.1 VOICE

The Greek voice system has become a much-discussed topic in the past decade. Some of the challenges to its elucidation are a result of historical accidents, misinterpretations of distinctions in types of voice systems, and methodological flaws. Despite these, there is a growing consensus as to the nature of biblical Greek voice that has sought to break with tradition and correct the mistakes of the past.

Voice may be defined broadly as involving the relationship between the verb and its subject. There are many different voice systems in the world. In order to understand Greek voice, it is necessary to understand a few differences between these different types of voice systems. English-type voice systems are active-passive systems. Such systems assume that in a basic "transitive" clause, the subject takes the semantic role of agent, and the object takes the role of patient. English voice, then, involves the alternation of this basic transitive clause so that the patient semantic role that is normally associated with the object may be used as the subject. An active sentence such as "John broke the window" would be used to talk about John and what he has done.

What if the speaker and audience are primarily interested not in John, but in the broken window? The passive voice makes this possible. The patient is promoted from the position of grammatical object, and the agent is demoted either into a prepositional phrase or removed entirely. Thus, it becomes possible to talk about the patient as the subject of the sentence: "The window was broken." In English, this might be necessary if no one knows who the agent was, as in, "The Jeffersons arrived home and saw that the window was broken." Or people might use the passive voice if they are intentionally trying to avoid drawing attention to their role as the agent of the action. This strategy for using the English passive is often associated with politicians: "Mistakes were made in the running of the campaign." Neither of these uses are inherent to the passive voice. They are merely practical results of how speakers have taken advantage of the English voice system.

This background is important for understanding how English grammarians and language teachers have misunderstood the Greek voice system. Greek does not have an active-passive voice system like English does. Rather, Greek has what has become known as a "middle system."[7] Active–passive systems are known as derived voice systems since they involve a semantic-syntactic alternation. Middle systems are basic voice systems. Neither the active voice nor the middle voice can be derived from the other. Before we examine the nature of the Greek middle system, it is important to note that, historically, grammarians have struggled to squeeze Greek voice into the paradigm of English voice, essentially forcing a square peg into a round hole. We have been living with the results for quite some time now. This has resulted in two primary problems. First, most traditional grammars talk about three voices: active, middle, and passive. The second problem arises from the first. This tripartite division of voices by traditional grammars necessitated the creation of an additional category for the leftovers that they could not fit into the English conceptualization of voice. These have become known as deponent verbs.

Deponency refers to a mismatch in form and function.[8] While deponency is a real phenomenon in language, and it is generally accepted that deponency exists in biblical Greek voice morphology, the actual language evidence suggests otherwise. This is especially true if we take seriously the difference between the English voice and the Greek voice systems.[9]

---

7. The analysis of middle-voice systems only began to receive serious interest from linguists in the past few decades. The seminal research was only published in the early 1990s: M. H. Klaiman, *Grammatical Voice* (Cambridge: Cambridge University Press, 1991); Suzanne Kemmer, *Middle Voice* (Amsterdam: John Benjamins, 1993). Both Klaiman and Kemmer dealt with a variety of languages, including ancient Greek.

8. See Matthew Baerman et al., eds., *Deponency and Morphological Mismatches* (Oxford: Oxford University Press, 2007).

9. This is despite the fact that most introductory grammars assume and teach the category. There are a few exceptions, such as Stanley Porter, Matthew Brook O'Donnell, and Jeffrey Reed, *Fundamentals of New Testament Greek* (Grand Rapids: Eerdmans, 2010); and Micheal Palmer's excellent online grammar, available at www.greek-language.com/grammar/.

The traditional account states that these "deponent" verbs are active in meaning, but middle/passive in form. But when we examine examples of the verbs themselves, we find that these so-called "deponent" verbs do not actually follow that definition. Consider the following examples, organized into categories.[10]

Direct Reflexive Middle		Indirect Reflexive Middles	
ἐγκαυχάομαι	boast (pride oneself in)	ἐργάζομαι	work, perform
μιμέομαι	imitate	κτάομαι	acquire
κάθημαι	sit		
Reciprocal Middle		**Body Motion Middles**	
ἐναγκαλίζομαι	embrace	ἀφικνέομαι	arrive
χαρίζομαι	forgive	ἐξάλλομαι	leap up
μάχομαι	fight	ἔρχομαι	come, go
ἐμπορεύομαι	buy and sell	ὀρχέομαι	dance
Speech-Act Middles		**Perception Middles**	
ἀποκρίνομαι	answer	αἰσθάνομαι	perceive
διηγέομαι	tell, convey	θεάομαι	notice, see
ψεύδομαι	lie, speak falsely	ἐπισκέπτομαι	to look after
Mental Process Middles		**Mental Activity Middles**	
ἐνυπνιάζομαι	dream	διαλογίζομαι	ponder
ἐπιλανθάνομαι	forget	ἐπίσταμαι	understand
εὐλαβέομαι	feel reverence for	πυνθάνομαι	learn
Spontaneous Process			
διαγίνομαι	pass/elapse (of time)		
διαδέχομαι	inherit		
γίνομαι	become		
κοιμάομαι	fall asleep, die		

---

10. These verbs are taken from Neva Miller, "A Theory of Deponent Verbs," in *Analytical Lexicon of the Greek New Testament*, ed. Timothy Friberg, Barbara Friberg, and Neva Miller (Grand Rapids: Baker, 2000), 423–31. However, the categories here are those of Rutger J. Allan, *The Middle Voice in Ancient Greek: A Study in Polysemy* (Amsterdam: J.C. Gieben, 2003). This is perhaps the most accessible set of middle categories because Allan's dissertation is freely available online, and his categories were adopted in the intermediate Greek grammar by Albert Rijksbaron, *The Syntax and Semantics of the Classical Greek*, 3rd ed. (Chicago: University of Chicago Press, 2007).

All these verbs are traditionally categorized as deponent. However, they all involve the same sort of semantic distinctions that all other verbs that appear in the middle voice have. If the usages of these middle-only verbs are identical to other middles, then there is no principled reason why we should distinguish between verbs that appear only in the middle and verbs in the middle that also have an active form. They are all semantically middle.

At this point the question becomes: What ties verbs in the middle voice together? Is there some relationship between these various categories of usage? On this question, observe that all these verbs involve situations in which the grammatical subject participates in the action, process, or state expressed by the verb. We label this "semantic constraint subject affectedness."[11] This is the unifying factor that ties together all of these categories semantically, and it has been recognized by traditional grammars for quite some time, even if middle-only verbs (formerly "deponent") had not received that definition. Notably from this perspective, the passive can then be easily subsumed within the category of middle voice: Passives fundamentally involve subject affectedness to the highest degree.[12]

More recently, Rachel Aubrey has put forward a model for understanding middle voice that builds on Allan and also the broader linguistic literature on voice.[13] Her analysis goes beyond merely subject affectedness. She demonstrates how the apparently disparate categories of usage for middle verbs (direct reflexive, speech act, perception, mental and spontaneous processes, passives, etc.) can be motivated on the basis of their meaning in conjunction with transitivity.

---

11. See especially Allan, *Middle Voice*, 39–41.

12. This is, in fact, precisely what Kemmer does in her analysis: The passive-middle is a function within middle systems (*Middle Voice*, 202). She draws a distinction between languages with middle systems that mark passives separate from middles and those that subsume passive within the middle. Greek does the latter. Contrary to the discussion in most introductory grammars, the -θη suffix is not an aorist passive marker. It is an alternative middle marker and is used for the very same categories of middle usage that the other sigmatic aorist middle does. To explore this topic further, see §7.5 Resources for Further Study.

13. Rachel Aubrey, "Motivated Categories, Middle Voice, and Passive Morphology," in *The Greek Verb Revisited: A Fresh Approach for Biblical Exegesis*, ed. Steven E. Runge and Christopher J. Fresch (Bellingham, WA: Lexham Press, 2016).

In light of all of this, it might be practical to note the proposal of Carl Conrad.[14] He suggests referring to the active voice as the "default voice," making no explicit claim one way or another about the status of the subject or the transitivity of the clause. The default voice then alternates with the "subject-focused voice"—that is, the middle. These labels would make the semantic and grammatical function of Greek voice more transparent to students.

7.2.2 TENSE AND ASPECT

Research on the Greek verb at the end of the twentieth century produced a renewed interest in the grammatical categories of tense and aspect. A few different perspectives were put forth, but none received consensus. While there is agreement on a few issues, such as the basic aspectual values of the present, imperfect, and aorist forms, debate continues over the nature of aspect as a category, the existence of grammaticalized tense, and the semantic value of the Greek perfect. The different approaches are represented by Porter, Fanning, McKay, and Campbell, and they all diverge on these points.[15] Porter and Campbell rejected the idea that the Greek verb is marked morphologically for tense (i.e. the location of an event in time).[16] Fanning has followed the standard (and still prevailing view) that the tense is marked morphologically in the verb. And between these two positions falls McKay, who rejects the extreme view of Porter while still emphasizing the importance of aspect over against tense within the verbal system.

---

14. Carl Conrad, "Active, Middle, and Passive: Understanding Ancient Greek Voice" (unpublished manuscript, 2003). Available online at https://pages.wustl.edu/files/pages/imce/cwconrad/undancgrkvc.pdf.

15. Stanley E. Porter, *Verbal Aspect in the Greek of the New Testament with Reference to Tense and Mood* (New York: Peter Lang, 1989); Buist Fanning, *Verbal Aspect in New Testament Greek* (Oxford: Oxford University Press, 1990); K. L. McKay, *A New Syntax of the Verb in New Testament Greek* (New York: Peter Lang, 1994); Constantine Campbell, *Verbal Aspect, the Indicative Mood, and Narrative* (New York: Peter Lang, 2007).

16. It should be emphasized, however, that Porter and Campbell do not see eye to eye on this issue. Campbell views the Greek future as a true, future-tense-referring morphological form, while Porter claims that the future "grammaticalizes the semantic (meaning) feature of expectation" (*Idioms of the Greek New Testament*, 2nd ed. [Sheffield: Sheffield Academic, 1999], 44).

In order to gain a grasp on the issues here, it might be helpful to look at the various tense and aspect markers in the Greek verb. We find that the relationship between these two categories is clear in the morphological oppositions. The semantic relationships between tense-aspect forms can be organized easily based on their internal morphological structure, as shown in the table below.[17]

	Present & Imperfect	Aorist & Future	Perfect & Pluperfect
Augment	ἔλυον	ἔλυσα	ἐλελύκειν
No Augment	λύω	λύσω	λέλυκα
	Imperfective	Perfective	Perfect
Past	ἔ-∅-λυ-∅-ο-ν	ἔ-∅-λυ-σ-α-∅	ἐ-λε-λύ-κ-ει-ν
Nonpast	∅-∅-λύ-∅-ω-∅	∅-∅-λύ-σ-ω-∅	∅-λέ-λυ-κ-α-∅

The first half of this table provides the first-person singular active indicative of the verb λύω ("I loosen") as we normally might see it in an introductory grammar with the traditional labels: present, imperfect, aorist, future, perfect, and pluperfect. The second half of the table shows how we might break down the Greek verb into morphemes and the semantic features those morphemes represent. A number of observations can be made here. First, we can see a clear relationship between the augment (ἐ- prefix) and past tense, since it occurs with all the forms that are prototypically past-referring: imperfect, aorist, and pluperfect. Similarly, an augment does not appear on those verb forms on which past tense is unmarked: The future has future-time reference, the present has present-time reference, and the perfect may have either present or past reference. Likewise, the

---

17. This chart is only representative of the most productive Greek verbal paradigm during the Koine period, the first aorist. The future perfect, which was productive in the classical period and the early Hellenistic period, was no longer productive for nonliterary (i.e. non-Atticizing) Greek in the first century AD. Classical Greek structured the relationship between the future and other forms quite differently. Nicholas Ellis ("Aspect-Prominence, Morpho-Syntax, and a Cognitive-Linguistic Framework for the Greek Verb," in Runge and Fresch, *Greek Verb Revisited*) has a helpful summary of these issues, though his choice of the term "combinative" for the perfect is an unusual one. Also, note that the null marker is being used here simply for clarity and convenience. We are not making theoretical claims about the existence of "null morphemes," a topic of much debate in linguistic morphology.

morphological markers for aspect are also consistent. The present and the imperfect are imperfective and have no morphological marker. The aorist and the future are perfective in aspect, and they share the sigma marker. Finally, the perfect and pluplerfect share reduplication and the kappa suffix, and both involve perfect aspect.[18] Because of this aspectual pairing of two forms, each differentiated by the augment, we must also recognize that the primary morphological distinction for tense is not past, present, future, but rather past and nonpast. That is, the central morphological tense marking is the combination of the ἐ- prefix, the augment, and the distinction between primary and secondary subject agreement suffixes. The augment always coincides with the secondary endings and the lack of the augment with the primary endings.[19]

Also, we can note that the past tense marking augment (ἐ-) consistently parallels itself with the secondary personal endings. This grammatical redundancy means that even when the augment is missing, the past tense is still differentiated from the distinct personal endings. This is an important argument against those promoting a tenseless analysis of Greek. Scholars such as Porter and others rely heavily on the optionality of the augment in Homer and the papyri and its more consistent disappearance from the aorist and especially the pluperfect.[20] Yet this argument fails because the augment duplicates the same semantic information conveyed by the primary (nonpast) and secondary (past) personal endings. We can take the division of the verb into morphemes above and label the position as in the table below.

---

18. Some grammarians might say "stative" rather than "perfect" here.

19. In the classical period, this was not the case: The subjunctive used the primary endings, and the optative used the secondary endings. Because of this, the concept of remoteness is perhaps more useful for Classical Greek, where the primary/secondary distinction marked the remoteness that then aligned with nonpast/past in the indicative. The optative was still relatively viable during the time of the Septuagint, but by the first century, it was all but gone in the spoken language with the exception of a few fossilized forms (Robertson, *Grammar of the Greek New Testament*, 935–37).

20. Porter, *Verbal Aspect*, 208–11; Rodney J. Decker, *Temporal Deixis of the Greek Verb in the Gospel of Mark with Reference to Verbal Aspect* (New York: Peter Lang, 2001), 39–40.

Traditional Label	Tense	Aspect (Perfect)	Lexical Root[21]	Aspect	Personal Endings[22]
Present	∅	∅	λυ	∅	ω (Primary)
Imperfect	ε-	∅	λυ	∅	-ον (Secondary)
Future	∅	∅	λυ	σ	-ω (Primary)
Aorist	ε-	∅	λυ	σ	-α (Secondary)
Perfect	∅	λε ([C]+ε)	λυ	κ	-α (Primary)
Pluperfect	ε-	λε ([C]+ε)	λυ	κ	-ειν (Secondary)

In terms of semantics, tense and aspect cannot be separated from each other on a formal basis. First of all, the table suggests that the relationship between the future and the aorist is probably one of perfective aspect, differing only in tense: past versus nonpast. Very few languages have a perfective present tense, and those that do invariably use that form to express some other semantic feature.[23] This view of the future is in perfect alignment with the ancient grammarians.[24]

Porter suggests that ancient and modern scholars have been deceived by the morphological parallel between the aorist and future.[25] Why he views this as a deception is not clear. One reason might be that the sigmatic future has no historical relationship to the sigmatic aorist. The former arose from the Proto-Indo-European desiderative affix.[26] But to think the origin of the

---

21. We use the word "root" not to refer to a historical root, but to the most basic morphological portion of a word.

22. The personal endings involve a conglomerate of semantic features, not only tense and aspect, but also person, number, voice, and mood. Since our interest here is primarily in tense and aspect, we do not articulate them here.

23. Consider the English present perfective: "walk," "am walking," "walked." When the first of these is used in speech, it rarely (if ever) actually has present meaning, but instead defaults to a universal or habitual interpretation: "I walk on a regular basis." In Koine Greek, habitual meaning is already covered by the imperfective, thus the future, λύσω, is readily available for future reference. And in fact, perfective aspect is one of two common sources for future tenses, the other being epistemic modality (possibility/necessity). See D. N. S. Bhat, *The Prominence of Tense, Aspect and Mood* (Amsterdam: John Benjamins, 1999), 176–77.

24. R. H. Robins, *The Byzantine Grammarians: Their Place in History* (Berlin: Mouton de Gruyter, 1993).

25. Porter, *Verbal Aspect*, 19–20.

26. Benjamin W. Fortson, *Indo-European Language and Culture* (Oxford: Blackwell, 2004), 91; Andrew Sihler, *New Comparative Grammar of Greek and Latin* (Oxford: Oxford University Press, 1995), 507–9; 556–57. Porter wrongly views the future as having its origin in the subjunctive (*Verbal Aspect*, 404).

form determines its meaning is to commit an etymological fallacy. Every generation of speakers of a language reinterprets the morphological forms with their own conceptualization. It is a natural development alongside the regularization of the thematic -ω conjugation that eventually replaced even the -μι verbs entirely. Importantly, that the Stoics and the ancient grammarians made this supposed "mistake" is strong historical evidence that just such a re-analysis took place.

Nevertheless, the categories of tense and aspect continue to be a fertile area of research and discussion. While those who follow the tenseless model are a minority, they are a fairly vocal one. Thankfully, this has only encouraged the continued discussion of this important subject. For example, Constantine Campbell has stepped beyond the ideas of Porter to suggest that the augment prefix traditionally associated with past tense could instead be conceived as denoting the grammatical category of remoteness instead.[27] In this explanation, the past time reference we see in the use of the augment (with the imperfect, pluperfect, and aorist) is not tense per se, but functions as one particular realization of the category of remoteness. The field continues to evaluate these proposals with cautious suspicion. In the meantime, the model held by the majority of scholars—that Greek does indeed grammaticalize tense on the verb—continues to receive argument and analysis.[28]

7.3 SEMANTICS AND LEXICOGRAPHY

We observed previously, in our discussion of problems with the data, that biblical Greek is in a unique situation in which having too much available data and text to work with has actually hindered the development of resources. Nowhere is this more clearly visible than in the realm of lexicography. The task of lexicography for both classical and biblical Greek is simply so vast that very few fresh and completely original lexical works exist, and none can claim to be comprehensive. In fact, there is a tradition of simply re-editing older lexicons that goes back hundreds of years, even back to the earliest Latin-Greek glossaries. In a few cases, this habit of re-editing and copying has resulted in wrong meanings being attributed

---

27. Campbell, *Verbal Aspect*, 88–90.
28. See especially the essays brought together in Runge and Fresch, *Greek Verb Revisited*.

to words hundreds of years ago that have been promulgated without reevaluation and being corrected only recently.

Does all of this mean that our lexicons for the NT and Septuagint are completely unreliable and inaccurate? Thankfully, the answer to that question is still a resounding, "No." In the majority of cases, we know quite precisely the meanings for individual Greek words. It does not mean we cannot trust our lexicons. Rather, it suggests that we cannot view our lexicons as the last word on the meaning of words.[29] It also means that we need to be reading lexical entries carefully and comparing the entries for particular words across multiple lexicons and evaluating their analyses on the basis of the context of where these words appear in Scripture.

Surveys of the strengths and weaknesses of biblical Greek lexicons are available in a number of places.[30] Rather than duplicate the discussions that are readily available elsewhere, the examination that follows here attempts to examine biblical Greek lexicons in terms of the development of semantic theory over the past century.

7.3.1 ISSUES IN LEXICAL SEMANTICS

The NT has enjoyed a rich tradition of lexicography over the past two centuries. Intent interest in the text and meaning of the NT has encouraged the production of detailed lexicons and dictionaries. The most significant have been the theological dictionaries produced in the nineteenth and twentieth centuries, the various editions of Bauer's lexicon produced in German and English, and the lexicon created for Bible translators by J. P. Louw and Eugene Nida, published in 1989.[31] These three are ordered chronologically

---

29. This is, in fact, true of lexicons in general for any language. For NT Greek, these issues are dealt with most compellingly in John Lee's *A History of New Testament Lexicography* (New York: Peter Lang, 2003).

30. See especially Frederick Danker, *Multi-purpose Tools for Bible Study*, rev. and exp. ed. (Minneapolis: Fortress, 1993), 116–31; Lee, *History of New Testament Lexicography*.

31. e.g., Gerhard Kittel, Gerhard Friedrich, and Geoffrey W. Bromiley, eds., *Theological Dictionary of the New Testament*, electronic ed. (Grand Rapids: Eerdmans, 1964-1973); Walter Bauer et al., eds., *A Greek-English Lexicon of the New Testament and Other Early Christian Literature*, 3rd ed. (Chicago: University of Chicago Press, 2000); Johannes Louw and Eugene A. Nida, *Greek-English Lexicon of the New Testament: Based on Semantic Domains*, 2nd ed. (New York: United Bible Societies, 1989). Note that Kittel's theological dictionary derives from German work begun in the late nineteenth century and continued into the first half of the twentieth century, with English versions appearing in the 1960s. Similarly, the first English edition of Bauer's lexicon appeared in 1957, based on the fourth German edition.

here for an important reason: The debates that exist within the realm of biblical Greek lexicography are directly tied to the theoretical and methodological approaches representative of their eras.

The nineteenth century represents the era in which lexical semantics began to come into its own as a field of study. Alongside it, the practice of lexicography was emerging out of glossaries culled from translations into its own scientific discipline. The approach of historical philology that developed during that time provided the basis for the majority of lexicons, combining the terminology and concepts from ancient rhetorical theory (e.g. metaphor, metonymy, synecdoche, etc.) and the empirical basis of the lexicological data.[32] Max Hecht helpfully summarized the state of lexical semantics toward the end of the nineteenth century:

> Semantics is linguistically valuable to the extent that it chronologically classifies meanings in the interest of lexicography, and writes down the laws of semantic change in the interests of etymology. To the extent, however, that it derives these laws from the nature of the mind and that it writes a history of ideas—meanings are ideas—it falls within the realm of empirical psychology.[33]

While Hecht does not focus on or express an interest specifically in biblical Greek lexicography, his statement is significant for understanding the mindset of biblical lexicographers from the nineteenth century, whose efforts have formed the foundation for the majority of Greek lexicons used today. These words represent the theoretical orientation that motivated the efforts of scholars such as Walter Bauer, Henry Liddell, Robert Scott, and Joseph Thayer, for example. We can note a few specific observations here. First, lexicographers from this period viewed the classification of semantic change and etymology as central to their work. Second—and quite significantly—this quote demonstrates that these lexicographers viewed their work as involving a *psychological* component: The lexicographers viewed the meaning of words and the processes that drive the semantic change of the meaning of words as providing insights into the nature of the human

---

32. Dirk Geeraerts, *Theories of Lexical Semantics* (Oxford: Oxford University Press, 2010), 2–9.

33. Max Hecht, *Griechische Bedeutungslehre* (Leipzig: Teubner, 1888), 5; cited and translated by Dirk Geeraerts, *Theories of Lexical Semantics*, 9.

mind. Dirk Geeraerts argues that this fact and the development of classification systems for describing semantic change "demarcate the domain
of historical-philological semantics."[34]

These two prongs of historical-philological semantics form the back
bone for the two primary semantic traditions that arose out of this period
in biblical Greek: The standard descriptive lexicons such as those of Thayer,
Bauer, and Liddell and Scott arose out of the interests in semantic change
and etymology of the era. Their focus was empirical in nature. This was a
natural development from older glossaries and lexicons. On the other side
of things, the tradition of theological lexicons also finds its origin in the
methodology of historical-philological semantics.[35] The secular linguists
and lexicographers of this period had quite clearly recognized an important fact about the nature of language that was lost (or ignored) during
much of the twentieth century: "The linguistic phenomena under study
are seen as revealing characteristics of the human mind."[36] Scholars of
biblical Greek picked up on the significance of this relationship between a
word and the larger cultural and psychological associations with that word.
Consider, for example, the following two phrases/compounds: "garage sale."
If we were to ask a group of American English speakers what a garage
sale was, they would all likely respond along the following lines: a sale of
unwanted used items sold from in and around the garage over the course
of a day or two.

At the same time, there are significant cultural and social factors or
features that correlate with garage sales. Garage sales tend to take place
in the spring or the fall. Cities or local communities might establish desig-
nated weekends for garage sales. The items on sale are generally expected
to be quite low in price. Bartering is acceptable, if not encouraged. Prices
might be reduced toward the end of the day (or weekend), when the sale is
coming to a close. There might even be a box of items being given away for
free. The purpose is as much about getting rid of excess stuff as it is about

---

34. Hecht, *Griechische Bedeutungslehre*, 10.

35. This tradition more or less began in English with Hermann Cremer's *Biblico-Theological
Lexicon of New Testament Greek*, 3rd Eng. ed., trans. from the 2nd ed., with additional matter
and corrections by the author (Edinburgh: T&T Clark, 1880).

36. Geeraerts, *Theories of Lexical Semantics*, 10. The psychological nature of language,
which has again come to be appreciated in the past few decades in linguistics, was disregarded
during the reign of structuralist linguistics that lasted up to the 1960s.

making money. Perhaps most striking, linguistically speaking, the term "garage sale" has been extended such that if a sufficient number of these features are present, the term does not need to refer to a sale taking place in a garage. A youth group might do a garage sale in the parking lot of their church with items donated by the congregation. In such a case, there is not even a garage present, and yet the term is still contextually appropriate.

We might call this type of cultural, social, and contextual information *associative* meaning.[37] Linguists at the turn of the nineteenth century viewed associative meaning as highly valuable for developing an understanding of language, semantic change in language, and the human mind. In our example here, "garage sale" does not *mean* all this corollary information in a denotative sense. However, in our minds, this information, either in whole or in part, is evoked by "garage sale." It is cultural baggage. Scholars such as Cremer and Kittel, who produced theological dictionaries, were working within this theoretical framework. They sought to bring together and articulate the social, cultural, and theological information that is associated with individual lexemes. They recognized that words are not self-contained phonetic vessels, but complex mental representations of human knowledge.

It is important here to emphasize this methodological and theoretical background to the theological dictionaries. This is because over the past several decades the popular trend has been to degrade them, particularly since the publication of James Barr's *Semantics of Biblical Language*.[38] This is not to say that James Barr was wrong when he wrote his heavy critique of theological lexicography in general or of the *Theological Dictionary of the New Testament* in particular.[39] Barr's *Semantics of Biblical Language* was a criticism of theologians using poor linguistics. This was certainly an accurate criticism,[40] as there were a number of significant linguistic failures here. For one, these theological dictionaries went well beyond the

---

37. This is following Eugene Nida and J. P. Louw, *Lexical Semantics of the Greek New Testament* (Atlanta: Scholars Press, 1992), 31–34.

38. James Barr, *The Semantics of Biblical Language* (Oxford: Oxford University Press, 1961).

39. Kittel et al., *Theological Dictionary of the New Testament*.

40. Biblical scholars at the time were making a number of extreme claims about how much they could get into the mind of Hebrew and Greek speakers on the basis of the meaning of individual words (see Thorleif Boman, *Hebrew Thought Compared with Greek* [New York: W. W. Norton, 1960]).

documentation of sociocultural assumptions implicit in biblical Greek lexemes into making significant theological claims about those particular lexemes.

They also encouraged the lexical fallacy of illegitimate totality trans-fer,[41] making the assumption that *all* the associative meanings that might be evoked by a particular lexeme are *always* all evoked by a particular lexeme. In the case of our "garage sale" example above, a youth group garage sale fundraiser at the church would not evoke a garage or even necessarily the sale of unwanted items. A good Greek example is the noun υἱοθεσία (*huiothesia*, "adoption"). Would a Jew writing a letter to a group of Gentiles in the first century have a mental representation of *huiothesia* that was primarily Jewish in nature, as James M. Scott would argue?[42] Or would it involve more Graeco-Roman associations, as Trevor Burke has proposed?[43] Both are justifiably a part of the mental representation evoked by *huiothesia* in the mind of a first-century Jew. But they are also extremely distinct representations: Graeco-Roman adoption involves legal expecta-tions and requirements for establishing an heir, while Jewish adoption is theological and political, grounded in the OT background of God adopting the king of Israel.

At its most basic level the critique leveled against *TDNT* was that words cannot be equated with ideas/concepts. As Silva writes in his discussion of Barr's critique, "The confusion [of words and concepts] may be inher-ent in the nature of *TDNT*, which seeks to deal with conceptual history (*Begriffsgeschichte*) in the form of a dictionary of words."[44] This is certainly a valid criticism. And it is one with significant exegetical implications. If one is interested in studying the concept of reconciliation in Paul's let-ters, for example, an exegete certainly must examine his use of the word ἀποκαταλλάσσω (*apokatallassō*, "I reconcile"); but if the exegete does not fur-ther examine all the various examples of reconciliation where no actual

---

41. See Moises Silva, *Biblical Words and Their Meaning*, rev. and exp. ed. (Grand Rapids: Zondervan, 1996), 25–27.

42. James M. Scott, *Adoption as Sons of God: An Exegetical Investigation into the Background of ΥΙΟΘΕΣΙΑ in the Corpus Paulinum* (Tübingen: J. C. B. Mohr, 1992).

43. Trevor Burke, *Adopted into God's Family: Exploring a Pauline Metaphor* (Downers Grove, IL: InterVarsity, 2006).

44. Silva, *Biblical Words and Their Meaning*, 27.

reference to the individual lexeme occurs, then the study will result in an inadequate picture of the term. Concepts are much larger than words. Moreover, the tendency to move from attempting to document the mental representation evoked by words found in biblical Greek to theologizing about the nature of biblical Greek must be viewed as highly problematic.[45]

At the same time, Barr's criticisms also reflect that the structuralist linguistic ideas of the 1940s and 1950s were fundamentally at odds with the psychological perspective on language that existed in the nineteenth and early twentieth centuries. In the early to mid-twentieth century, lexical semantics had begun to move away from the psychological orientation that we observed above.[46] If the failure of theological dictionaries was the assumption that words and concepts are identical, then the failure of the structuralist semantics that dominated the field when James Barr wrote his critique was the assumption that words and concepts are dramatically different. If words mean anything at all, then there must be a substantive relationship between them and the concepts (both associative and denotative) they evoke mentally.

The dominant scholars in structuralist semantics for Greek were Johannes Louw and Eugene Nida, who together produced *A Greek-English Lexicon of the New Testament based on Semantic Domains*.[47] Lexical semantics during this period went too far in the other direction, placing essentially no emphasis on the mental representations that are evoked by particular lexical items. Words became little more than bundles of semantic features related to other bundles of semantic features (see §2.3.2.a Componential Analysis). Moisés Silva provides the following example.[48]

---

45. On this front, Cremer was highly criticized. See, for example, Adolf Deissmann and Lionel Richard Mortimer Strachan, *Light from the Ancient East: The New Testament Illustrated by Recently Discovered Texts of the Graeco-Roman World* (London: Hodder & Stoughton, 1910), 69–117.

46. That is to say, it is not entirely clear whether the theological dictionary actually confused words and concepts in the manner that they are accused or whether they were simply misunderstood by proponents of structuralist semantics. It is entirely possible that the accusation itself was a result of the great theoretical and methodological chasm that existed between historical-philological semantics and structuralist semantics.

47. Louw and Nida, *Greek-English Lexicon of the New Testament Based on Semantic Domains*. Louw and Nida were the dominant scholars for structuralist semantics in Greek. Beyond the realm of Greek studies, there were numerous other scholars along with them, though Nida in particular played a significant role in structuralist semantics both in Greek and in linguistics generally.

48. Silva, *Biblical Words and Their Meaning*, 135.

	man	woman	boy	girl
human	+	+	+	+
adult	+	+	-	-
male	+	-	+	-

This type of feature analysis is certainly useful for developing an understanding of how various vocabulary items are connected and also for understanding the denotative meaning of lexical items, or in the words in Nida and Louw, "The meanings of verbal signs are determined by other verbal signs."[49] Within structuralist semantics, the meaning of a given word is fundamentally grounded in its relationship with other words. Such an approach to understanding how words have meaning is useful, particularly for recognizing that there are nontrivial relationships between words: that the concept of a semantic domain is a very useful and meaningful one. On the other hand, if the meaning of words is, as Nida and Louw (and structuralists in general) claim, grounded in their relationships to other words, then we must wonder exactly how the relationship between language and reality functions. Geeraerts put the problem this way:

> The structuralist tenet that it is possible to identify an entirely language-internal level of semantic structure may be difficult to maintain. The crucial problem is one of demarcation: if there is an essential distinction between linguistic semantic knowledge as part of the language, and the conceptual knowledge in general, as part of our knowledge of the world, where exactly do we find the boundary? How easy would it actually be to draw a neat boundary around the structures that constitute semantic knowledge according to the structuralist point of view?[50]

For Nida and Louw, the answer to this question is twofold. They hold to a theory of lexical meaning as naming.

> The principle function of lexemes is naming. ... This process of naming applies to both the linguistic and nonlinguistic worlds of

---

49. Nida and Louw, *Lexical Semantics*, 18.
50. Geeraerts, *Theories of Lexical Semantics*, 93.

entities, activities, characteristics (including states), and relations. But the naming capacity of a lexeme (whether inflectional morpheme, word, or idiom) depends upon its being a part of a system of such units, in which the various units serve to define each other.[51]

Unfortunately, Nida and Louw give no explanation for why language should be this way. The simple question is: When someone says the word "shoe," do you immediately call to mind all the sense relations that exist within the same domain? Or do you project a mental image of a shoe in your mind? To put it another way, if Nida and Louw were correct about the nature of meaning here, then it would become necessary that a person learn the sense relationships that exist between shoe, sandal, high heel, boot, and so forth in order to actually grasp the meaning of "shoe." For Nida and Louw, meaning only exists as names within a system.[52] But the reality is that the system is not necessary to grasp the meaning of "shoe." Rather, what is necessary is simply *experience* with a shoe.

In the end, according to structuralist perspectives on semantics, lexical items have no relationship to concepts at all. Those who practice structuralist semantics claim meaning is found in the system of verbal signs, which for our purposes are lexical items or words. We have seen that this view has its own problems. To repeat what we said above: If the failure of the theological dictionaries was the assumption that words and concepts

---

51. Nida and Louw, *Lexical Semantics*, 24.

52. And while this sounds rather odd, they make it quite clear that this is the case. Consider their analogy:

In order to better understand the significance of this relationship between a verbal sign, its reference, and the system of verbal signs, it may be useful to compare the structure of a very simple code such as traffic signals. In order to signal the meanings of "go," "stop," and "prepare to stop," there are three different colors: green, red, and yellow. But red does not mean anything in and of itself. Its meaning of "stop" depends upon the code in which the contrasting color green means "go" and the color yellow means "prepare to stop." Not only do the colors occur in a particular sequence, but each color serves a distinctive function in regulating traffic. (Nida and Louw, *Lexical Semantics*, 25)

There are a number of accurate points here. Each color does, indeed, serve a distinctive function and has a specific meaning, and an individual color has no meaning in and of itself. But we must question whether the meaning the colors receive is gained from the system of three colors or whether the meaning is gained by human experience and social interaction. The system is not an autonomous entity that imbues meaning to its constituent parts. Rather, the system is itself motivated by human experience. People had a specific need for traffic regulation, and it is that specific need that motivates the system and by extension the meaning of its parts. Systems do not create meaning; humans do.

were equated, the failure of structuralist semantics is that words and concepts have no relationship at all. Fundamentally, we can view the approach put forward by grammarians and linguists such as Barr, Silva, Louw, and Nida as a reaction against the historical-philological tradition that produced dictionaries like *TDNT*. But perhaps they threw the baby out with the bathwater. Perhaps there is a way to reconcile these two approaches.

At the end of the day, we find ourselves in roughly the same spot. The central problem in biblical Greek lexical semantics lies with the relationship between lexical items like words and the concepts or ideas to which they refer. We can, perhaps, make a few statements with some confidence. Words are not concepts. They are distinct. Structural semantics is correct on this point, and its emphasis on the relationships between lexical items is highly valuable. However, words have a nontrivial relationship with the external world and human knowledge. And on that point, historical philology has still made an important contribution—even if there has been an unfortunate tendency to overtheologize the meaning of words.

Little has been done in biblical Greek lexical semantics and lexicography to move beyond this theoretical impasse. We can, however, imagine a solution that could bring together the valuable insights of both historical–philological semantics and also structuralist semantics. Recall two important concepts within cognitive linguistics discussed previously: prototype theory and semantic frames (see §5.6.2 Important Concepts). Prototype theory provides us with an approach to understanding both how individual lexical items are related to each other and how multiple senses of a lexical item (polysemy) are related to each other in a similar, but more nuanced, way to structuralist semantics. Similarly, the concept of semantic frames recognizes that the meaning of individual lexical items is encyclopedic in nature. This encyclopedic meaning is grounded in our shared human experience of the world.

A popular metaphor that cognitive linguists have used when talking about the encyclopedic nature of meaning in lexical semantics and the relationship between words and concepts has been the metaphor of an iceberg. If we conceive of a concept as an iceberg, we could then also imagine that a word or lexical item exists as the tip of the iceberg that is visible above the surface of the water. In this schema, the word is not identical to the concept, but its use evokes a variety of associations. The full iceberg exists as a personal total mental representation of potential associations that one has with the lexical item in question.

Thus far, there has been no significant, much less comprehensive, work in biblical Greek lexical semantics using cognitive linguistics. This limits our ability to discuss specific proposals or ideas. We can, however, make a few suggestions for how we might approach using existing tools with what we have learned about semantics and cognitive linguistics.

7.3.2 GREEK LEXICONS AND DICTIONARIES

7.3.2.a Theological Dictionaries

The three English theological dictionaries still used in biblical Greek studies are *TDNT*, *NIDNTT*, and the *EDNT*.[53] The latter two are more recent works that attempted to take more seriously the critique of James Barr and others, more or less successfully. *EDNT* is, perhaps, the most successful in this regard since it is more exegetically oriented rather than theological. We noted above that the central problem with the theological dictionaries was their tendency to confuse words and concepts and treat them as more or less identical. Whether or not this was an accurate criticism or merely a misunderstanding of the goals of historical-philological semantics as psychological in nature is less relevant to how we use them today.

If meaning is encyclopedic in the manner that cognitive linguistics suggests, then there is a gap in information when we look at the standard lexicons. Even if theological dictionaries themselves might actually be confusing words and concepts, we as users do not need to fall into that trap while using them. Rather, we can consider them repositories for the kind of encyclopedic information that words evoke: cultural, sociological, theological, and so forth. A normal dictionary does not provide the sort of associative meaning that all words have. Biblical Greek words evoke mental representations just as our English example of "garage sale" did above. Theological dictionaries, such as *TDNT*, *NIDNTT*, and *EDNT*, are unique in the way they have collected similar information for us. Nevertheless,

---

53. Kittel et al., *Theological Dictionary of the New Testament*; Colin Brown, ed., *New International Dictionary of the New Testament Theology*, 3 vols. (Grand Rapids: Zondervan, 1975–86); Horst Balz and Gerhard Schneider, *Exegetical Dictionary of the New Testament* (Grand Rapids: Eerdmans, 1990).

we still must use them critically, since such efforts still represent modern attempts to understand the associative meanings of ancient words and are still fraught with the historical challenges that have always made research results for biblical Greek tentative and provisional.[54]

7.3.2.b Louw & Nida

Louw and Nida's *A Greek-English Lexicon of the New Testament based on Semantic Domains* is the central structuralist contribution to biblical Greek lexicography. Its most significant contribution is its ordering of biblical Greek lexical items according to their meanings rather than the traditional alphabetical order. Despite the methodological issues with structuralist semantics, the major contribution of understanding lexical items in terms of how they relate to each other is still infinitely useful. Louw and Nida's organizational structure allows us to easily and quickly evaluate what lexical options were available to the biblical authors. Louw and Nida's lexicon is also the only ancient Greek lexicon that provides independent entries for Greek idiomatic expressions directly alongside individual words. The primary practical flaw of the lexicon is its limited corpus. Since it only covers NT vocabulary, we do not have access to the full semantic relations available in Koine Greek. Synonyms, antonyms, and other related words that do not appear in the NT receive no treatment. This also makes the lexicon far less useful for examining the Septuagint and other early Christian and Jewish writers.

7.3.2.c BDAG

The most recent edition of Bauer's lexicon, abbreviated BDAG and edited by Danker and others, is probably the most important Greek lexicon for the NT.[55] It is unique among NT lexicons in that it covers not only the NT but also other early Christian writings. BDAG and the rest of the lexicons mentioned below technically exist within the historical-philological tradition,

---

54. In fact, one of the reasons that structuralist linguists shifted so far away from making psychological or cognitive claims about language was simply that such claims were too messy or complicated to be dealt with in a manner that they found scientifically satisfactory. For a comprehensive overview of the history of structural linguistics, see P. H. Matthews, *Grammatical Theory in the United States: From Bloomfield to Chomsky* (Cambridge: Cambridge University Press, 1993).

55. Bauer et al., *Greek-English Lexicon.*

though in a different way from the theological dictionaries because they are all more descriptive in nature. Since the mid-twentieth century, there has also been decreasing focus on etymology and increasing focus on synchronic description. This is a direct result of influence from structuralist linguistics. In its third edition, BDAG, following the lead of Louw and Nida, introduced full definitions in addition to the standard translation glosses that pervaded earlier editions. This was a significant methodological improvement and contributes to the lexicon's great value.

7.3.2.d LSJ

The standard lexicon for ancient Greek in general is the ninth edition of Liddell and Scott's *A Greek-English Lexicon* (LSJ).[56] Because of its nature as a lexicon that provides broad coverage of the language over the course of several centuries, LSJ is important for both the Septuagint and the NT. Providing citations from a much larger corpus makes it useful for understanding Greek words over their history, both before and after the period of biblical Greek. Care must be taken, however, for using LSJ for work in the Septuagint. While the revised supplement in the 1996 edition certainly improves the situation to a large degree, LSJ continues to occasionally assume the meaning of the Hebrew words behind the Greek in their references to the Septuagint. This is methodologically problematic and occasionally results in misinterpretations of the data.

7.3.2.e LEH

This concise lexicon of the Septuagint edited by Lust, Eynikel, and Hauspie is one of only two contemporary resources devoted specifically to the Septuagint.[57] Its primary strength lies in its bibliographic references. While LEH is an original work, occasionally its glosses are pulled directly from LSJ.

---

56. Henry George Liddell et al., *A Greek-English Lexicon: With a Revised Supplement*, 9th ed. (Oxford: Clarendon, 1996).

57. Johan Lust, Erik Eynikel, and Katrin Hauspie, eds., *A Greek-English Lexicon of the Septuagint*, rev. ed. (Stuttgart: Deutsche Bibelgesellschaft, 2003).

7.3.2.f GELS

Takamitsu Muraoka's *Greek-English Lexicon of the Septuagint* (*GELS*) is the most comprehensive contemporary lexicon of the Septuagint.[58] Methodologically, Muraoka follows BDAG and Louw and Nida in providing actual definitions of lexical items rather than merely providing glosses for translation. *GELS* provides helpful citations and bibliographies for each entry, though unfortunately not comprehensively. LEH often has bibliographic items not available in *GELS*. Last, while Muraoka's lexicon is ordered alphabetically, his work is unique in that, when relevant, the editor provides cross-references to related words, both synonyms and antonyms. This allows for the comparison of vocabulary in a way that has not been previously feasible for other Septuagint lexicons.

7.4 WORD ORDER

The study of biblical Greek word order has grown significantly in the past decade. While a few studies have focused primarily on statistical analyses of word order, few have been received with much satisfaction.[59] Just as with Hebrew, traditional accounts of word order have generally assumed that the ordering of constituents is quite free, though some have put effort into how various particles order themselves, particularly postpositives and enclitics.[60]

In terms of the ordering of sentence constituents, efforts to better understand their positioning began in earnest in the 1990s, when classicist Helma Dik published *Word Order in Ancient Greek*.[61] Dik evaluated ancient Greek in terms of Functional Grammar. She developed the following template:[62]

Setting—Topic—Focus—Verb—Remainder

---

58. Takamitsu Muraoka, *Greek-English Lexicon of the Septuagint* (Leuven: Peeters, 2010).

59. Most representative of this is Ivan Shing Chung Kwong, *The Word Order of the Gospel of Luke: Its Foreground Messages* (London: T & T Clark, 2005).

60. See especially Kenneth Dover, *Greek Word Order* (Oxford: Oxford University Press, 1960).

61. Helma Dik, *Word Order in Ancient Greek* (Leiden: Brill, 1995).

62. Helma Dik, *Word Order in Greek Tragic Dialogue* (Oxford: Oxford University Press, 2007), 38.

In this scheme, the setting establishes the frame of reference for the clause, the topic presents the participant that the speaker/writer desires to convey as a particular piece of information, and the focus is the constituent containing the information that the speaker/writer most urgently desires to convey to the audience. The verb predicates that information, and the remainder consists of constituents that provide relevant information for proper interpretation of the focus.[63]

Other scholars studying biblical Greek have reached essentially the same conclusion. Steven Runge and Stephen Levinsohn are in essential agreement with Dik.[64] Levinsohn's analysis is generally more detailed and complicated, but nevertheless, the basic principles of ordering are the same. Runge helpfully provides a survey of how word order and information structure have been dealt with from a variety of theoretical perspectives and has shown that the work being done in biblical Greek is very much in line with the broader trends in the study of constituent ordering.[65]

7.5 RESOURCES FOR FURTHER STUDY

Allan, Rutger J. *The Middle Voice in Ancient Greek: A Study in Polysemy.* Leiden: Brill, 2003.

> While Allan's analysis of middle voice is focused on Homeric and classical Greek, his work is the most comprehensive and useful analysis of Greek voice available today. His conclusions are equally relevant to our understanding of biblical Greek, both in the Septuagint and the NT. The dissertation version of his work is also freely available online.

Bortone, Pietro. *Greek Prepositions from Antiquity to the Present.* Oxford: Oxford University Press, 2010.

> Bortone's monograph *Greek Prepositions* provides the most thorough and accessible discussion of contemporary semantic theory as related to ancient Greek, including biblical Greek.

---

63. Dik, *Word Order in Greek Tragic Dialogue*, 31–37.

64. Steven Runge, *Discourse Grammar of the Greek New Testament* (Peabody, MA: Hendrickson, 2010), 181–83; Stephen Levinsohn, *Discourse Features of New Testament Greek* (Dallas: SIL, 2000), 29–47.

65. Runge, *Discourse Grammar*, 200.

While his book is principally about prepositions, the first
half of the book effectively functions as an introduction to
semantics and cognitive linguistics for students of ancient and
biblical Greek.

Lee, John. *A History of New Testament Greek Lexicography*. New York: Peter
Lang, 2003.

Lee's survey of the history of NT Greek lexicography is one of
the most compelling books available on Greek lexicons. Lee
demonstrates the challenges of compiling a lexicon while
crafting a brilliant narrative that details how we got our lexicons.
This book should be required reading for anyone who has ever
used a lexicon for biblical Greek.

Levinsohn, Stephen H. *Discourse Features of the Greek New Testament*. 2nd
ed. Dallas: SIL International, 2000.

Levinsohn's introduction provides a hands-on treatment of the
various challenges that exist in analyzing Greek discourse. He
provides particularly detailed studies of conjunctions, tense and
aspect, and word order. Full of useful exercises, the book is an
excellent learning tool.

Miller, Neva. "A Theory of Deponent Verbs." Pages 423–31 in *Analytical
Lexicon of the Greek New Testament*. Edited by Friberg, Timothy,
Barbara Friberg, and Neva F. Miller. Grand Rapids: Baker, 2000.

Miller was one of the first contemporary researchers focusing
specifically on biblical Greek to make a formal proposal
for moving beyond the concept of deponency in the mid-
1990s. Her work provides a helpful account of the difficulties
of the traditional view of deponency but does not provide
a comprehensive model for understanding how supposed
"deponent verbs" relate to voice more generally.

Nida, Eugene, and J. P. Louw. *Lexical Semantics of the Greek New Testament*.
Atlanta: Scholars Press, 1992.

While Nida and Louw's discussion of lexical semantics is
somewhat out of date, it remains the most helpful introduction to

the challenges of doing lexical semantics in biblical Greek. With brief problem sets and exercises, the book makes for a practical guide to various issues with the study of words in biblical Greek. It is especially helpful for understanding the work that went into their lexicon based on semantic domains.

Rijksbaron, Albert. *The Syntax and Semantics of the Verb in Classical Greek: An Introduction.* 3rd ed. Chicago: University of Chicago Press, 2007.

Albert Rijksbaron's brief discussion of the syntax and semantics of the Greek verb primarily focuses on classical Greek rather than biblical Greek. Nevertheless, it represents the most up-to-date discussion of tense and aspect for ancient Greek. Ignoring his discussion of the optative mood, the rest of the book is still highly relevant to the student of biblical Greek, particularly for tense, aspect, and voice.

Runge, Steven E. *Discourse Grammar of the Greek New Testament: A Practical Introduction for Teaching and Exegesis.* Peabody, MA: Hendrickson, 2010.

Runge provides an accessible and practical treatment of how word order affects the exegesis of biblical Greek. His manual is a good starting place, especially for students and pastors interpreting the Greek NT.

Runge, Steven E., and Christopher J. Fresch. *The Greek Verb Revisited: A Fresh Approach to Biblical Exegesis.* Bellingham, WA: Lexham Press, 2016.

This is a collection of essays from the Cambridge Greek Verb Conference at Tyndale House from 2015. The purpose of the volume was to establish a broadly consensus perspective on the Greek verb that functions as an alternative to those who have, in recent years, argued for a tenseless model of the verb. The volume covers theoretical issues and practical application to a number of topics, with contributions from scholars working on the NT, classics, and general linguistics. Several essays will likely come to be viewed as seminal for their contribution.

8

THE VALUE OF LINGUISTICALLY INFORMED EXEGESIS

Michael Aubrey

E xegesis is and has always been, fundamentally, an intersection of history, theology, and language. As such, linguistics must invariably play a key role in the task. Through most of the nineteenth century, advancements in the study of language went hand in hand with exegetical work. The work of scholars such as A. T. Robertson and James Hope Moulton for Greek, or Wilhelm Gesenius and Samuel Driver for Hebrew, functioned as some of the cutting-edge language research of the day. It was only into the first couple decades of the twentieth century that linguistics and biblical studies diverged. Thus throughout this volume we have been discussing linguistics as it has developed since then. At no point has language become any less significant for exegetical work, and the ideas and approaches developed in linguistics in the past several decades have significant import to the exegetical enterprise.

At the same time, biblical studies and linguistics have only recently begun to converge once again. In fact, it is this recent convergence that necessitated this volume. Our purpose in this final chapter is to summarize some of the recent advances in linguistics in terms of their relevance to exegetical work. We can lump these advances into a few specific areas: (1) The field of linguistics provides us a greater level of precision in making grammatical decisions with a higher degree of explanatory power than past approaches. (2) The advances in the study of larger chunks of texts (discourse) have improved our understanding of the nature of grammar and language above the sentence level. (3) And lastly, the subfield in linguistics of language typology (the study of similarities and differences across many languages) has dramatically increased our knowledge of the limits of language variation. This has significant import for evaluating the reasonableness of alternative interpretations within texts. We survey each of these topics below, each with a brief example.

8.1 GREATER PRECISION AND EXPLANATORY POWER

Some ideas within the field of linguistics that allow greater precision for making exegetical decisions are, at times, theory specific. These are ideas that exist within some, but not all, linguistic frameworks. Sometimes this is a result of differing points of view on a debated subject. But more often than not, these situations are a result of the specific research aims of a particular framework. Not all linguistic frameworks or theories are seeking to answer the same questions. Other linguistic ideas are universally accepted, but have not received much attention in exegesis.

One striking example of the latter involves how we go about making exegetical decisions about the meaning of clauses: verbs and their noun phrases. Most textbooks dealing with Greek exegesis have students evaluating the function and meaning of words and grammatical elements one at a time in a linear order. This is essentially how grammar is laid out in Daniel Wallace's *Greek Grammar Beyond the Basics: An Exegetical Syntax of the New Testament*.[1] Many, if not most, Greek exegesis classes in North America follow this approach. This tends to involve exegetical observations that move one word at a time. Thus, at Eph 1:22, for example, we might look at the Greek text:

καὶ πάντα ὑπέταξεν ὑπὸ τοὺς πόδας αὐτοῦ, καὶ αὐτὸν ἔδωκεν κεφαλὴν ὑπὲρ πάντα τῇ ἐκκλησίᾳ (*kai panta hypetaxen hypo tous podas autou, kai auton edōken kephalēn hyper panta tē ekklēsia*)

---

1. Daniel B. Wallace, *Greek Grammar Beyond the Basics: An Exegetical Syntax of the New Testament* (Grand Rapids: Zondervan, 1996).

"and [the Father] subjected all things under his feet and gave him as head over all things to the church" (LEB)

From here, we would locate the verb, examine its possible meanings and make a decision. Then we would move on to examine the meaning of the nouns and the function of the case markers. This is, in fact, precisely how Harold Hoehner in his well-respected commentary on Ephesians goes about the question. He spends a substantial amount of time considering whether ἔδωκεν (edōken) is best understood as meaning "he appointed" or "he gave," concluding that because the latter meaning is the primary sense and because it fits contextually, it should be preferred here.[2] From there, Hoehner proceeds to discuss the meaning of the four phrases in the clause and the functions of the Greek cases. Hoehner treats αὐτὸν (auton) as the object of the verb and κεφαλὴν ὑπὲρ πάντα (kephalēn hyper panta) as a single phrase functioning as an adverbial accusative. Lastly, he spends a substantial amount of time discussing what kind of dative τῇ ἐκκλησίᾳ (tē ekklēsia) may be. Is it a dative of respect/reference (i.e., "with reference to the church")? Could it be a dative of advantage (i.e., for the benefit of the church)? Or is it a dative of indirect object (i.e., to the church)? Hoehner concludes that the third option is to be preferred.[3]

All of this is rather standard fare for learning how to do exegesis. However, the approaches to syntax and semantics developed over the past few decades offer a more practical alternative that is more precise and has more explanatory power. Nearly all linguistic frameworks have a mechanism for integrating the relationships between verbs and phrases within a clause. For example, Paul Danove has approached these relationships within the framework of Construction Grammar, a framework within the family of cognitive linguistics (see §5.6 Cognitive Linguistics).[4] He has, over the past two decades, worked hard on developing a lexicon of the kinds of phrases individual verbs require and their semantic roles. This allows us

---

2. Harold W. Hoehner, *Ephesians: An Exegetical Commentary* (Grand Rapids: Baker Academic, 2002), 285.

3. Hoehner, *Ephesians*, 289.

4. While the discussion that follows focuses on Construction Grammar, virtually all linguistic frameworks and theories have a similar approach to what we are describing.

to constrain the various senses of a given verb dramatically. Consider his four senses for the verb δίδωμι (didōmi).[5]

1. Transference, Active, Ditransitive

   a) Transference, Active, Ditransitive (Agent, Theme, Goal+dat), give

   b) Transference, Active, Ditransitive (Agent, Theme, Locative+P), give/put

2. Effect, Active, Transitive (Agent, Patient), give forth, produce

3. Delegation, Active, Ditransitive (Agent, Event+ ἵνα , Goal), give, delegate

4. Disposition, Active, Ditransitive (Agent, Patient, Event+inf/ ἵνα), make, dispose

Here we have four senses. Sense 1 involves the transference of an object (a theme) from an "Agent" to either a "Goal" (sense 1a) or a "Location" (sense 1b). Sense 2 involves an "Agent" causing an action and affecting a participant that is a "Patient." The other two senses are irrelevant since they involve causal complements with either ἵνα or an infinitive, which means our options are either sense 1a or sense 2.[6]

The important point here is that once the decision of which sense of δίδωμι (didōmi) is made, there is no need to discuss the function of the case. Those are determined by the verb itself. If one decides that sense 1a is correct, then the only option for the dative τῇ ἐκκλησίᾳ (tē ekklēsia) is an indirect object with the semantic role of recipient. Conversely, if one decides that sense 2 is the better one, then the dative τῇ ἐκκλησίᾳ (tē ekklēsia) must then, by definition, function in an adverbial manner, and thus must either be a dative of advantage ("for the church's benefit") or a dative of reference. All three options have been chosen by some translation or commentator at

5. Adapted from Paul Danove, *A Grammatical and Exegetical Study of New Testament Verbs of Transference: A Case Frame Guide to Interpretation and Translation* (London: T&T Clark, 2009), 168, 185–87. Note also that this is a substantial simplification of the usage as presented in BDAG. The Construction Grammar approach is also quite significant for lexicography.

6. Sense 1b is irrelevant also since there is no locative prepositional phrase.

some point. And we will not advocate one over the other here. That is not our focus. What we want to do instead is observe the difference in orientation between the traditional method and the approach of Construction Grammar. The traditional method is focused first and foremost upon the individual words themselves. Each word is evaluated on its own. Within this approach, all semantic functions of the dative case are viewed as potential options. Depending on which Greek grammar is consulted, that list of options could be extremely daunting.[7]

Conversely, within the Construction Grammar approach, the focus is first and foremost upon the clause as a whole. Focusing upon how verbs license their noun phrases, prepositional phrases, and subordinate clauses constrains the interpretation from the start. We end up being more precise than we otherwise would. Moreover, the decision of the particular category for the case of the noun phrase, in this case the dative, allows for a stronger explanation: the case category is now defined by the lexical semantics of the verb, rather than merely a list in a grammar. Contemporary linguistic theory provides an explanation for how case categories in Greek relate to their contexts in a manner that traditional approaches do not, simply by expanding our focus in terms of how we relate individual words to each other.

8.2 DISCOURSE FEATURES

The study of discourse and discourse features has significant import (see §5.5 Discourse Analysis). In previous chapters, we discussed the nature of information structure and word order. We saw that the ordering of words or constituents was directly related to how information flows from one sentence to the other. In other words, constituent order functions as a feature of discourse. This fact tended to be overlooked in traditional grammars simply because the idea of examining grammatical structure above the level of the clause or sentence was not within their purview. But there are numerous other discourse features as well that provide similar functions for understanding the structure of larger portions of text. Logos Bible Software has two excellent resources in this regard: the *Lexham Discourse*

---

7. Daniel Wallace, for example, provides nearly 30 different dative categories (*Greek Grammar Beyond the Basics*, 137).

Greek New Testament and the *Lexham Discourse Hebrew Bible*.[8] Both of these databases provide a thorough analysis of numerous discourse features and details across Scripture, oftentimes providing information that would otherwise be ignored.

One of the most striking features is the charting of how participants are referred to, whether by proper names, pronouns, or titles. The tracking of participants in discourse allows for a means of understanding why the author or speaker chose to refer to someone else in a particular way. Oftentimes, this is in order to highlight a participant or character in a certain way. This allows the speaker or author to influence the audience's impression and perspective toward that participant. For example, in 1 Samuel 24:7, after encountering Saul who is trying to kill him, David says to his men:

> Far be it from me in Yahweh that I do this thing to my lord, to Yahweh's anointed one, by stretching out my hand against him! For he is the anointed one of Yahweh.

David could have chosen any number of ways to refer to Saul. He might have said: "the king," "King Saul," "Jonathan's father," or any number of others. Each one would have evoked a different set of conceptualizations about who Saul is—recall our discussion about the encyclopedic nature of meaning (see §7.3.1 Issues in Lexical Semantics). But what David does is this: first he gives Saul his title as "lord" and places himself in a subservient position relative to Saul by referring to him as "my lord." This might have been a sufficient statement both in terms of referring to Saul—there is no debate now who Saul is and how David views their relationship, despite all that has happened. But that is not enough for David. He wants to drive the point home. So he says more than he needs to for the purposes of referring to Saul. He over-specifies the participant: "to my lord, to Yahweh's anointed one." In doing so, David provides a second reason for why he did not kill Saul when he had a chance. And by placing that characterization of Saul directly after the first, after his audience has already connected

---

8. Steven E. Runge, ed., *Lexham Discourse Greek New Testament* (Bellingham, WA: Lexham Press, 2008–2014); Steven E. Runge and Joshua R. Westbury, eds., *Lexham Discourse Hebrew Bible* (Bellingham, WA: Lexham Press, 2012–2014).

the reference to the actual person of Saul, David gives greater significance to the second characterization. The fact that David still views Saul as his lord would have been a sufficient explanation, but the fact that Saul is also chosen by God is the most important reason of all.

This sort of analysis is not always obviously more profound than the traditional approaches. This example could just as easily be paralleled in a traditional exegetical discussion. However, what needs to be emphasized here is our point above. Examining how participants are characterized and presented within the text from the perspective of the linguistic analysis of discourse is fundamentally grounded in the nature of human language more generally. Steven Runge explains this quite helpfully:

> Although there is tremendous diversity among languages, every language has to accomplish certain basic tasks. For instance, if I want to tell you a story about the first time I went rock climbing, I need to accomplish several tasks, such as:
>
> - introduce the people involved in the story;
>
> - set the time, place, and situation;
>
> - provide background information that I think you might need (e.g., I have a fear of heights).
>
> [...]
>
> Regardless of whether I am speaking or writing, I need some means of accomplishing these tasks. Since there is a common set of tasks that need to be accomplished across all languages, the task list can inform our description of what the different grammatical choices accomplish. The tasks provide an organizational framework to help us understand the meaningful difference between choosing X versus Y or Z.[9]

Fundamentally, discourse features involve the basic needs of humans for communicating with each other in conjunction with the diversity of language. These basic tasks for communication ground the linguistic

---

9. Steven E. Runge, *Discourse Grammar of the Greek New Testament: A Practical Introduction for Teaching and Exegesis* (Peabody, MA: Hendrickson, 2010), 6–7.

analysis of discourse features in a manner that traditional exegesis does not. The fact that these are features that are relevant to all language brings us to our final topic: language typology.

8.3 LANGUAGE TYPOLOGY

If there is any topic that can make traditional biblical scholars uncomfortable or suspicious, it is language typology (see §4.1 Language Universals and Typology). There is a general skepticism on the part of many biblical scholars toward the idea of using other languages, whether related or not, as a guide for how we might understand the grammar of Greek or Hebrew. From the perspective of a guild that is still operating under the linguistic assumptions that were in place at the turn of the twentieth century, this is perfectly logical. Language appears to vary endlessly. And to some extent this is true. Individual languages are infinitely unique. There are no two languages that are exactly the same, whether in their lexicon, their morphology, or syntax. But this does not mean that there are no limits to language variation. All languages, no matter how unique they are, are all *human* languages. And the human nature of language is an important element that they all share in common.

A useful metaphor that we could use for talking about language variation would be trees. There are no trees that are perfectly identical to each other. And yet we can delineate them into clear types with well-defined features and structures. All oak trees share features in common, even if two oaks are on opposite sides of the world. All maples share features in common. We can draw comparisons and similarities across varieties of trees at the level of individual species and we can also draw comparisons at higher, more abstract levels. Conifers share many features in common, whether we are talking about redwoods or Douglas firs. Over the past century, linguists have been examining and comparing the languages of the world to each other. They have been analyzing features, structures, and patterns across many languages and have an ever-growing knowledge of what is possible and what is probable with respect to language variation. This information about typology can be extremely useful as a starting point for knowing what we might expect to find when we study Hebrew and Greek. In this respect, D. N. S. Bhat suggests a very useful approach. He writes:

We may compare the distinction between typological studies ... and in-depth studies of individual languages with the distinction between areal [sic; aerial] or satellite pictures of a countryside and an architect's drawing of a town or a dam. A satellite picture would only show patches of colour and vague lines and curves that an expert can interpret as indicating the location of a possible earthquake or deposits of mineral wealth, whereas an architect's drawings would show locations of various buildings, parks, canals, etc. in very precise terms.

It would be a mistake, however, to discard the former merely on the basis of the fact that they are not as precise and specific as the latter. The two complement one another, with the satellite pictures giving a warning to the builder of dams so that they can avoid certain cites [sic; sites] as possible disaster areas. Typological studies and in-depth studies of language can also complement one another in a similar fashion. The general tendencies that one can perceive through a comparison of hundreds of different languages can be helpful in avoiding certain conclusions and in raising certain questions that might not have been raised otherwise while carrying out in-depth studies of individual languages.[10]

If we were to extend Bhat's analogy here, we could say that the task of exegesis is an up-close and personal task. Language typology is a satellite image and we as exegetes are working at ground level in the details of the terrain.

In that sense, language typology cannot tell us how many trees there are or what kinds there are, but it can give us an idea of what to expect on the other side of the interpretive or exegetical ridge. The satellite map might show us where the rivers are, or where potential fault lines are. And perhaps most importantly, it gives us a set of standards by which we can evaluate new proposals and research into the structure of Hebrew and Greek. When a scholar, for example, claims that Koine Greek does not have the grammatical category of tense, we can ask: Are there other languages

---

10. D. N. S. Bhat, *The Prominence of Tense, Aspect, and Mood* (Amsterdam: John Benjamins, 1999), 98.

of the world that lack the category of tense? We can dig through library resources to find the answer to that: Yes, there are languages that lack the category of tense. We can also ask a follow-up question: Do any of those languages that lack tense look anything like Greek in terms of the structure of its verbal system? The answer is not as definite as the first question, but when we look at the information available in a resource such as *The World Atlas of Language Structures*,[11] it certainly appears to not be the case. Tenseless languages do not look like Koine Greek.

Language typology has the potential to provide us with safeguards in our analysis of the biblical languages. Without knowing the bounds of variation that human language can and cannot have, we as exegetes and students of the biblical languages might be tempted to make Greek and Hebrew into something they are not. We can only hope that typology will begin to play a larger role in the efforts of biblical scholars who study the grammar of biblical Greek and Hebrew.

8.4 RESOURCES FOR FURTHER STUDY

Comrie, Bernard. *Language Universals and Linguistic Typology*. 2nd ed. Chicago: University of Chicago Press, 1989.

> Comrie gives a short introduction to language typology, providing beneficial overview of various grammatical phenomena and an introduction to important principles involved in the study of language.

Levinsohn, Stephen H. *Discourse Features of New Testament Greek*. 2nd ed. Dallas: SIL International, 2000.

> Stephen Levinsohn's helpful book is more advanced than Runge's and functions as a useful workbook, including exercises that allow students to practice what they have learned from both Runge and Levinsohn.

Runge, Steven E. *Discourse Grammar of the Greek New Testament: A Practical Introduction for Teaching and Exegesis*. Peabody, MA: Hendrickson; Bellingham, WA: Lexham Press, 2010.

---

11. "The World Atlas of Language Structures Online," http://wals.info/.

A highly practical introduction to the linguistic study of
discourse for biblical Greek. This grammar functions as a useful
starting point for students of Greek who are interested in the
insight that the field of linguistics has to offer the analysis of
Greek discourse.

Runge, Steven E., and Joshua R. Westbury, eds. *Lexham Discourse Hebrew
Bible*. Bellingham, WA: Lexham Press, 2012–2014.

The *Lexham Discourse Hebrew Bible* is a thorough analysis of
numerous discourse features throughout the Old Testament.
The database is accompanied by a brief but useful introduction
and glossary.

Van Valin, Robert D., Jr. *An Introduction to Syntax*. Cambridge: Cambridge
University Press, 2001.

Robert Van Valin Jr.'s introductory text on syntactic analysis
provides a useful tool for studying syntactic structure. Covering
a wide variety of grammatical phenomena, the book is quite
accessible to the non-specialist.

BIBLIOGRAPHY

Akmajian, Adrian, Richard A. Demers, Ann K. Farmer, and Robert
  M. Harnish. *Linguistics: An Introduction to Language and
  Communication.* 5th ed. Cambridge, MA: The MIT Press, 2001.
———. *Linguistics: An Introduction to Language and Communication.* 6th ed.
  Cambridge, MA: The MIT Press, 2010.
Allan, Rutger J. *The Middle Voice in Ancient Greek: A Study in Polysemy.*
  Amsterdam: J.C. Gieben, 2003.
Andersen, Francis I. "Review Article and Responses: The Dictionary
  of Classical Hebrew. Vol. 1 א." *Australian Biblical Review* 43
  (1995): 50–75.
Andrason, Alexander W. *El sistema verbal hebreo en su contexto semítico:
  una visión dinámica.* Estella: Editorial Verbo Divino, 2013.
———. "The Complexity of Verbal Semantics—An Intricate Relationship
  Between *Qatal* and *Wayyiqtol*." *JHS* 16 (2016): art. 4. doi:10.5508/
  jhs.2016.v16.a4
Andrews, Edna. *Markedness Theory.* Durham, NC: Duke University
  Press, 1990.
Anstey, Matthew, and J. Lachlan Mackenzie. "Introduction." In *Crucial
  Readings in Functional Grammar,* edited by Matthew Anstey and J.
  Lachlan Mackenzie, vii–xiv. Berlin: Mouton de Gruyter, 2005.
Aronoff, Mark, and Janie Rees-Miller. *The Handbook of Linguistics.*
  Malden, MA: Blackwell, 2000.
Aubrey, Rachel. "Motivated Categories, Middle Voice, and Passive
  Morphology." In *The Greek Verb Revisited: A Fresh Approach for
  Biblical Exegesis,* edited by Steven E. Runge and Christopher J.
  Fresch. Bellingham, WA: Lexham Press, 2016.

Austin, J. L. *How to Do Things with Words*. Edited by J. O Urmson and
    Marina Sbisà. 2nd ed. Cambridge, MA: Harvard University
    Press, 1975.

Baerman, Matthew, Greville G. Corbett, Dunstan Brown, and Andrew
    Hippisley, eds. *Deponency and Morphological Mismatches*. Oxford:
    Oxford University Press, 2007.

Balz, Horst, and Gerhard Schneider, eds. *Exegetical Dictionary of the New
    Testament*. Grand Rapids: Eerdmans, 1990.

Bandstra, Barry L. "Word Order and Emphasis in Biblical Hebrew
    Narrative: Syntactic Observations on Genesis 22 from a Discourse
    Perspective." In *Linguistics and Biblical Hebrew*, edited by Walter R.
    Bodine, 108–23. Winona Lake, IN: Eisenbrauns, 1992.

Barr, James. *Comparative Philology and the Text of the Old Testament*.
    Winona Lake, IN: Eisenbrauns, 1987.

———. "Hebrew Lexicography: Informal Thoughts." In *Linguistics and
    Biblical Hebrew*, edited by Walter R. Bodine, 137–51. Winona Lake,
    IN: Eisenbrauns, 1992.

———. *The Semantics of Biblical Language*. Oxford: Oxford University
    Press, 1961.

Barr, James M. "Hebrew Lexicography." In *Studies in Semitic Lexicography*,
    edited by P. Fronzaroli, 103–26. Quarderni Di Semiti. Florence:
    Istituto di Linguistica, Università di Firenze, 1973.

Battistella, Edwin L. *Markedness: The Evaluative Superstructure of
    Language*. New York: State University of New York Press, 1990.

———. *The Logic of Markedness*. New York: Oxford University Press, 1996.

Bauer, Walter, Frederick W. Danker, William Arndt, and F. Wilbur
    Gingrich, eds. *A Greek-English Lexicon of the New Testament and
    Other Early Christian Literature*. 3rd ed. Chicago: University of
    Chicago Press, 2000.

Belsey, Catherine. *Poststructuralism: A Very Short Introduction*. Oxford:
    Oxford University Press, 2002.

Benton, Richard C. "Aspect and the Biblical Hebrew Niphal and Hitpael."
    Ph.D. diss., University of Wisconsin-Madison, 2009.

Bergen, Robert, ed. *Biblical Hebrew and Discourse Linguistics*. Dallas:
    SIL, 1994.

Bergen, Robert D. "Text as a Guide to Authorial Intention: An
    Introduction to Discourse Criticism." *JETS* 30, no. 3 (1987): 327-36.

Berlin, Adele. *Dynamics of Biblical Parallelism*. Rev. and exp. ed. Grand
    Rapids: Eerdmans, 2008.

Berlin, Brent, and Paul Kay. *Basic Color Terms: Their Universality and
    Evolution*. Berkeley, CA: University of California Press, 1969.

Bhat, D. N. S. *The Prominence of Tense, Aspect and Mood*. Amsterdam: John
    Benjamins, 1999.

Binnick, Robert I. *Time and the Verb: A Guide to Tense and Aspect*. Oxford:
    Oxford University Press, 1991.

Birner, Betty. *Introduction to Pragmatics*. Blackwell Textbooks in
    Linguistics. Malden, MA: Wiley, 2013.

Black, David Alan. *Linguistics for Students of New Testament Greek: A
    Survey of Basic Concepts and Applications*. 2nd ed. Grand Rapids:
    Baker, 1995.

Blau, Joshua. *Phonology and Morphology of Biblical Hebrew: An Introduction*.
    Linguistic Studies in Ancient West Semitic 2. Winona Lake, IN:
    Eisenbrauns, 2010.

Block, Daniel I. "How Many Is God? An Investigation into the Meaning of
    Deuteronomy 6:4-5." *JETS* 74, no. 2 (2004): 193-212.

Blois, Reinier de. "Lexicography and Cognitive Linguistics: Hebrew
    Metaphors from a Cognitive Perspective." Toronto, 2002. http://
    www.sdbh.org/documentation/Paper_SBL_2002.pdf.

———. "Semantic Dictionary of Biblical Hebrew." *Semantic Dictionary of
    Biblical Hebrew*, n.d. www.sdbh.org.

———. "Semantic Domains for Biblical Hebrew." In *Bible and Computer;
    the Stellenbosch Aibi-6 Conferences; Proceedings of the Association
    Internationale Bible et Informatique "from Alpha to Byte,"* 209-29.
    Leiden: Brill, 2002.

———. "Towards a New Dictionary of Biblical Hebrew Based on
    Semantic Domains." Ph.D. diss., Free University, 2000.

———. "Towards a New Dictionary of Biblical Hebrew Based on
    Semantic Domains." Nashville, TN, 2000. http://www.sdbh.org/
    documentation/Paper_SBL_2000.pdf.

Bodine, Walter R., ed. *Discourse Analysis of Biblical Literature: What It Is
    and What It Offers*. Atlanta: Scholars Press, 1995.

———. "How Linguists Study Syntax." In *Linguistics and Biblical Hebrew*, edited by Walter R. Bodine, 89–107. Winona Lake, IN: Eisenbrauns, 1992.

———, ed. *Linguistics and Biblical Hebrew*. Winona Lake, IN: Eisenbrauns, 1992.

———. "Linguistics and Biblical Studies." In *Anchor Yale Bible Dictionary*, edited by David Noel Freedman. New York: Doubleday, 1992.

———. "Linguistics and Philology in the Study of Ancient Near Eastern Languages." In *Working With No Data: Semitic and Egyptian Studies Presented to Thomas O. Lambdin*, edited by David M. Golomb, 39–54. Winona Lake, IN: Eisenbrauns, 1987.

Boman, T. *Hebrew Thought Compared with Greek*. Translated by Jules L. Moreau. London: SCM Press, 1960.

Bortone, Pietro. *Greek Prepositions: From Antiquity to the Present*. Oxford: Oxford University Press, 2010.

Bransford, John, and Marcia Johnson. "Contextual Prerequisites for Understanding: Some Investigations of Comprehension and Recall." *Journal of Verbal Learning and Behavior* 11 (1972): 722–25.

Brown, Colin, ed. *New International Dictionary of New Testament Theology*. Grand Rapids: Zondervan, 1986.

Brown, F., S. R. Driver, and C. A. Briggs, eds. *A Hebrew and English Lexicon of the Old Testament, with an Appendix Containing the Biblical Aramaic*. Oxford: Oxford University Press, 1906.

———, eds. *The Enhanced Brown-Driver-Briggs Hebrew-English Lexicon: A Hebrew and English Lexicon of the Old Testament, with an Appendix Containing the Biblical Aramaic*. Electronic ed. Oak Harbor, WA: Logos Research Systems, 2000.

Burke, Trevor. *Adopted into God's Family: Exploring a Pauline Metaphor*. Downers Grove, IL: InterVarsity Press, 2006.

Buth, Randall. "The Hebrew Verb in Current Discussions." *Journal of Translation and Textlinguistics* 5 (1992): 91–105.

Buttrick, David. "Interpretation and Preaching." In *The Renewal of Sunday Worship*, edited by Robert E. Webber. Nashville, TN: Star Song, 1993.

Campbell, Constantine. *Verbal Aspect, the Indicative Mood, and Narrative*. New York: Peter Lang, 2007.

Campbell, Lyle. *Historical Linguistics: An Introduction*. 2nd ed. Cambridge, MA: The MIT Press, 2004.

———. "The History of Linguistics." In *The Handbook of Linguistics*, edited by Mark Aronoff and Janie Rees-Miller, 81–104. Malden, MA: Wiley Blackwell, 2002.

Carson, D. A. *Exegetical Fallacies*. 2nd ed. Carlisle, UK: Paternoster, 1996.

Chomsky, Noam. *Aspects of the Theory of Syntax*. Cambridge, MA: MIT Press, 1965.

———. *On Language*. New York: New Free Press, 2007.

———. *Reflections on Language*. London: Fontana, 1976.

———. *Syntactic Structures*. 2nd ed. Berlin: Mouton de Gruyter, 2002.

Clines, David J. A., ed. *The Dictionary of Classical Hebrew*. 8 vols. Sheffield: Sheffield Academic Press, 1993-2011.

Cohen, Ohad. *The Verbal Tense System in Late Biblical Hebrew Prose*. Winona Lake, IN: Eisenbrauns, 2013.

Cole, Michael, and Sylvia Scribner. "Culture and Language." In *Issues in Cultural Anthropology: Selected Readings*, edited by David W. McCurdy and James P. Spradley, 78–92. Boston: Little, Brown and Company, 1979.

Comrie, Bernard. *Language Universals and Linguistic Typology*. 2nd ed. Chicago: University of Chicago Press, 1989.

Conrad, Carl. "Active, Middle, and Passive: Understanding Ancient Greek Voice." Unpublished manuscript, December 16, 2003. https://pages.wustl.edu/files/pages/imce/cwconrad/undancgrkvc.pdf.

Cook, John A., "Current Issues in the Study of the Biblical Hebrew Verbal System." *KUSATU* 17 (2014): 79-108.

———. "The Finite Verbal Forms in Biblical Hebrew Do Express Aspect." *Journal of the Ancient Near Eastern Society* 30 (2006): 21–35.

———. *Time and the Biblical Hebrew Verb: The Expression of Tense, Aspect, and Modality in Biblical Hebrew*. Linguistic Studies in Ancient West Semitic 7. Winona Lake, IN: Eisenbrauns, 2012.

Cotterell, Peter, and Max Turner. *Linguistics & Biblical Interpretation*. Downers Grove, IL: InterVarsity Press, 1989.

Coulmas, Florian, ed. *The Handbook of Sociolinguistics*. Oxford: Blackwell, 1998.

Cremer, Hermann. *Biblico-Theological Lexicon of New Testament Greek*. 3rd
    Eng. ed. Edinburgh: T & T Clark, 1880.
Croft, William. *Typology and Universals*. 2nd ed. Cambridge: Cambridge
    University Press, 2003.
Croft, William, and D. A. Cruse. *Cognitive Linguistics*. Cambridge
    Textbooks in Linguistics. Cambridge: Cambridge University
    Press, 2004.
Cruse, Alan. "Language as a Sign System: Some Basic Notions of
    Semiotics." In *Meaning in Language: An Introduction to Semantics
    and Pragmatics*, 3rd ed. Oxford: Oxford University Press, 2011.
Cruse, D. A. *Meaning in Language: An Introduction to Semantics and
    Pragmatics*. 2nd ed. Oxford Textbooks in Linguistics. Oxford:
    Oxford University Press, 2004.
———. *Meaning in Language: An Introduction to Semantics and Pragmatics*.
    3rd ed. Oxford Textbooks in Linguistics. Oxford: Oxford
    University Press, 2011.
Crystal, David. *A Dictionary of Linguistics and Phonetics*. 6th ed. Malden,
    MA: Blackwell Publishing, 2008.
Danker, Frederick W. *Multipurpose Tools for Bible Study*. Rev. ed.
    Minneapolis: Augsburg Fortress, 1993.
Danove, Paul. *A Grammatical and Exegetical Study of New Testament
    Verbs of Transference: A Case Frame Guide to Interpretation and
    Translation*. London: T & T Clark, 2009.
Dawson, David Allan. *Text-Linguistics and Biblical Hebrew*. Sheffield:
    Sheffield Academic Press, 1994.
DeCaen, Vincent. "A Unified Analysis of Verbal and Verbless Clauses
    within Government-Binding Theory." In *The Verbless Clause in
    Biblical Hebrew: Linguistic Approaches*, edited by Cynthia L. Miller-
    Naudé, 109–31. Winona Lake, IN: Eisenbrauns, 1999.
Decker, Rodney J. *Temporal Deixis of the Greek Verb in the Gospel of Mark
    with Reference to Verbal Aspect*. New York: Peter Lang, 2001.
Deissmann, Adolf, and Lionel Richard Mortimer Strachan. *Light
    from the Ancient East the New Testament Illustrated by Recently
    Discovered Texts of the Graeco-Roman World*. London: Hodder &
    Stoughton, 1910.
Dik, Helma. *Word Order in Ancient Greek*. Leiden: Brill, 1995.

———. *Word Order in Greek Tragic Dialogue*. Oxford: Oxford University Press, 2007.

Dik, Simon C. *The Theory of Functional Grammar, Part 1: The Structure of the Clause*. Edited by Kees Hengeveld. 2nd ed. Berlin: Mouton de Gruyter, 1997.

Dooley, Robert A., and Stephen H. Levinsohn. *Analyzing Discourse: A Manual of Basic Concepts*. Dallas: SIL, 2001.

Dover, Kenneth. *Greek Word Order*. Oxford: Oxford University Press, 1960.

Dryer, Matthew S. "Significant and Non-Significant Implicational Universals." *Linguistic Typology* 7 (2003): 108–28.

Edwards, John. *Sociolinguistics: A Very Short Introduction*. Oxford: Oxford University Press, 2013.

Eggins, Suzanne. *An Introduction to Systemic Functional Linguistics*. 2nd ed. London: Continuum, 2004.

Ellis, Nicholas. "Aspect-Prominence, Morpho-Syntax, and a Cognitive-Linguistic Framework for the Greek Verb." In *The Greek Verb Revisited: A Fresh Approach for Biblical Exegesis*, edited by Steven E. Runge and Christopher J. Fresch. Bellingham, WA: Lexham Press, 2016.

Erteschik-Shir, Nomi. *Information Structure: The Syntax-Discourse Interface*. Oxford: Oxford University Press, 2007.

Evans, Vyvyan, and Melanie C. Green. *Cognitive Linguistics: An Introduction*. Edinburgh: Edinburgh University Press, 2006.

Fanning, Buist. *Verbal Aspect in New Testament Greek*. Oxford: Oxford University Press, 1990.

Fellbaum, Christiane. "Introduction." In *WordNet: An Electronic Lexical Database*, edited by Christiane Fellbaum, 1–19. Cambridge, MA: The MIT Press, 1998.

———, ed. *WordNet: An Electronic Lexical Database*. Cambridge, MA: The MIT Press, 1998.

Fortson, Benjamin W. *Indo-European Language and Culture*. Oxford: Blackwell, 2004.

Fromkin, Victoria, Robert Rodman, and Nina M. Hyams. *An Introduction to Language*. 9th ed. Boston: Wadsworth, Cengage Learning, 2011.

Geeraerts, Dirk. "Introduction: A Rough Guide to Cognitive Linguistics." In *Cognitive Linguistics: Basic Readings*, edited by Dirk Geeraerts. The Hague: Mouton de Gruyter, 2006.

———. *Theories of Lexical Semantics.* Oxford: Oxford University Press, 2010.

Geisler, Norman L., and William E. Nix. *A General Introduction to the Bible.* Chicago: Moody, 1968.

Gesenius, Wilhelm. *Gesenius' Hebrew and Chaldee Lexicon to the Old Testament Scriptures.* Translated by Samuel Prideaux Tregelles. London: Samuel Bagster and Sons, 1857.

———. *Gesenius' Hebrew Grammar.* Edited by E. Kautzsch. Translated and edited by A. E. Cowley. 2nd Eng. ed. Oxford: Clarendon Press, 1910.

———. *Hebräisches Und Aramäisches Handwörterbuch Über Das Alte Testament.* Edited by Rudolf Meyer and Herbert Donner. 6 vols. Berlin: Springer, 1987–2010.

———. *Hebräisches und aramäisches Handwörterbuch über das Alte Testament.* Edited by Rudolf Meyer and Herbert Donner. 18th ed. Berlin: Springer, 2013.

———. *Lexicon Manuale Hebraicum et Chaldaicum in Veteris Testamenti Libros.* Leipzig, 1833.

Givón, Talmy. *Syntax: A Functional-Typological Introduction.* Vol. 2. Amsterdam: John Benjamins, 1990.

Greenberg, Joseph H. *Language Universals.* The Hague: Mouton, 1966.

———. "Some Universals of Grammar with Particular Reference to the Order of Meaningful Elements." In *Universals of Language*, edited by Joseph H. Greenberg. Cambridge, MA: MIT Press, 1963.

Groom, Susan Anne. *Linguistic Analysis of Biblical Hebrew.* Carlisle, UK: Paternoster, 2003.

Habel, Norman C. *Literary Criticism of the Old Testament.* Philadelphia: Fortress, 1971.

Haspelmath, Martin. "Against Markedness (and What to Replace It with)." *Journal of Linguistics* 42 (2006): 1–37.

Hecht, Max. *Griechische Bedeutungslehre.* Leipzig: Teubner, 1888.

Hecke, Pierre van. *From Linguistics to Hermeneutics: A Functional and Cognitive Approach to Job 12–14.* Leiden: Brill, 2011.

Heimerdinger, Jean-Marc. *Topic, Focus and Foreground in Ancient Hebrew Narratives*. Sheffield: Sheffield Academic Press, 1999.

Hendel, Ronald S. *The Book of Genesis: A Biography*. Princeton: Princeton University Press, 2013.

Hoehner, Harold W. *Ephesians: An Exegetical Commentary*. Grand Rapids: Baker Academic, 2002.

Hoffmeier, James K., and A. R. Millard, eds. *The Future of Biblical Archaeology: Reassessing Methodologies and Assumptions*. Grand Rapids: Eerdmans, 2004.

Holmstedt, Robert D. "The Typological Classification of the Hebrew of Genesis: Subject-Verb or Verb-Subject?" *JHS* 11, no. 14 (2011).

———. "Word Order and Information Structure in Ruth and Jonah: A Generative Typological Analysis." *Journal of Semitic Studies* 54, no. 1 (2009): 111–39.

Horsley, G. H. R. *New Documents Illustrating Early Christianity*. Linguistic Essays 5. Grand Rapids: Eerdmans, 2005.

Huang, Yan. *Pragmatics*. Oxford. Oxford: Oxford University Press, 2007.

Huehnergard, John. "Languages: Introductory Survey." In *Anchor Yale Bible Dictionary*, edited by David Noel Freedman. New York: Doubleday, 1992.

Jakobson, Roman. *Six Lectures on Sound and Meaning*. Translated by John Mepham. Cambridge, MA: MIT Press, 1978.

Joosten, Jan. *The Verbal System of Biblical Hebrew: A New Synthesis Elaborated on the Basis of Classical Prose*. Jerusalem: Simor Ltd., 2012.

Joüon, Paul, and T. Muraoka. *A Grammar of Biblical Hebrew*. Revised. Roma: Pontificio istituto biblico, 2006.

Kemmer, Suzanne. *Middle Voice*. Amsterdam: John Benjamins, 1993.

King, Philip J., and Lawrence E. Stager. *Life in Biblical Israel*. Louisville, KY: Westminster John Knox, 2001.

Kittel, Gerhard, Gerhard Friedrich, and Geoffrey W. Bromiley, eds. *Theological Dictionary of the New Testament*. Electronic ed. Grand Rapids: Eerdmans, 1964–1973.

Klaiman, M. H. *Grammatical Voice*. Cambridge: Cambridge University Press, 1991.

Koehler, Ludwig, Walter Baumgartner, and Johann Jakob Stamm, eds. *The Hebrew and Aramaic Lexicon of the Old Testament*. Translated by M.E.J. Richardson. Electronic ed. Leiden: Brill, 1994–2000.

Koerner, Konrad. "Linguistics vs Philology: Self-Definition of a Field or Rhetorical Stance?" *Language Sciences* 19, no. 2 (1997): 167–75.

Kroeger, Paul. *Analyzing Grammar: An Introduction*. Cambridge: Cambridge University Press, 2005.

Kwong, Ivan Shing Chung. *The Word Order of the Gospel of Luke: Its Foreground Messages*. London: T & T Clark, 2005.

Lakoff, George. *Women, Fire, and Dangerous Things: What Categories Reveal about the Mind*. Chicago: University of Chicago Press, 1987.

Lakoff, George, and Mark Johnson. *Metaphors We Live By*. Chicago: University of Chicago Press, 1980.

Lambrecht, Knud. *Information Structure and Sentence Form: A Theory of Topic, Focus, and the Mental Representations of Discourse Referents*. Cambridge: Cambridge University Press, 1994.

Langacker, Ronald. *Cognitive Grammar: A Basic Introduction*. Oxford: Oxford University Press, 2008.

Lee, John. *A History of New Testament Lexicography*. New York: Peter Lang, 2003.

Levinsohn, Stephen H. *Discourse Features of New Testament Greek: A Coursebook on the Information Structure of New Testament Greek*. 2nd ed. Dallas: SIL, 2000.

Liddell, Henry George, Robert Scott, Henry Stuart Jones, and Roderick McKenzie, eds. *A Greek-English Lexicon*. 9th ed. Oxford: Clarendon, 1996.

Longacre, Robert E. *Joseph: A Story of Divine Providence: A Text Theoretical and Textlinguistic Analysis of Genesis 37 and 39–48*. 2nd ed. Winona Lake, IN: Eisenbrauns, 2003.

Louw, Johannes. *Sociolinguistics and Communication*. London: United Bible Societies, 1986.

Louw, Johannes, and Eugene A. Nida. *Greek-English Lexicon of the New Testament: Based on Semantic Domains*. 2nd ed. New York: United Bible Societies, 1989.

Lunn, Nicholas P. *Word-Order Variation in Biblical Hebrew Poetry: Differentiating Pragmatics and Poetics*. Milton Keynes, UK: Paternoster, 2006.

Lust, Johan, Erik Eynikel, and Katrin Hauspie, eds. *A Greek-English Lexicon of the Septuagint*. Rev. ed. Stuttgart: Deutsche Bibelgesellschaft, 2003.

Lyons, John. *Language and Linguistics*. Cambridge: Cambridge University Press, 1981.

MacDonald, Peter J. "Discourse Analysis and Biblical Interpretation." In *Linguistics and Biblical Hebrew*, edited by Walter R. Bodine, 153–75. Winona Lake, IN: Eisenbrauns, 1992.

Matthews, P. H. *Grammatical Theory in the United States: From Bloomfield to Chomsky*. Cambridge: Cambridge University Press, 1993.

Matthews, Peter H. *Linguistics: A Very Short Introduction*. Oxford: Oxford University Press, 2002.

Matthews, Victor Harold. *More than Meets the Ear: Discovering the Hidden Contexts of Old Testament Conversations*. Grand Rapids: Eerdmans, 2008.

McCurdy, David W., and James P. Spradley, eds. *Issues in Cultural Anthropology: Selected Readings*. Boston: Little, Brown and Company, 1979

McFall, Leslie. *The Enigma of the Hebrew Verbal System: Solutions from Ewald to the Present Day*. Sheffield: Almond Press, 1982.

McKay, K. L. *A New Syntax of the Verb in New Testament Greek*. New York: Peter Lang, 1994.

McWhorter, John. *Language Interrupted: Signs of Non-Native Acquisition in Standard Language Grammars*. Oxford: Oxford University Press, 2007.

———. *The Language Hoax: Why the World Looks the Same in Any Language*. Oxford: Oxford University Press, 2014.

———. *The Power of Babel: A Natural History of Language*. New York: Perennial, 2003.

Miller, Neva. "A Theory of Deponent Verbs." In *Analytical Lexicon of the Greek New Testament*, edited by Timothy Friberg, Barbara Friberg, and Neva Miller, 423–31. Grand Rapids: Baker, 2000.

Miller-Naudé, Cynthia L. "A Linguistic Approach to Ellipsis in Biblical Hebrew Poetry (Or, What to Do When Exegesis of What Is There Depends on What Isn't)." *BBR* 13 (2003): 251–70.

———. "A Reconsideration of 'Double-Duty' Prepositions in Biblical Poetry." *Journal of the Ancient Near Eastern Society* 31 (2008): 99–110.

———. "Methodological Issues in Reconstructing Language Systems from Epigraphic Fragments." In *The Future of Biblical Archaeology: Reassessing Methodologies and Assumptions*, edited by James Karl Hoffmeier and A. R. Millard, 281–305. Grand Rapids: Eerdmans, 2004.

———. "Pivotal Issues in Analyzing the Verbless Clause." In *The Verbless Clause in Biblical Hebrew: Linguistic Approaches*, 3–17. Winona Lake, IN: Eisenbrauns, 1999.

———., ed. *The Verbless Clause in Biblical Hebrew: Linguistic Approaches*. Linguistic Studies in Ancient West Semitic 1. Winona Lake, IN: Eisenbrauns, 1999.

Miller-Naudé, Cynthia L., and C. H. J. van der Merwe. "הִנֵּה and Mirativity in Biblical Hebrew." *Hebrew Studies* 52 (2011): 53–81.

Miller-Naudé, Cynthia L., and Ziony Zevit, eds. *Diachrony in Biblical Hebrew*. Linguistic Studies in Ancient West Semitic 8. Winona Lake, IN: Eisenbrauns, 2012.

Moshavi, Adina. *Word Order in the Biblical Hebrew Finite Clause: A Syntactic and Pragmatic Analysis of Preposing*. Linguistic Studies in Ancient West Semitic 4. Winona Lake, IN: Eisenbrauns, 2010.

Moulton, James H., and George Milligan. *The Vocabulary of the Greek Testament*. London: Hodder & Stoughton, 1930.

Moulton, James Hope, Wilbert Francis Howard, and Nigel Turner. *A Grammar of New Testament Greek*. 4 vols. Edinburgh: T & T Clark, 1906–1976.

Muraoka, T. *Emphatic Words and Structures in Biblical Hebrew*. Jerusalem: Magnes, 1985.

Muraoka, Takamitsu. "A New Dictionary of Classical Hebrew." *Abr-Nahrain Supplement* 4 (1995): 87–101.

———. *Greek-English Lexicon of the Septuagint*. Leuven: Peeters, 2010.

Mussies, Gerhard. *The Morphology of Koine Greek as Used in the Apocalypse of St. John: A Study in Bilingualism*. Leiden: Brill, 1971.

Næss, Åshild. *Prototypical Transitivity*. Amsterdam: John
    Benjamins, 2007.

Naudé, Jacobus. "A Perspective on the Chronological Framework of
    Biblical Hebrew." *JNSL* 30, no. 1 (2004): 87–102.

Naudé, Jacobus A. "The Transitions of Biblical Hebrew in the
    Perspective of Language Change and Diffusion." In *Biblical
    Hebrew: Studies in Chronology and Typology*, edited by Ian Young,
    369:189–214. London: T & T Clark, 2003.

Nerlich, Brigitte, and David Clarke. "Cognitive Linguistics and the
    History of Linguistics." In *The Oxford Handbook of Cognitive
    Linguistics*, edited by Dirk Geeraerts and H. Cuyckens. Oxford:
    Oxford University Press, 2007.

Newmeyer, Frederick J. *Language Form and Language Function*.
    Cambridge, MA: MIT Press, 1998.

Niccacci, Alviero. *The Syntax of the Verb in Classical Hebrew Prose*.
    Sheffield: JSOT Press, 1990.

Nida, Eugene A., and J. P. Louw. *Lexical Semantics of the Greek New
    Testament*. Atlanta: Scholars Press, 1992.

O'Conner, Patricia. "Language: Learning to Like Like." *New York Times*.
    July 15, 2007. http://www.nytimes.com/2007/07/15/opinion/15iht-
    edoconnor.1.6661788.html?_r=0.

O'Connor, M. "Discourse Linguistics and the Study of Biblical Hebrew."
    In *Congress Volume Basel 2001*, edited by A. Lemaire, 92:17–42.
    Supplements to Vetus Testamentum. Leiden: Brill, 2002.

———. "Semitic Lexicography: European Dictionaries of Biblical Hebrew
    in the Twentieth Century." In *Semitic Linguistics: The State of
    the Art at the Turn of the Twenty-First Century*, edited by Shlomo
    Izre'el, 173–212. Winona Lake, IN: Eisenbrauns, 2002.

O'Grady, William. *Contemporary Linguistics: An Introduction*. Harlow, UK:
    Longman, 1997.

Palmer, Micheal. "Hellenistic Greek." Accessed November 16,
    2016. http://www.greek-language.com/grammar/.

Pavey, Emma L. *The Structure of Language: An Introduction to Grammatical
    Analysis*. Cambridge: Cambridge University Press, 2010.

Peays, Ben. "Fantasy Funerals and Other Designer Ways of Going
    Out in Style." In *Everyday Theology: How to Read Cultural Texts*

and Interpret Trends, edited by Kevin J. Vanhoozer, Charles A. Anderson, and Michael J. Sleasman. Grand Rapids: Baker, 2007.

Pinker, Steven. *The Language Instinct: How the Mind Creates Language.* New York: Morrow, 1994.

———. *The Stuff of Thought: Language as a Window into Human Nature.* New York: Viking, 2007.

Polak, Frank. "Sociolinguistics: A Key to the Typology and the Social Background of Biblical Hebrew." *Hebrew Studies* 47 (January 1, 2006): 115–62.

Porter, Stanley E. *Idioms of the Greek New Testament.* 2nd ed. Sheffield: Sheffield Academic Press, 1999.

———. *Verbal Aspect in the Greek of the New Testament with Reference to Tense and Mood.* New York: Peter Lang, 1989.

———. "What More Shall I Say? A Response to Steve Runge and Benjamin Merkle." *BBR* 26, no. 1 (2016): 75–79.

Porter, Stanley E., and D. A. Carson, eds. *Biblical Greek Language and Linguistics: Open Questions in Current Research.* Sheffield: Sheffield Academic Press, 1993.

———, eds. *Discourse Analysis and Other Topics in Biblical Greek.* Sheffield: Sheffield Academic Press, 1995.

———, eds. *Linguistics and the New Testament: Critical Junctures.* Sheffield: Sheffield Academic Press, 1999.

Porter, Stanley E., and Jeffrey T. Reed, eds. *Discourse Analysis and the New Testament: Approaches and Results.* Sheffield: Sheffield Academic Press, 1999.

Porter, Stanley, Matthew B. O'Donnell, and Jeffrey T. Reed. *Fundamentals of New Testament Greek.* Grand Rapids: Eerdmans, 2010.

Poythress, Vern S. *In the Beginning Was the Word: Language—A God-Centered Approach.* Wheaton, IL: Crossway, 2009.

Pratt, Mary Louise. *Toward a Speech Act Theory of Literary Discourse.* Bloomington, IN: Indiana University Press, 1977.

Princeton University. "About WordNet." *WordNet: A Lexical Database for English*, 2016. http://wordnet.princeton.edu/.

Radford, Andrew. *Minimalist Syntax: Exploring the Structure of English.* Cambridge: Cambridge University Press, 2004.

—————. *Minimalist Syntax Revisited*. University of Essex, 2006. http://
www.public.asu.edu/~gelderen/Radford2009.pdf.

Rijksbaron, Albert. *The Syntax and Semantics of Classical Greek*. 3rd ed.
Chicago: University of Chicago Press, 2007.

Robar, Elizabeth. *The Verb and the Paragraph in Biblical Hebrew: A
Cognitive-Linguistic Approach*. Leiden: Brill, 2014.

Robertson, A. T. *A Grammar of the Greek New Testament in the Light of
Historical Research*. 3rd ed. London: Hodder & Stoughton, 1919.

—————. *A Grammar of the Greek New Testament in the Light of Historical
Research*. 4th ed. London: Hodder & Stoughton, 1923.

Robins, R. H. *A Short History of Linguistics*. 2nd ed. London:
Longman, 1979.

Robins, R. H. *The Byzantine Grammarians: Their Place in History*. Berlin:
Mouton de Gruyter, 1993.

Rocine, Bryan M. *Learning Biblical Hebrew: A New Approach Using
Discourse Analysis*. Macon, GA: Smyth & Helwys, 2000.

Runge, Steven E. *Discourse Grammar of the Greek New Testament: A
Practical Introduction for Teaching and Exegesis*. Electronic ed.
Bellingham, WA: Lexham Press, 2010.

—————. *Discourse Grammar of the Greek New Testament: A Practical
Introduction for Teaching and Exegesis*. Peabody, MA:
Hendrickson, 2010.

—————, ed. *Lexham Discourse Greek New Testament*. Bellingham, WA:
Lexham Press, 2008.

—————. "Markedness: Contrasting Porter's Model with the Linguists
Cited as Support." *BBR* 26, no. 1 (2016): 43–56.

—————, ed. *The Lexham High Definition New Testament: ESV Edition*.
Bellingham, WA: Lexham Press, 2008.

Runge, Steven E., and Christopher J. Fresch, eds. *The Greek Verb Revisited:
A Fresh Approach for Biblical Exegesis*. Bellingham, WA: Lexham
Press, 2016.

Runge, Steven E., and Joshua R. Westbury, eds. *Lexham Discourse Hebrew
Bible*. Bellingham, WA: Lexham Press, 2012.

—————, eds. *The Lexham High Definition Old Testament: ESV Edition*.
Bellingham, WA: Lexham Press, 2012.

Sampson, Geoffrey. *The Language Instinct Debate*. Rev. ed. London: Continuum, 2005.

Sapir, Edward. "The Status of Linguistics as a Science." *Language* 5, no. 4 (1929): 207–14.

Saussure, Ferdinand de. *Cours de linguistique générale*. Edited by Charles Bally, Albert Secheye, and Albert Reidlinger. Paris: Payot, 1916.

———. *Course in General Linguistics*. Edited by Charles Bally, Albert Secheye, and Albert Reidlinger. Translated by Wade Baskin. New York: Philosophical Library, 1959.

———. *Course in General Linguistics*. Translated by Roy Harris. Chicago: Open Court, 1986.

Schriffin, Deborah. *Handbook of Discourse Analysis*. Malden, MA: Blackwell, 2001.

Scott, James M. *Adoption as Sons of God: An Exegetical Investigation into the Background of ΥΙΟΘΕΣΙΑ in the Corpus Paulinum*. Tübingen: J. C. B. Mohr, 1992.

Searle, John R. *Expression and Meaning: Studies in the Theory of Speech Acts*. Cambridge: Cambridge University Press, 1979.

Seuren, Pieter. *Western Linguistics: An Historical Introduction*. Malden, MA: Blackwell, 1998.

Shepard, Jon. *Sociology*. 9th ed. Belmont, CA: Wadsworth/Thompson Learning, 2005.

Siewierska, Anna. *Word Order Rules*. London: Routledge, 1988.

Sihler, Andrew. *New Comparative Grammar of Greek and Latin*. Oxford: Oxford University Press, 1995.

Silva, Moisés. *Biblical Words and Their Meaning: An Introduction to Lexical Semantics*. Rev. exp. ed. Grand Rapids: Zondervan, 1994.

———. *God, Language, and Scripture: Reading the Bible in the Light of General Linguistics*. Foundations of Contemporary Interpretation 4. Grand Rapids: Zondervan, 1990.

———. *Philippians*. 2nd ed. Baker Exegetical Commentary on the New Testament. Grand Rapids: Baker, 2005.

Silzer, Peter James, and Thomas John Finley. *How Biblical Languages Work: A Student's Guide to Learning Hebrew and Greek*. Grand Rapids: Kregel, 2004.

Stassen, Leon. *Intransitive Predication*. Oxford: Clarendon, 1997.

Stubbs, Michael. "Language and the Mediation of Experience: Linguistic Representation and Cognitive Orientation." In *The Handbook of Sociolinguistics*, edited by Florian Coulmas, 358–73. Oxford: Blackwell, 1998.

Tannen, Deborah, Heidi E. Hamilton, and Deborah Schiffrin, eds. *The Handbook of Discourse Analysis*. 2nd ed. Malden, MA: Wiley Blackwell, 2015.

Taylor, John R. *Linguistic Categorization*. 3rd ed. Oxford Textbooks in Linguistics. New York: Oxford University Press, 2003.

Thatcher, Adrian. "Living Together Before Marriage: The Theological and Pastoral Opportunities." In *Celebrating Christian Marriage*, edited by Adrian Thatcher. Edinburgh: T & T Clark, 2001.

"The World Atlas of Language Structures Online." *The World Atlas of Language Structures Online*. Accessed September 6, 2016. http://wals.info/.

Thiselton, Anthony C. "Semantics and New Testament Interpretation." In *New Testament Interpretation: Essays on Principles and Methods*, edited by I. Howard Marshall, 74–100. Milton Keynes, UK: Paternoster, 1997.

Thompson, Jeremy. *Bible Sense Lexicon: Dataset Documentation*. Bellingham, WA· Faithlife Corporation, 2015.

———. "The Bible Sense Lexicon: WordNet Theory Adapted for Biblical Languages." Baltimore, MD, 2013. http://jeremythompson.ws/docs/BSLLexicographyThompsonSBL2013.pdf.

Tomasello, Michael. "Language Is Not an Instinct." *Cognitive Development* 10 (1995): 131–56.

Trubetzkoy, Nikolai. *Principles of Phonology*. Translated by Christiane A. M. Baltaxe. Berkeley, CA: University of California Press, 1969.

Tucker, Gene M. *Form Criticism of the Old Testament*. Philadelphia: Fortress, 1971.

Ullendorff, Edward. "Is Biblical Hebrew a Language?" *Bulletin of the School of Oriental and African Studies* 34 (1971): 241–55.

Van der Merwe, Christo H. J., "Some Recent Trends in Biblical Hebrew Linguistics: A Few Pointers Towards a More Comprehensive Model of Language Use." *Hebrew Studies* 44 (2003): 7–24.

———. Jackie A. Naudé, and Jan H. Kroeze. *A Biblical Hebrew Reference Grammar*. Sheffield: Sheffield Academic Press, 1999.

———. "Towards a Principled Model for Biblical Hebrew Lexicology." *JNSL* 30, no. 1 (2004): 119-37.

Van Valin, Robert D., Jr. "A Brief Overview of Role and Reference Grammar." Unpublished paper. Department of Linguistics & Center for Cognitive Science, State University of New York at Buffalo, 2002. http://www.acsu.buffalo.edu/~vanvalin/rrg/RRGpaper.pdf.

———. "A Summary of Role and Reference Grammar." Unpublished paper. Department of Linguistics & Center for Cognitive Science, State University of New York at Buffalo, 2008. http://www.acsu.buffalo.edu/~vanvalin/rrg/RRGsummary.pdf.

———. *An Introduction to Syntax*. Cambridge: Cambridge University Press, 2001.

Van Voorst, Robert E. *Building Your New Testament Greek Vocabulary*. 3rd ed. Atlanta: Society of Biblical Literature, 2001.

van Wolde, Ellen. "Linguistic Motivation and Biblical Exegesis." In *Narrative Syntax and the Hebrew Bible*, edited by Ellen van Wolde, 21-50. Leiden: Brill, 1997.

———. *Reframing Biblical Studies: When Language and Text Meet Culture, Cognition, and Context*. Winona Lake, IN: Eisenbrauns, 2009.

van Wyk, W. C. "The Present State of OT Lexicography." In *Lexicography and Translation*, edited by J. P. Louw, 82-96. Cape Town, South Africa: Bible Society of South Africa, 1985.

Vazquez-Orta, Ignacio. "Doing Things with Words." In *Cognitive Exploration of Language and Linguistics*, edited by R. Dirven and M. Verspoor. Philadelphia: John Benjamins, 2004.

Wallace, Daniel B. *Greek Grammar Beyond the Basics: An Exegetical Syntax of the New Testament*. Grand Rapids: Zondervan, 1996.

Waltke, Bruce K., and Michael Patrick O'Connor. *An Introduction to Biblical Hebrew Syntax*. Winona Lake, IN: Eisenbrauns, 1990.

White, Hugh C., ed. *Semeia 41: Speech Act Theory and Biblical Criticism*. Decatur, GA: Society of Biblical Literature, 1987.

Whorf, Benjamin Lee. "The Relation of Habitual Thought and Behavior to Language." In *Issues in Cultural Anthropology: Selected Readings*, edited by David W. McCurdy and James P. Spradley, 51–67. Boston: Little, Brown and Company, 1979.

Widder, Wendy L. *"To Teach" in Ancient Israel: A Cognitive Linguistic Study of a Biblical Hebrew Lexical Set*. Berlin: De Gruyter, 2014.

Wilson, Deirdre, and Dan Sperber. *Meaning and Relevance*. Cambridge: Cambridge University Press, 2012.

Winters, Margaret. "Languages Across Time." In *Cognitive Exploration of Language and Linguistics*, edited by R. Dirven and M. Verspoor. Cognitive Linguistics in Practice. Philadelphia: John Benjamins, 2004.

Winther-Nielsen, Nicolai. "Biblical Hebrew Parsing on Display: The Role-Lexical Module (RLM) as a Tool for Role and Reference Grammar." *Hiphil Novum* 6 (2009): 1–51.

Young, Ian, ed. *Biblical Hebrew: Studies in Chronology and Typology*. London: T & T Clark, 2003.

———. "Introduction: The Origin of the Problem." In *Biblical Hebrew: Studies in Chronology and Typology*, edited by Ian Young, 1–6. London: T & T Clark, 2003.

Young, Richard A. *Intermediate New Testament Greek: A Linguistic and Exegetical Approach*. Nashville, TN: Broadman & Holman, 1994.

Zevit, Ziony. "Review of Biblical Hebrew: Studies in Chronology and Typology by Ian Young." *RBL*, no. 6 (2004): 1–16.

Zwicky, Arnold M. "On Markedness in Morphology." *Die Sprache: Zeitschrift Für Sprachwissenschaft Wien* 24, no. 2 (1978): 130.

SUBJECT INDEX

A

Akkadian, 5, 90, 149
Akmajian, Adrian, 9, 114
Allan, Rutger J., 168, 187
ambiguity, 3, 30, 45–46, 54–55
    syntax, 116–17
anachronism, semantic, 36–37
Andrason, Alexander W., 137n8
antonymy, 96–98
apophony, 17, 19
apostle, 36–37
Arabic, 5, 91–92, 148
Aramaic, 5, 90, 148, 156
Aristotle, 33
articulation, 12–17
aspect, 23–24
    Greek, 169–73, 189
    Hebrew, 144–46, 158
Aubrey, Rachel, 168–69
audience, original, 28–29, 54
Austin, John L., 51–52, 55–56
authors, 28–29, 54, 124, 196–97

B

Barr, James, 37, 88, 89, 91–93, 150, 158
    theological lexicography, 177–78, 179
Battistella, Edwin L., 75, 77, 78, 85
Bauer, Walter, 174, 175–76, 184–85
Baumgartner, Walter, 148
Bergen, Robert, 60, 122–23, 126
Berlin, Adele, 120

Bhat, D. N. S., 198–99
Binnick, Robert I., 146
binyanim / stems, 138, 140–44, 160
Birner, Betty, 56–57
Black, David Alan, 4, 11, 19, 20, 27,
        37–38, 48–49
    generative grammar, 119–20
Blau, Joshua, 20, 27, 145
Bloomfield, Leonard, 95
Bodine, Walter R., 6, 9, 126
Bortone, Pietro, 187
Bransford, John, 57–58
*Brown-Driver-Briggs Hebrew and
        English Lexicon, Enhanced*
        (BDB), 89, 148–49, 150, 151–52
Burke, Trevor, 178
Buth, Randall, 84n39, 137n8

C

Campbell, Constantine, 169, 173
Carson, D. A., 30–31, 35–37, 38, 125, 129
case endings, Greek, 22–23, 193–95
categorizing, 22–24, 32–33, 34, 62
characterization, 196–97
children, acquisition of language, 1–2,
        9, 68–69, 112–13
Chomsky, Noam, 85, 102–03, 105, 119
    competence, 98–99,
    syntax, 95–96, 122
    universal grammar, 68, 112–13
Chronicles, 156–57

Chrysostom, 162–63
Clarke, David, 103
Clines, David J. A., 151
cognitive linguistics, 95–96, 99,
    100–01, 103, 111, 153
  Construction Grammar, 193–95
  Greek lexicons and, 182–83, 187
  Hebrew lexicons and, 152–53
  meaning, 127–33
  semantics, 34–35, 131–32
Cohen, Ohad, 137n8
comparative philology, 88–94, 147–49,
    151, 198–200
Comrie, Bernard, 67, 71, 110, 200
Construction Grammar, 193–95
context, 32, 51, 53–55
  discourse, 54–55, 56–57
  frames and, 57–58
  meaning, 30–31, 52–53, 131, 176–77
  pragmatics, 53–55
  social, 56, 61
Cook, John A., 72–73, 137n8, 158
Cotterell Peter, 9, 28–29, 38, 49
Courtenay, Jan Baudouin de, 95
Cremer, Hermann, 177
Croft, William, 76–77, 109
crosslinguistic universals, 69–70
Cruse, Alan, 52, 53–55
culture, 62–64, 132, 176–77

D

Danove, Paul, 193
David, 196–97
Dead Sea Scrolls, 148, 150, 152
de Blois, Reinier, 100–01, 151, 153
DeCaen, Vincent, 121
Demers, Richard A., 9
deponent verbs, 166–68, 188
diachrony, 89, 91
Dictionary of Classical Hebrew, 100,
    151–53
Dik, Helma, 186–87
Dik, Simon, 104–05
discourse analysis, 56–59, 60, 121–26
  context, 54–55, 56–57

exegesis, 195–97
grammar, 59–60, 66, 85–86, 110,
    125–26, 197, 200–01
  Greek, 60, 124–26
  Hebrew, 58–59, 60, 124–25, 126
  markers, 57, 58–59
Dooley, Robert A., 126
Doron, Edit, 84n39
Driver, Samuel, 191
Dryer, Matthew S., 70

E

Edwards, John, 61
Eggins, Suzanne, 103, 105
ellipsis, 45–47
encyclopedic meaning, 96, 128, 131,
    182–83, 196
Erteschik-Shir, Nomi, 108–09
exegesis, 65, 66, 80–81, 84–85, 126,
    191–92
  clauses, meaning of, 192–95
  discourse analysis, 195–97
  Greek, 192–95
  typology, 198–00
  word order, 159, 189
  word study, 35, 178–79
*Exegetical Dictionary of the New
    Testament (EDNT)*, 183
Eynikel, Erik, 185

F

Fanning, Buist, 169
Farmer, Ann K., 9
figurative language / metaphoric, 30,
    33–34, 132–33
Fillmore, Charles, 128
Finley, Thomas John, 20, 27–28, 38, 49
formalist approach, 102, 104
frames, 57–58, 131–32, 182
Fresch, Christopher J., 189
functionalism, 102–05, 107–10, 110–11,
    122
  Role and Reference Grammar (RRG),
    105–06, 110
  word order, 107–08, 111

G

Geeraerts, Dirk, 96, 101, 127, 176, 180

gender, grammatical, 22–23, 73–74, 78–79, 83

generative grammar, 95–96, 99, 102–03, 109, 111–13, 122, 128
  ambiguous syntax, 116–17
  structure, deep and surface, 114–15, 120
  transformations, 114–19
  universal grammar, 113–14, 115

Gesenius, Wilhelm, 142, 149, 191

Givón, Talmy, 76–77

glosses, 150–51

grammar, 9, 28, 39
  Construction, 193–95
  discourse, 59–60, 66, 85–86, 110, 125–26, 197, 200–01
  Hebrew, 11–12, 24, 120
  parts of speech, 39–40
  Role and Reference (RRG), 105–06, 110
  universal, 68–69, 113–14, 115

Greek, Classical, 6, 170n17, 171, 173, 187, 189

Greek-English Lexicon (LSJ), 185

Greek-English Lexicon of the New Testament Based on Semantic Domains, 152–53, 184

Greek-English Lexicon of the New Testament and Other Early Christian Literature (BDAG), 184–85

A Greek-English Lexicon of the Septuagint (LEH), 185–86

Greek-English Lexicon of the Septuagint (GELS), 185–86

Greek fathers, 162–63

Greek, Koine, 6, 164, 184, 199–00

Greek lexicons / lexicography, 153, 173–74, 184–86
  cognitive linguistics, 182–83, 187
  historical philology, 175–76, 182, 184–85

lexical semantics, 174–76, 179, 182

meaning of words, 175–77, 178–81

naming, 180–81

Septuagint, 185–86

signs, verbal, 180–81

structural semantics, 179–84

theological dictionaries, 174, 177–78, 181–82, 183–86

Greek, New Testament, 24, 41, 66, 83
  cases, 22–23, 193–95
  comparative philology, 88, 93
  data issues, 161–64
  discourse analysis, 60, 124–26
  exegesis, 192–95
  functionalism, 110, 111
  grammars, 41, 59, 166, 168
  interpretation, 162–63
  leipō λείπω (I leave), 19–20
  markedness, 82–83, 84–85
  morphology, 26–27
  papyri, 163–64, 171
  patterns, 48, 72–73
  phonology, 19–20
  semantics, 36–37, 153
  transformation, 119–20
  word order, 111, 186–87
  See also Greek lexicons / lexicography; Greek verbal system;

Greek verbal system, 24, 164–65, 189, 194–95
  deponent verbs, 166–68, 188
  historical present, 59
  middle voice, 166–69, 187
  past and nonpast, 171–72
  tense and aspect, 169–73, 189
  voice, 165–69

Greenberg, Joseph H., 74, 76–77, 110

Groom, Susan A., 93

H

Halliday, Michael, 105, 110

Harnish, Robert M., 9

Harris, Zellig, 119

Hauspie, Katrin, 185

The Hebrew and Aramaic Lexicon of the
    Old Testament (HALOT), 7, 148,
    149–52
Hebrew, Biblical, 24, 35, 36, 41, 64–65,
    72, 81, 110
  chronology, 155–56, 159–60
  comparative philology, 88–93,
    147–49, 151
  data issues, 135–37
  discourse analysis, 58–59, 60, 124–25,
    126
  ellipsis, 45–47
  glosses, 150–51
  grammar, 11–12, 24, 120
  grammars, 90, 101–02, 140, 145
  הִנֵּה (hinnē) / imperative, 7–8, 24
  lamed preposition, 25–26
  lē'mōr (to say), 58–59
  morphology, 25–26
  paradigms, 25–26
  patterns, 72–73
  philology, 5–6
  phonology, 12–13, 18–20
  poetry, 45–47, 158
  priestly jargon, 64–65
  Semitic languages and, 90–92, 144,
    147–51
  sociolinguistics, 61, 64–65, 66
  verbless clauses, 41, 44–45
  word order, 72–73, 84, 85, 154–55,
    158–59
  See also Hebrew lexicons /
    lexicography; Hebrew verbal
    system.
Hebrew, Classical, 151–53
Hebrew lexicons / lexicography,
    88–89, 100–01, 147–53, 158
    159–60
  cognitive linguistics and, 153
  Dictionary of Classical Hebrew, 100,
    151–53
  semantic domains and, 153
  traditional, 148–51, 152
Hebrew verbal system, 24, 72–73, 81,
    124–25, 137–38, 158–60

  binyanim / stems, 138, 140–44, 160
  modality, 144–46
  movement, 139–40
  qatal and yiqtol, 145–46
  tense and aspect, 144–46, 158
  voice, 138–39
  waw prefixed, 145–46
Hecht, Max, 175
Heimerdinger, Jean-Marc, 125, 155
הִנֵּה (hinnē), 7–8
historical linguistics, 88–89, 93,
    156–57, 159–60
historical philology, 175–76, 182,
    184–85
historical present, 59
Hoehner, Harold W., 193
Holmstedt, Robert, 84n39, 154n52
Homer, 171, 187

I
information structure, 108–09

J
Jackendoff, Ray, 96
Jakobson, Roman, 74, 77, 85, 104
Jenni, Ernst, 143
Johnson, Marcia, 57–58
Jones, William, 88
Joosten, Jan, 84n39, 137n8, 159

K
Khan, Geoffrey, 84n39
Kittel, Gerhard, 177
Koehler, Ludwig, 148
Koine Greek, 6, 164, 184, 199–00. See
    also Greek, New Testament.

L
Lakoff, George, 128, 131
Lambrecht, Knud, 109, 155, 158
Langacker, Ronald, 52, 103
language:
  children, acquisition of, 1–2, 9,
    68–69, 112–13
  codes, 123–24

culture and, 62–64, 132
definition, 1–3, 6–7
figurative / metaphoric, 30, 33–34,
    132–33
markedness, 67–68, 73–77
mentality / worldview and, 35–36,
    62–63, 129
psychology and, 96, 97–98, 103, 105,
    175–77, 179
universals, 67, 68–72, 73, 76–77,
    109–10
langue, 98–99, 113
Lee, John, 188
leipō λείπω (I leave), 19–20
Levinsohn, Stephen, 60, 110, 125, 126,
    187, 188, 200
lexical semantics, 31–35, 38, 98
  conceptual / cognitive semantics,
    34–35, 131–32
  Greek and, 174–76, 182, 188
lexicons / lexicography. *See* Greek
        lexicons / lexicography;
        Hebrew lexicons /
        lexicography.
Liddell, Henry George, 175, 185
linguistic determinism, 62–63
linguistics, definition, 2–4
Longacre, Robert, 124–25
Louw, Johannes, 64–66, 100, 148, 153,
    174, 179–81, 184, 188
Lunn, Nicholas, 155, 158
Lust, Johan, 185

M

Malmkjaer, Kirsten, 105
markedness, 67–68, 73–77, 78–81, 86,
    107
  grammatical application, 79–80
  Greek, 82–83, 84–85
  opposition, 75–77, 78–80, 84
  phonological application, 77–78
  privative, 75–76, 78, 80, 82
  qualitative, 75–76, 79, 84–85

quantitative / relative, 76–77, 79–80,
    81–83
syntactic / pragmatic application,
    80–81
Marty, Anton, 103
Mathesius, Vilém, 104, 108
Matthews, Peter, 101
Matthews, Victor H., 65
McFall, Leslie, 137n8
McKay, K. L., 169
melek מֶלֶךְ (king), 18–19
metaphors, 30, 33–34, 132–33
middle voice, 166–69, 187
Miller-Naudé, Cynthia L., 7–8, 44,
    46–47, 49, 88, 137
Miller, Neva, 188
Milligan, George, 163–64
mirativity, 7–8
meaning, 2–3, 34, 77, 122, 150–51, 177
  of author, 28–29, 54, 124, 196–97
  cognitive linguistics, 127–28
  context, 30–31, 131, 176–77
  culture and, 176–77
  encyclopedic, 96, 128, 131, 182–83, 196
  perceived, 28–29
  psychology and, 96, 97–98, 103, 105,
    175–77, 179
  structuralism, 94–95, 101
  of words, 20–22, 29–31, 33–34, 131,
    147–53, 175–81
moods, 24, 146
morphology, 20–26
Moshavi, Adina, 84n39, 85, 155, 158–59
Moulton, James H., 163–64, 191
Muraoka, Takamitsu, 84n39, 152, 155,
    185–86
Mussies, Gerhard, 83

N

Naudé, Jacobus, 159
Nerlich, Brigitte, 103
Niccacci, Alviero, 137n8, 145
Nida, Eugene A., 148, 153, 174, 179–81,
    188

nouns, 22–23, 42

O

O'Connor, Michael, 8 1n99, 102, 120, 125, 140, 143, 152, 160
opposition, 75–77, 78–80, 84

P

parole, 98–99, 113
Pavey, Emma, 106, 110–11
philology, 6
  comparative, 88–94, 148–51, 198–200
  definition, 5–8
  historical, 175–76, 182, 184–85
phonology, 11–13, 74
  application, 77–78
  articulation, 12–17
  consonants, 12–14
  Greek, 19–20
  Hebrew, 18–19
  sound change patterns, 15–17, 18–19
  vowels, 14–15
Pinker, Steven, 100, 102
poetry, Hebrew, 45–47, 158
Polak, Frank, 65
polysemy, 3, 30
Porter, Stanley E., 65–66, 82, 86, 125, 169, 171–73
Poythress, Vern Sheridan, 10, 66
pragmatics, 51–53, 80–81, 82
  context, 53–55
  discourse analysis, 56–60
  speech-act theory, 55–56, 66
Prague school, 74, 77, 103–04, 107–08
privative markedness, 75–76, 78, 80, 82
pronunciation / sound change patterns, 15–17, 18–19
pronouns, 22–23, 79
Prototype Theory / prototypes, 130, 132–33, 182
psychology, 96, 97–98, 103, 105, 175–77, 179

R

relevance theory, 52–53
Rijksbaron, Albert, 189
Robar, Elizabeth, 137n8, 159
Robertson, A. T., 93, 191
Rocine, Bryan, 60
Role and Reference Grammar (RRG), 105–06, 110
roots of words, 18–19, 21–22, 24, 27, 36–37, 149
Rosch, Eleanor, 130
Runge, Steven, 111, 187, 189
  discourse grammar, 59, 60, 66, 85–86, 110, 125–26, 197, 200–01
  exegesis, word order, 159, 189

S

Sapir, Edward, 62, 95, 129
Sapir-Whorf Hypothesis, 62, 129
Saussure, Ferdinand de, 77, 94–100, 103
Schniedewind, William, 65, 66
Scott, James M., 178
Scott, Robert, 175
Searle, John R., 56
semantics, 28–31, 35–37, 96, 127
  cognitive linguistics and, 34–35, 131–32
  See also lexical semantics.
Semitic languages, 5, 90–92, 144, 148–50
sentences, 40–43, 49
Septuagint, 162, 171n19, 174, 184–86, 187
Seuren, Pieter, 88, 94–95, 98, 101, 103, 108
Shema, 44–45
signs, 75, 99–100, 180–81
Silva, Moisés, 10, 31, 94, 162–63, 178, 179–80
Silzer, Peter James, 20, 27–25, 38, 49
sociolinguistics, 56, 61–65, 105
sounds, 11–12, 77
  change patterns, 15–17, 18–19
  See also phonology.

speech-act theory, 55–56, 66
Sperber, Dan, 52–53
Stassen, Leon, 72
structure, 66, 124
  deep and surface, 114–15, 120
  information, 108–09
  word order, 114–19
  See also structuralism / structural
    linguistics.
structuralism / structural linguistics,
    93, 94–98, 103, 113, 122, 128
  Greek lexicons, 179–82
  langue and *parole*, 98–99, 113
  meaning and, 94–95, 101
  signifier and signified, 99–100
  synonymy and antonymy, 96–98
synonymy and antonymy, 96–98
syntax, 39, 44–48, 80–81, 201
  ambiguous, 116–17
  clauses and sentences, 40–41
  organization, 41–43
  word order, 42–43
  words and phrases, 39–40
Systemic Functional Linguistics, 103,
    105

T

Taylor, John, 32–34, 132–33
tenses, verb, 24, 59, 72, 129
  Greek, 169–73, 189
  Hebrew, 144–46, 158
Thayer, Joseph, 175–76
*Theological Dictionary of the New
    Testament* (TDNT), 177–78
theological dictionaries, Greek, 174,
    177–78, 181–82, 183–86
Thiselton, Anthony, 38–39
transformations, 114–19, 120
transitivity, 42, 48, 130, 139–40, 165,
    169
translation, Bible, 7, 44, 46–47, 58–59,
    149–50, 174
Trier, Jost, 101
Trubetzkoy, Nikolai, 74, 77, 104

Turner, Max, 9, 28–29, 38, 49
Turner, Nigel, 164n6
typology, linguistic, 67, 71–73, 77,
    109–10, 155–57, 198–200

U

Ugaritic / Ugarit, 5, 90, 149–50
universals, language, 67, 68–72, 73,
    76–77, 109–10
  crosslinguistic, 69–70
  grammar, 68–69, 113–14, 115

V

van der Merwe, Christo H. J., 7–8,
    84n39, 101–02, 110, 151, 159–60
van Hecke, Pierre, 100, 111
Van Valin, Robert D. Jr., 105–06, 201
Van Voorst, Robert, 26–27, 28
van Wolde, Ellen, 81, 133
Vazques-Orta, Ignacio, 56
verbless clauses, 41, 44–45
verbs, 23–25, 42, 130
  aspect, 23–24, 144–46, 158, 169–73,
    189
  deponent, 166–68, 188
  mood, 24, 146
  predicates, 40–41, 72
  tenses, 24, 59, 72, 129, 144–46, 158,
    169–73, 189
  transitivity, 42, 48, 130, 139–40, 165,
    169
  verbless clauses, 41, 44–45
  voice, 23–25, 138–39, 165–69, 187
  See also Greek verbal systems;
    Hebrew verbal systems.
voice, verbal, 23–25, 138–39
  Greek, 165–69, 187
  Hebrew, 138–39

W

Wallace, Daniel, 192
Waltke, Bruce, 84n39, 102, 120, 140,
    143, 160
Westbury, Joshua R., 84n39, 201

White, Hugh C., 66
Whorf, Benjamin Lee, 62–63, 129
Wierzbicka, Anna, 96
Wilson, Deirdre, 50–59
Winther-Nielsen, Nicolai, 110
Wittgenstein, Ludwig, 34
WordNet, 96, 100–01
word order, 69–70, 71–73, 84
    exegesis, 158–59, 189
    functionalism and, 107–08, 111
    Greek, 111, 186–87
    Hebrew, 72–73, 84, 85, 154–55, 158–59
    sentences, 42–43
    structure and, 114–19
    syntax, 42–43
words, 32
    adjectives, 39–41, 72
    defining, 32–33
    meaning of, 20–22, 29–31, 33–34, 131,
        147–53, 175–81
    nouns / pronouns, 22–23, 42, 79
    organizing, 41–43
    parts of speech, 39–40
    roots, 18–19, 21–22, 24, 27, 36–37,
        149–150
    syntax, 39–40
    See also verbs.

Y

Young, Richard, 119

Z

Zevit, Ziony, 160

SCRIPTURE INDEX

Old Testament

Genesis

1:16 107
1:29 7
42:92 44

Exodus

7:17 7
9:25 142
19:22 142

Numbers

26:55 143

Deuteronomy

6:4 44–45
31:7 143

Judges

12:6 61

1 Samuel

24:3 64
24:7 196
25:22 64
26:24 7

2 Samuel

20:18 142

1 Kings

19:4 142

2 Kings

20:20 148

2 Chronicles

36:20–23 157

Job

12–14 111

Psalms

23 132
49:1–4 47
49:3 46–47
109:10 142

Isaiah

1:27 45
60:2 46

Jonah

4:8 142

New Testament

Mark

11.22 71

Luke

22:70 28–29
22:71 29

John

10:9 132

Acts

7:38 30–31

Romans

1:16 37

Ephesians

1:18–20 37
1:22 192–93

Philippians

1:7 54

Revelation

22:11 83